IMAGES
of America

MATTITUCK AND LAUREL

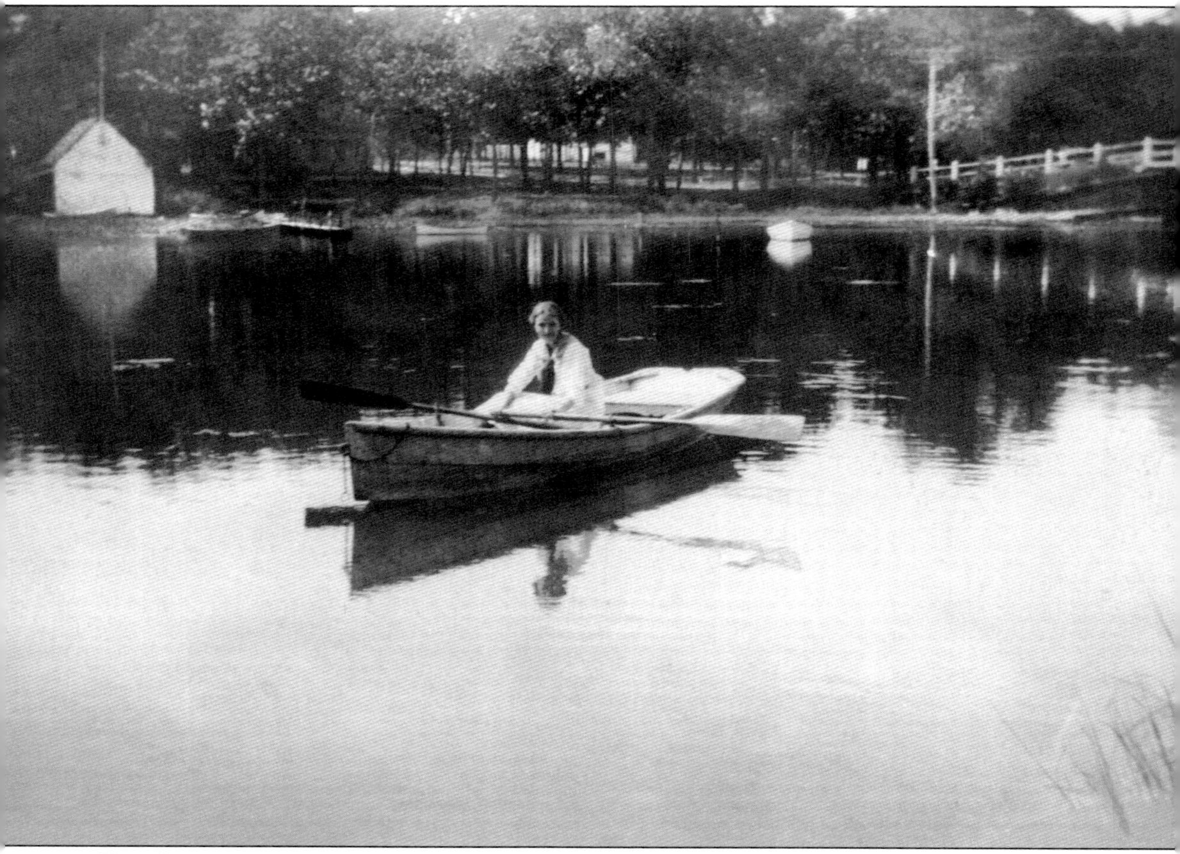

THE COVE, WEST OF WESTPHALIA BRIDGE, c. 1920. Edith Horton enjoys rowing on Mattituck Creek on a summer day. The Duryee boathouse and Westphalia Bridge are in the background. This portion of the creek, west of Westphalia Avenue, was filled in with silt when the county improved the waterway in 1956. (Courtesy of Carolyn Gillespie Markowitz.)

ON THE COVER: THE COVE ON MATTITUCK CREEK, c. 1910. From the Westphalia Bridge, people enjoy an easy summer day on the creek. (Courtesy of the Mattituck-Laurel Library.)

IMAGES
of America

MATTITUCK AND LAUREL

Norman Wamback, Jeffrey M. Walden,
and Gerard M. Matovcik

ARCADIA
PUBLISHING

ISBN 978-0-7385-9915-1

Published by Arcadia Publishing
Charleston, South Carolina

Printed in the United States of America

Library of Congress Control Number: 2012952540

For all general information, please contact Arcadia Publishing:
Telephone 843-853-2070
Fax 843-853-0044
E-mail sales@arcadiapublishing.com
For customer service and orders:
Toll-Free 1-888-313-2665

Visit us on the Internet at www.arcadiapublishing.com

Contents

ACKNOWLEDGMENTS

This book would not have been possible without the help and generosity of the many individuals and families who had the foresight to preserve and document the memories of past generations. We are especially grateful to those individuals who are no longer with us but who have contributed substantially to our knowledge of Mattituck and Laurel history through both pictures and words: Everett L. Conklin, Rev.Charles Craven, Larry DePetris, Nancy Duryee, Vivian Duryee, Charles Gildersleeve, Donald Gildersleeve, Jim A. Gildersleeve, Jim F. Gildersleeve, Louis "Chub" Gildersleeve, Charles Meredith, Elbert Hudson Reeve, Alma Suter, Parker Wickham, and Virginia Wines.

Thanks also go to the numerous individuals who have taken the time and effort to provide us with original photographs and oral histories of Mattituck and Laurel: Donald Bergen, Linda Bird, Fred Boutcher III, Ann DePetris, Charlotte Dickerson, Stephen and Beatrice Duke, Richard Ehlers, Maryann Fleischman, Alice Funn, Marilyn Gatz, Robert Gerdts, Diana Gibson, Pauline Gildersleeve, Robert Gildersleeve, Michael Huttenlocher, Robert Johnson, Peter Kren, Carolyn LaTulip, Carolyn Gillespie Markowitz, Doug and Deborah Massey, Frank McNulty, Michael J. Montgomery, Mary Jane Paul, George Penny, Robin Rambeau, Mike Richter, Donald Russo, Cliff Saunders III, Eleanor Scholtz, Gail and Robbie Sheets, John Sidor, John Traversa, Althea Travis, Anne and Joseph Traynor, John Tuthill, Jay Wickham, Richard Wines, Elberta Young, Myron Young, and Ron Ziel.

We would like to acknowledge our local historical societies and libraries for their assistance in providing images from their archives: director Geoffrey K. Fleming and archives assistant Daniel J. McCarthy, Southold Historical Society; director Kathryn M. Curran and librarian Edward H.L. Smith III, Suffolk County Historical Society; local history librarian Mariella Ostroski, Cutchogue-New Suffolk Library; executive director Herbert J. Strobel and assistant director Beth Motschenbacher, Hallockville Museum Farm; photo archivist Erik Huber, of the Queens Library Archives; Mattituck-Laurel Historical Society (MLHS); and Mattituck-Laurel Library (MLL).

We would also like to thank Kay Zegel, director of the Mattituck-Laurel Library, for her enthusiastic support of this project. Thank you, to Suzanne Conlin, Lynn Maaiki, Jill Tast, and Bev Wowak of the Mattituck-Laurel Library for their research assistance.

INTRODUCTION

In the Algonquin language, the name Mattituck had two meanings: "area of few trees" and "large waterway." In the case of our lovely community, either would apply. The Native Americans had been clearing land for thousands of years, using the wood to build huts and heat them; there are more trees in town today than there were in 1640. Mattituck Creek, James Creek, Deephole Creek, and Halls Creek originally had very large areas of salt marsh adjacent to their main gutters. Where no trees grew, the term "large waterway" would apply to Mattituck Creek, leading in from the Long Island Sound, and to James Creek, leading in from Great Peconic Bay. They come close to meeting each other at their ends, and both were used by the Native Americans to get from Connecticut to the South Fork of Long Island by canoe.

In 1661, allotments of land were given to the men of the Southold settlement based upon their service and their investment in the establishment of the town. William Purrier received the largest allotment in Mattituck, comprised of 400 acres. Mattituck remained a self-sustaining farming community until 1844, when a railroad line was established between Brooklyn and Greenport for the purpose of transporting freight to Boston for shipment to Europe. The peace treaty with England at the end of the Revolutionary War established Boston as the only port of export to Europe. In 1844, the original village center of Mattituck was growing along Kings Highway (Route 25) between Mill Lane and Manor Hill. The village center was comprised of two general stores, a school built in 1790, and two wind-driven gristmills.

The railroad changed the landscape of Mattituck and the North Fork forever. The village center shifted west around the railroad depot. Farmers increased their yield for export to New York City. Wealthy citizens from Brooklyn and Manhattan traveled two hours by rail to spend summer vacations on Mattituck Creek, the Long Island Sound, or Great Peconic Bay. They came by the hundreds, staying at the three hotels and many boardinghouses that were built in town. Many of their children chose to return to Mattituck-Laurel and put down roots as permanent residents, which increased economic growth and expanded light industry. Immigrants also arrived to work on the farms or establish their own businesses. Eventually, many Polish immigrants purchased farms and continued the renowned agricultural tradition of the community.

Just as the railroad changed the appearance and social nature of Mattituck and Laurel, so too did the emergence of the automobile at the beginning of the 20th century, which allowed people to make day trips to the North Fork from New York City. Farmers at the time realized that they could make more money selling waterfront lots for development along the sound shore and Great Peconic Bay than they could by raising potatoes on the land. Instead of boarding, visitors purchased lots to build summer cottages and bungalows, marking the demise of the Mattituck House and the other wood-frame hotels, inns, and boardinghouses that had characterized the hamlets for so many years.

In 1973, the first vineyard was established on the North Fork, in Cutchogue. The climate and soil were so well suited for grape-growing that the industry grew quickly. Today, there are

35 vineyards on the North Fork, with six in Mattituck and Laurel. Portions of the hamlets have preserved their agricultural landscapes, which, along with their beautiful watercourses, continue to make Mattituck-Laurel a cherished place to live.

—Norman Wamback, Village Historian

One

Summer Boarders

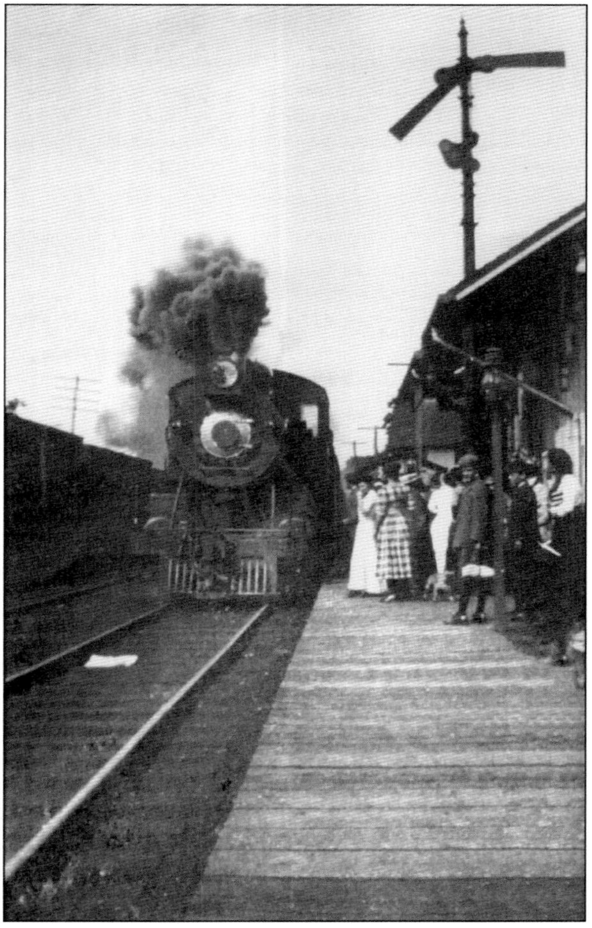

Mattituck Railroad Station, c. 1900. An 1898 brochure from the Long Island Rail Road lists 12 boardinghouses in Mattituck, not including the private homes that took in summer boarders from the city. Donald R. Gildersleeve recalled about the era: "Mattituck had much to offer, and visitors loved their outings here. There was fresh produce from the farm and a rich bounty of fish, crabs, clams and oysters from the sea; there was good boating and swimming in the creek, bay, and sound; there were sunburn and blisters to take back home; there were the Mattituck Literary Society meetings for entertainment and dancing; baseball games every Saturday; and stores to shop in. There was a rush for souvenir postcards immediately after arrival to send back to folks in the big city." (Courtesy of Gail and Robbie Sheets.)

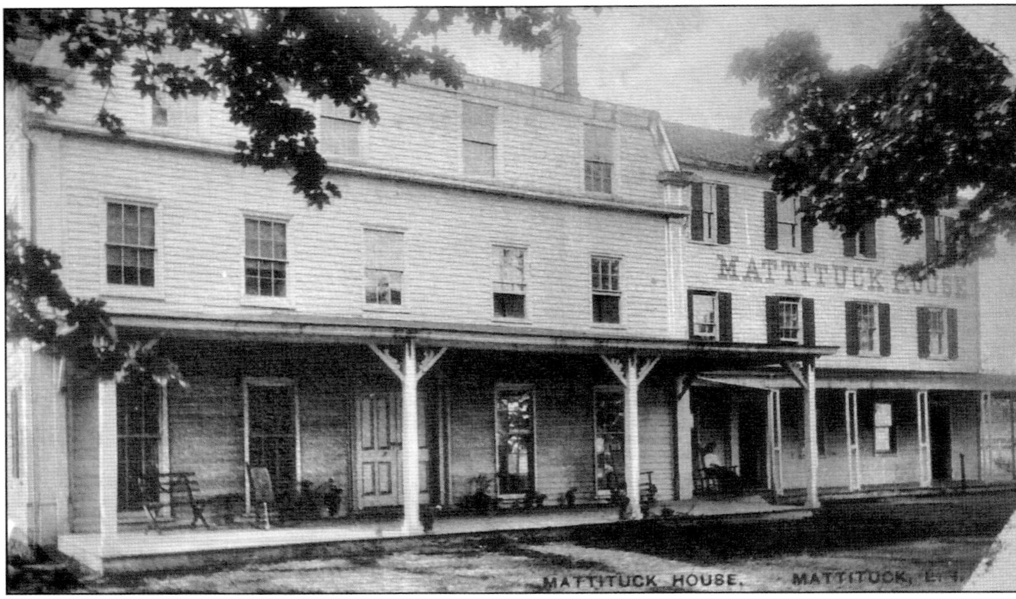

MATTITUCK HOUSE, 1881. Mattituck House was originally known as John Hubbard's Tavern in the 1700s. In 1826, a three-story addition was constructed on the east side. In 1881, a third story with nine rooms was added to the original building, creating 32 rooms overall. The dining room was large, the bar well stocked, and the poolroom a place for men to relax and smoke cigars. This impressive hotel was razed in 1938. (MLL.)

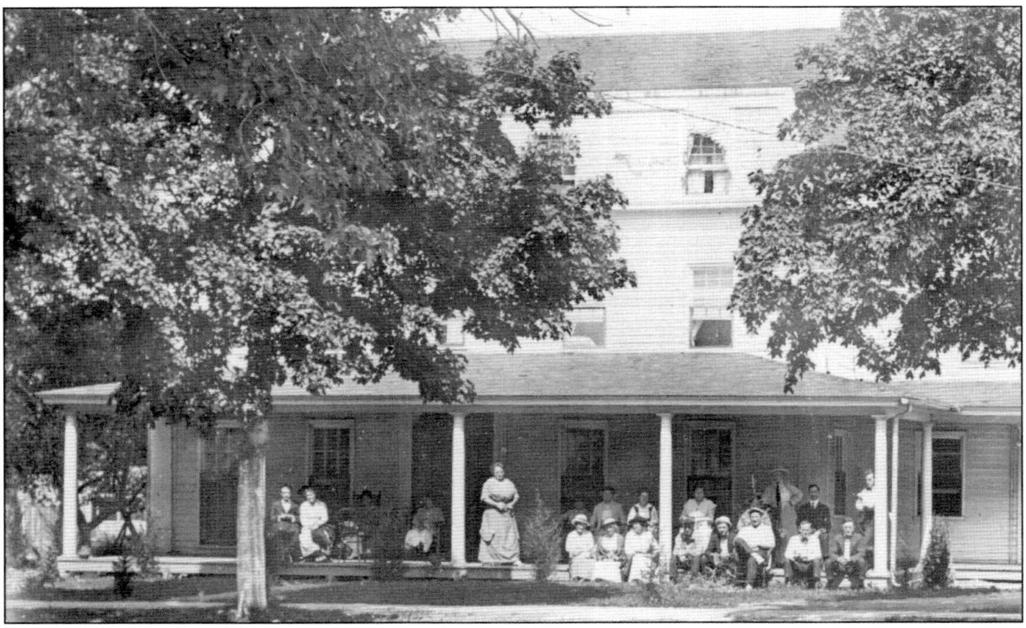

PORCH OF MATTITUCK HOUSE, C. 1910. The affluent visitors to Mattituck House came from Brooklyn with their servants to spend a month in the country. One of the owners put an arch opposite the railroad station advertising the hotel, and visitors could pass through the arch and along a path through a field to the hotel. Isaiah Reeve also transported guests from the hotel to Great Peconic Bay in his horse-drawn omnibus. (MLL.)

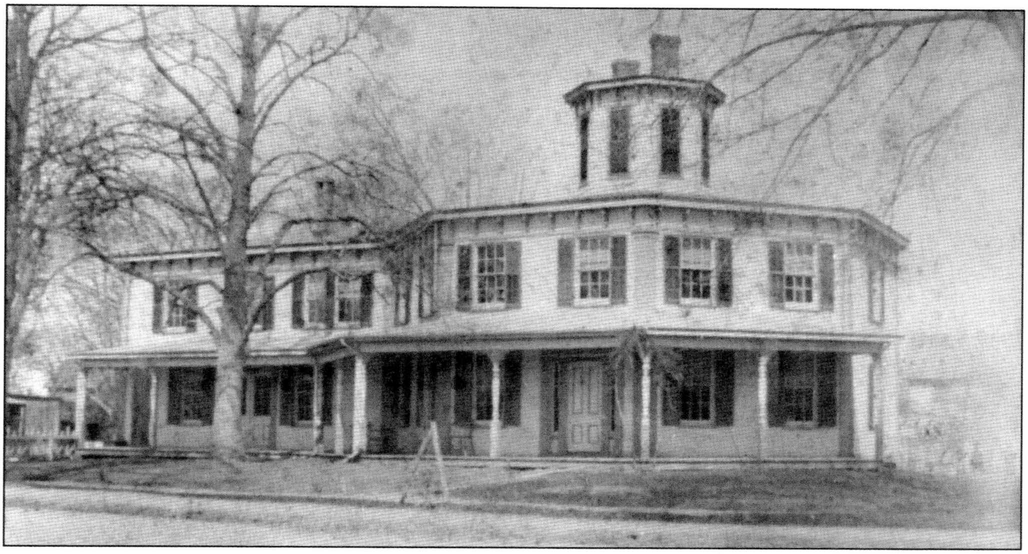

Octagon House, c. 1900. Andrew Gildersleeve built the Octagon House in 1854, inspired by the popularity of octagonal architecture at the time, which was itself inspired by phrenologist-architect Orson Fowler. In 1862, John Wells bought the Octagon House and made it into a store and residence. Unusual for Mattituck at the time, the building had a full basement, which was probably used to store produce. In one year, Wells shipped 51,000 quarts of strawberries from Mattituck to Boston for shipping to Eastern markets. (MLHS.)

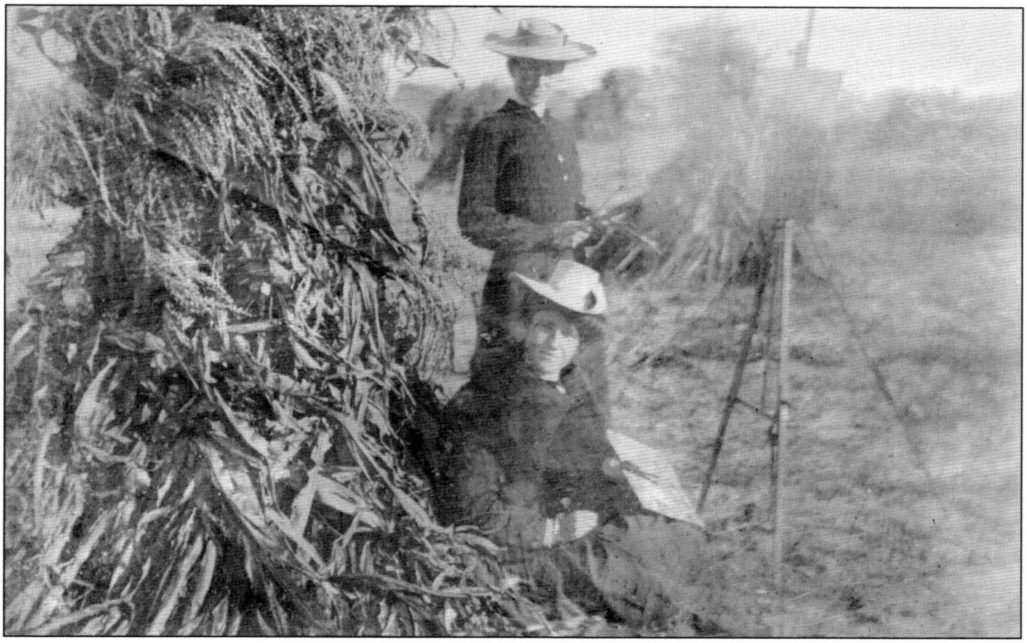

Plein Air Painting, c. 1900. From 1889 until 1922, Henrietta Wells ran the Octagon House, by then known as the Wells House, as a boardinghouse. Frequent guests included Letitia K. Bell and her daughter Caroline "Dolly" Bell, who became an Impressionist painter and influential teacher to many artists on the North Fork. Here, Dolly stands behind Julia Wickham. Bell eventually built a home and separate studio on Mattituck Creek. (Courtesy of the Southold Historical Society.)

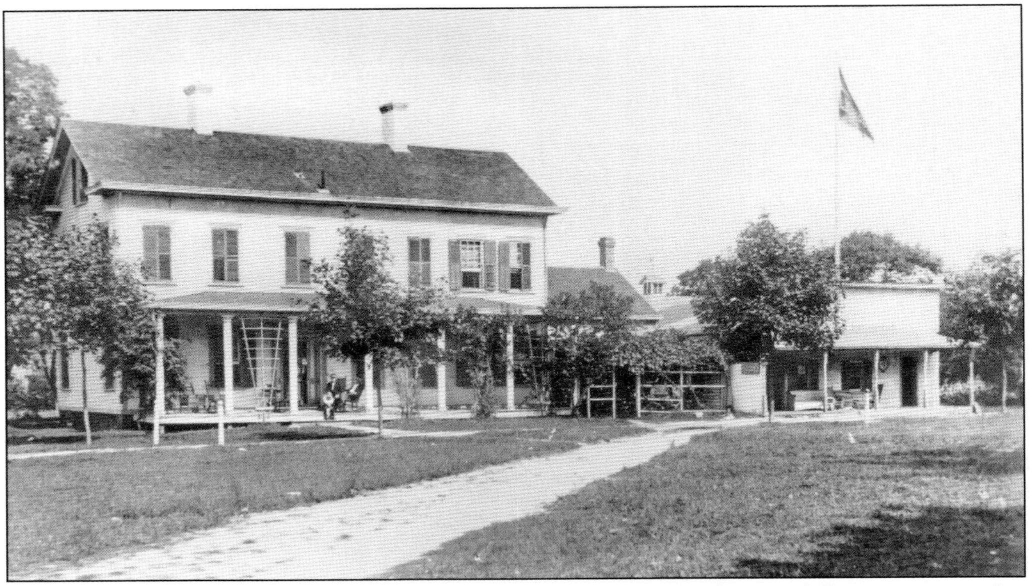

EUREKA HOUSE, C. 1900. In 1885, Clement McMillen bought the Randell House, named it Eureka House, and began taking in summer guests. It was next to Wines' general store. In July 1887, Prof. C.M. Dewey conducted a class for artists, about 30 young ladies in all, at the Eureka House. The next summer, in June 1888, Chief John Deer's Indian Show exhibited for a week in a large tent at the rear of the house. (MLL.)

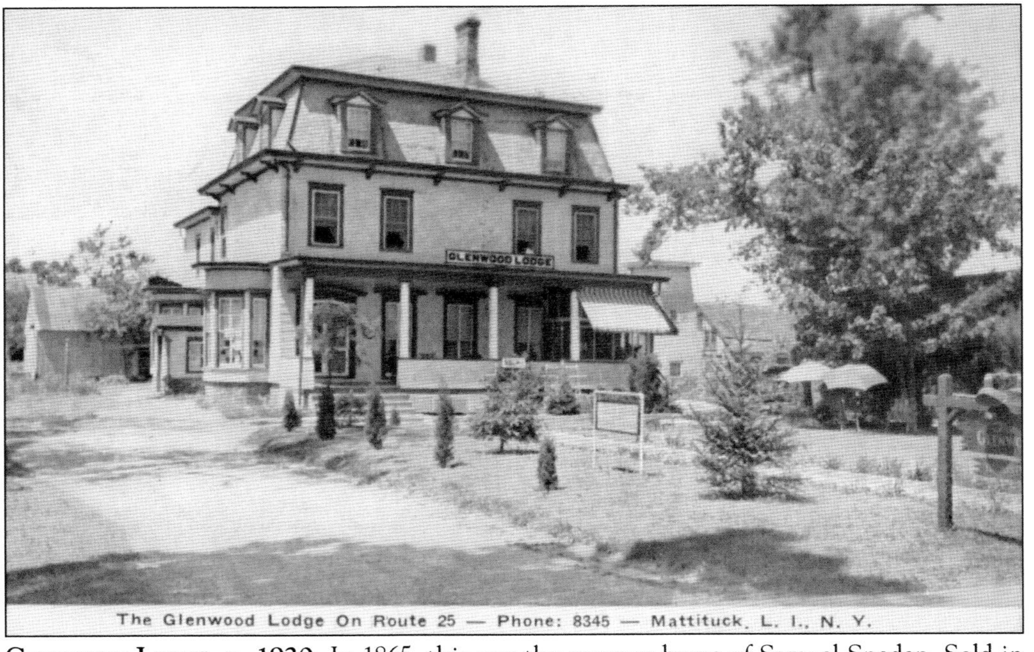

GLENWOOD LODGE, C. 1920. In 1865, this was the summer home of Samuel Sneden. Sold in 1892, it became the Hotel Glenwood, with a café in its basement. In 1897, the establishment was considered a Raines Law hotel, which meant it could serve alcohol on Sundays. The spacious hotel had between 15 and 20 rooms. In 1919, it was renamed the Glenwood Lodge. A fancy speakeasy operated in the basement during Prohibition. (MLL.)

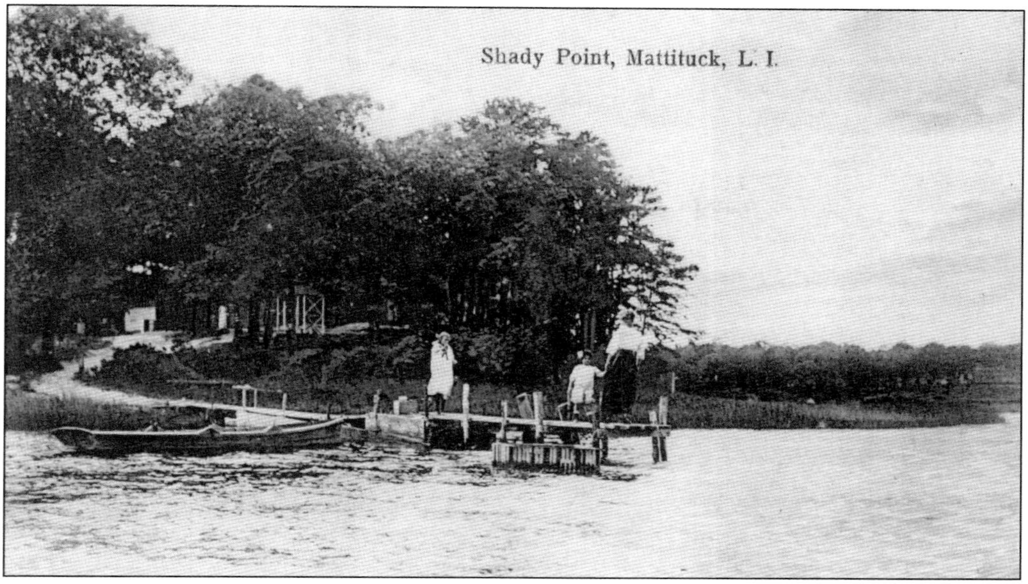

SHADY POINT HOUSE, C. 1900. Seymour Tuthill and William Dubois opened the Shady Point House on Mattituck Creek in 1881. At one point, they accommodated 45 guests, with a large piazza for a dancing floor. In August 1901, a euchre party was followed by a hop. For the party, the broad porch was lit with Japanese candles and decorated with tiny American flags, songs and recitations were performed, and couples did an excellent cakewalk. (MLL.)

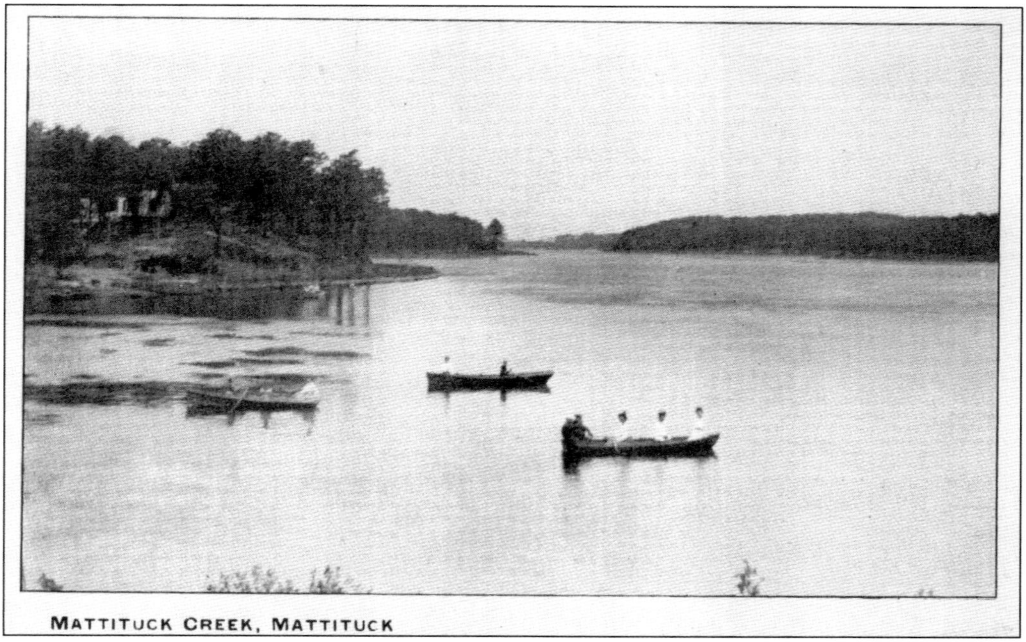

ROWING ON MATTITUCK CREEK, C. 1900. The May 6, 1881, edition of the *Long Island Traveler* describes a rowing contest in this way: "Last week the guests of Shady Point House made the tranquil waters of the creek echo with the splash of oars . . . The ladies of the house rowed for a silk umbrella . . . The gentlemen for a basket of champagne. The race was watched by a large crowd on shore and in boats on the creek, and afforded much amusement for our guests." (MLL.)

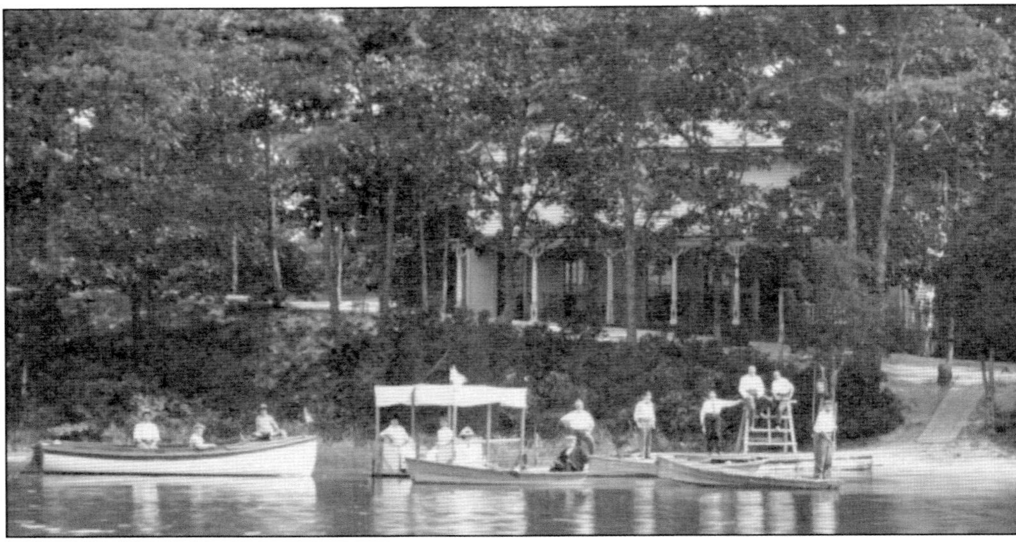

Ingleside Cottage, c. 1900. Next door to Shady Point was Ingleside Cottage, a boardinghouse established in 1884 by Ella and Seymour Tuthill. Boarders came back to Ingleside year after year. One such boarder, John Van Wagner of Brooklyn, spent 50 summers at Ingleside with Seymour Tuthill, his former boyhood chum. Van Wagner brought his wife, children, and grandchildren to the place before he built his own home in Mattituck in 1935. (MLL.)

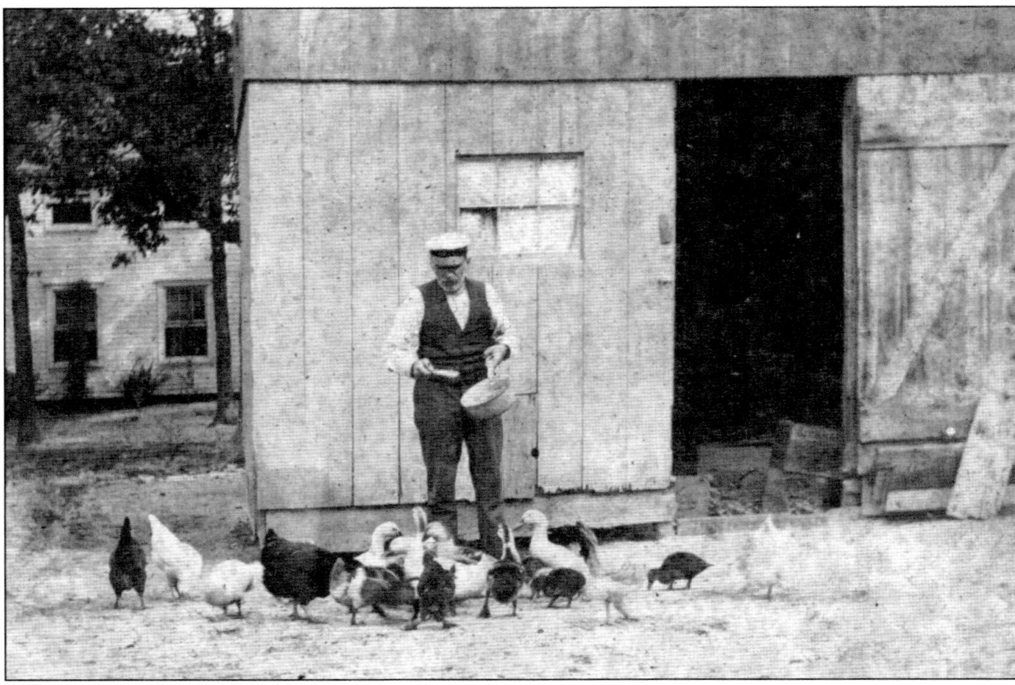

Seymour Tuthill, c. 1900. Seymour Tuthill feeds his chickens in the barn behind Ingleside Cottage. Board was $8 per week, and boarders were well fed. The Tuthills had one daughter, Jennie, who later conducted the boardinghouse with her husband, Doc Lester, a technician for Dr. William H. Drum, a dentist in Library Hall. Jennie was a renowned piano teacher with a large class of students. (Courtesy of Gail and Robbie Sheets.)

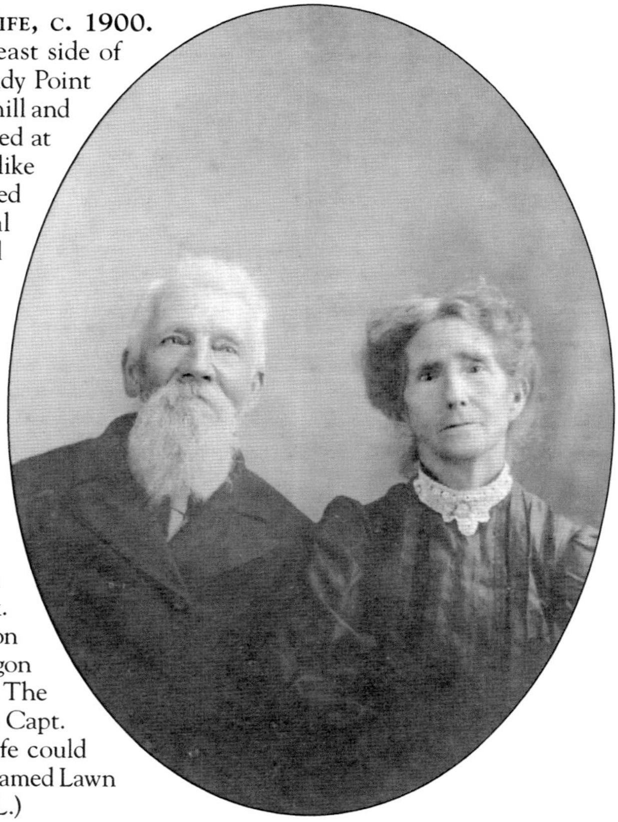

CAPT. BENJAMIN TUTHILL AND WIFE, C. 1900. Fairyland Cottage, located on the east side of Mattituck Creek across from the Shady Point House, was run by Capt. Benjamin Tuthill and his wife, Hannah. They accommodated at least 20 guests, including special guests like the Edward Ridley family. Ridley owned Edward Ridley & Sons, a monumental household goods store on Grand Street in Manhattan with 4.5 acres of floor room. (MLHS.)

MERMAID, C. 1895. Frank Moore Lupton, a native of Mattituck who became a famous publisher in New York, owned the naphtha launch *Mermaid*, seen here on Mattituck Creek. In June 1888, a group of 23 people went on an excursion on the *Mermaid* from Oregon and Mattituck village to Rose's Grove. The pilot of Lupton's naphtha launch was Capt. Warren Lewis Tuthill. He and his wife could accommodate 20 guests at their home, named Lawn Cottage after its extensive lawn. (MLL.)

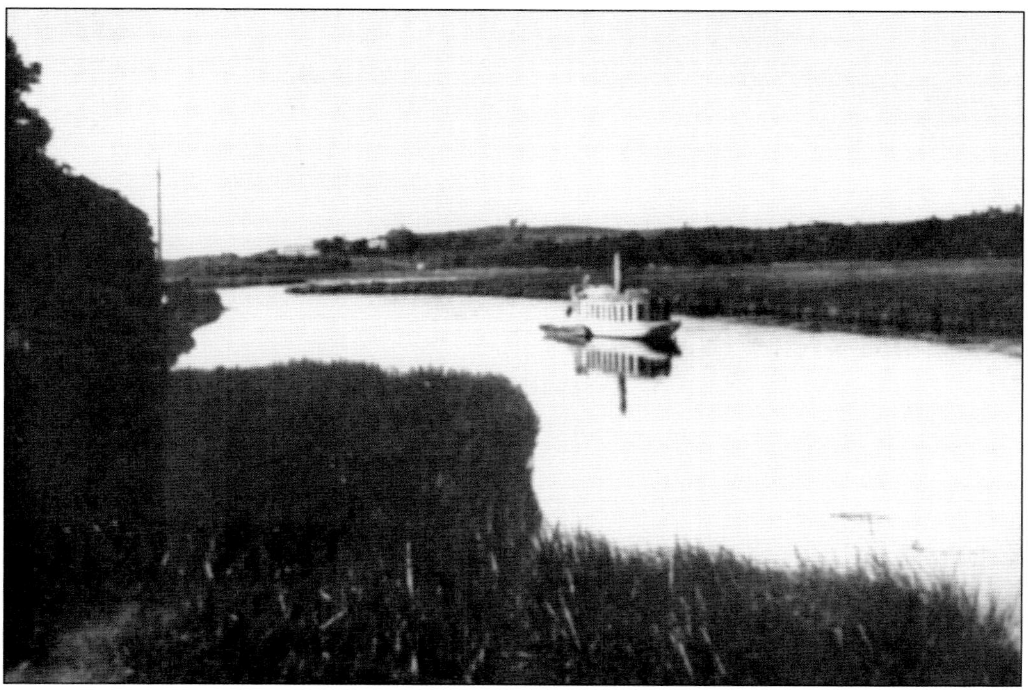

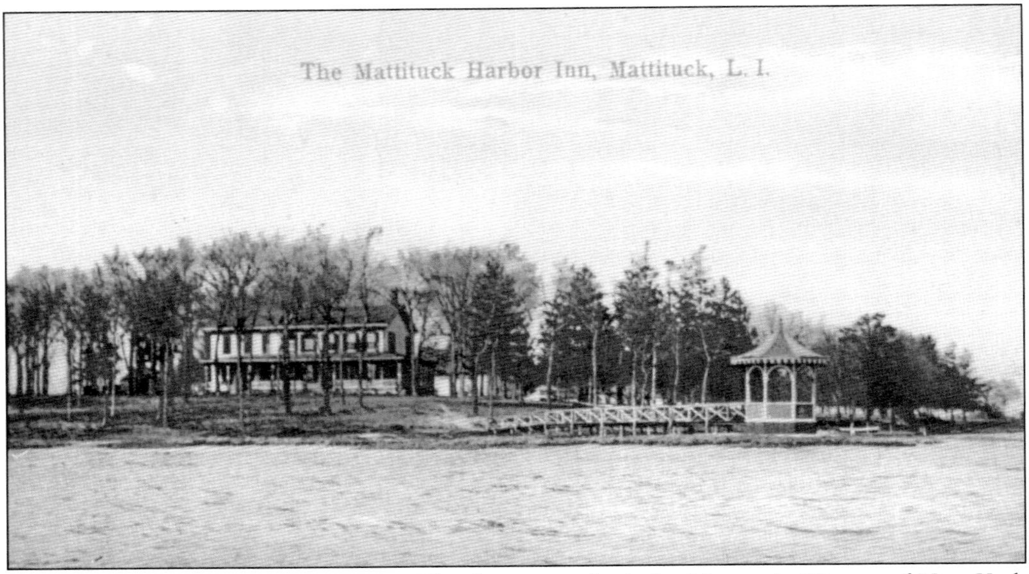

MATTITUCK HARBOR INN, c. 1900. This home was built for Henry A. Dingee of New York City as a summer home. Irad Gildersleeve was its second owner, and then Dr. Hubert W. Klein, Mattituck's first druggist, lived with his family in the spacious house on the creek, which he converted into a summer boardinghouse in 1896 and called the Windamere. The house later became the Mattituck Harbor Inn. (MLL.)

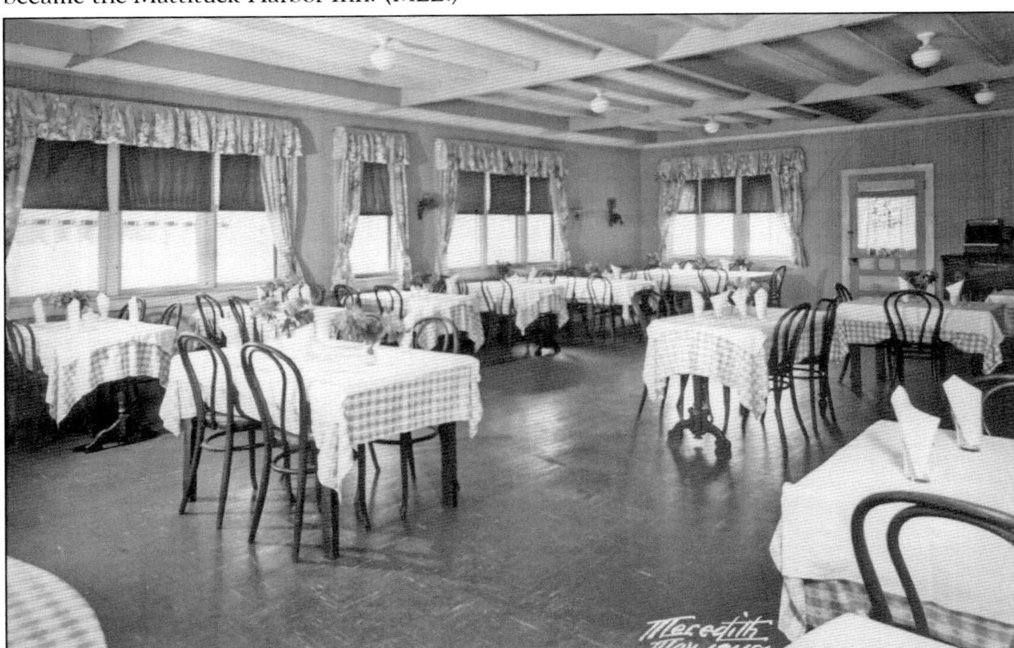

MATTITUCK HARBOR INN DINING HALL, 1948. Klein's Harbor Inn is advertised in an 1893 *Brooklyn Daily Eagle* as a private house with shady playgrounds for children. It offered boating, bathing, fishing, and crabbing; a stable; fruits; piano; and "the best German table," all for $7 to $10 per week. Appetizing meals were served in the dining hall, seen above in 1948 when it was called the Mattituck Harbor Inn. (Courtesy of the Southold Historical Society.)

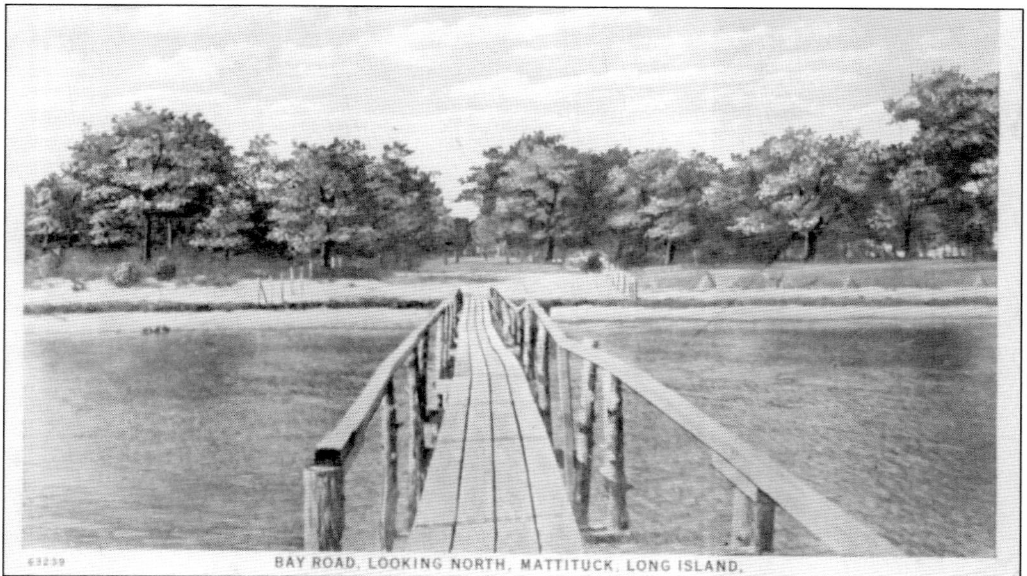

BAY AVENUE DOCK, C. 1910. Towards the end of Bay Avenue (then Bay Road) was Bay View Cottage, owned early on by Frederick Bicking, a Mattituck barber. From 1918 to 1952, Bessie Gaffney ran the cottage, renaming it the Gaffney House. Her father, Christopher, had a tailor shop in Cutchogue. After her passing in 1952, the boardinghouse became the Mattituck Motel. (MLL.)

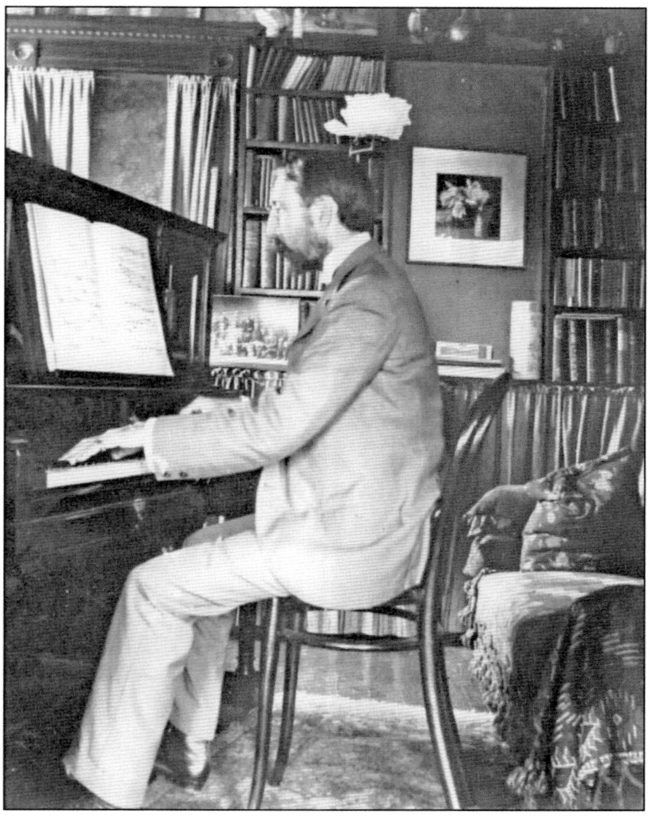

CHARLES FRANC GODDARD, C. 1910. A New York lawyer, Goddard (1862–1954) was also the president of the Long Island chapter of the New York Archaeology Society and a member of the Custer Institute. His chapter excavated one of the earliest Native American camps in the area, a burial ground on Shelter Island. His wife, Virginia Hargraves Wood, who studied at the Chase School, was a renowned portrait artist and a frequent visitor to the studio of Caroline "Dolly" Bell. (MLHS.)

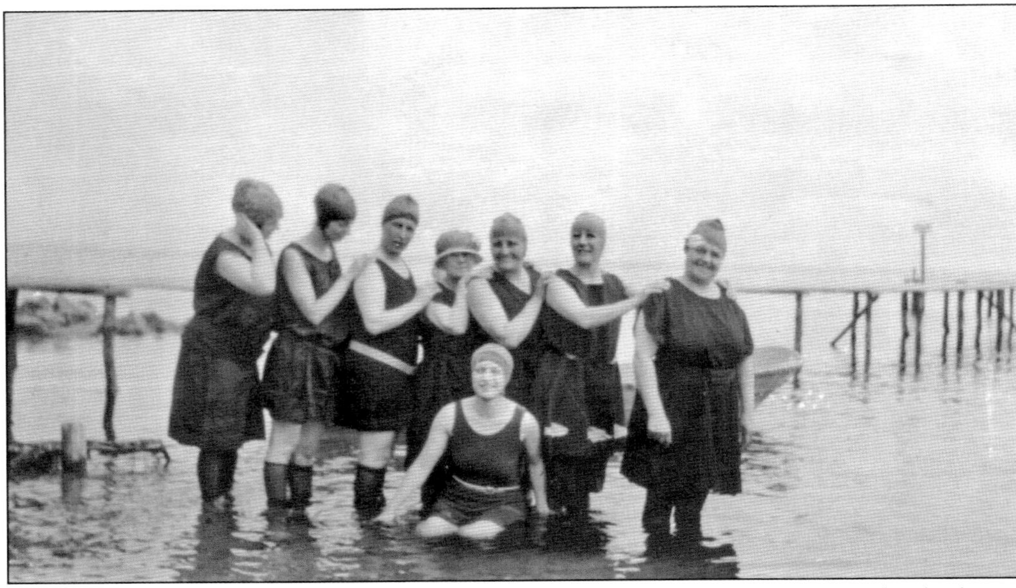

Order of the Eastern Star, 1918. An organization connected to Freemasonry that both men and women could join, the Order of the Eastern Star follows teachings based on the Bible and objectives that are charitable and benevolent. Here, members from a Brooklyn chapter of the Eastern Star visit Great Peconic Bay. (Courtesy of Mary Jane Paul.)

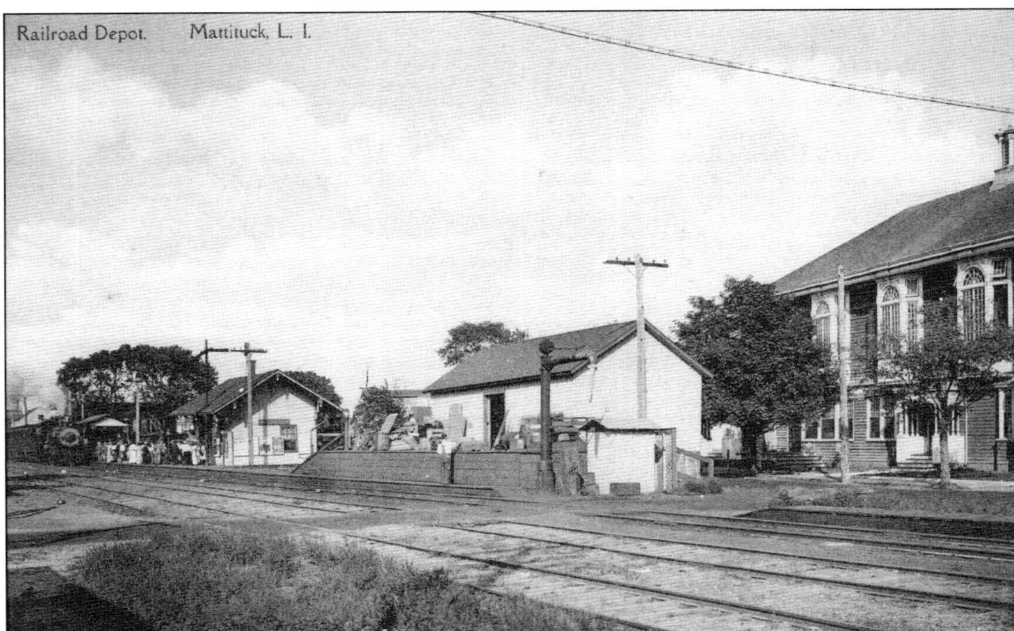

Railroad Depot, c. 1915. Afternoon passengers board the train for their trip back to the city. Most visitors, however, departed on the 9:00 p.m. Sunday train that took one-week boarders back home. Often, other boarders as well as townspeople came to the station to see them off. Conversations were known to be so loud that a station agent once compared the hubbub to the building of the Tower of Babel. (MLL.)

Two

The Sound and the Creek

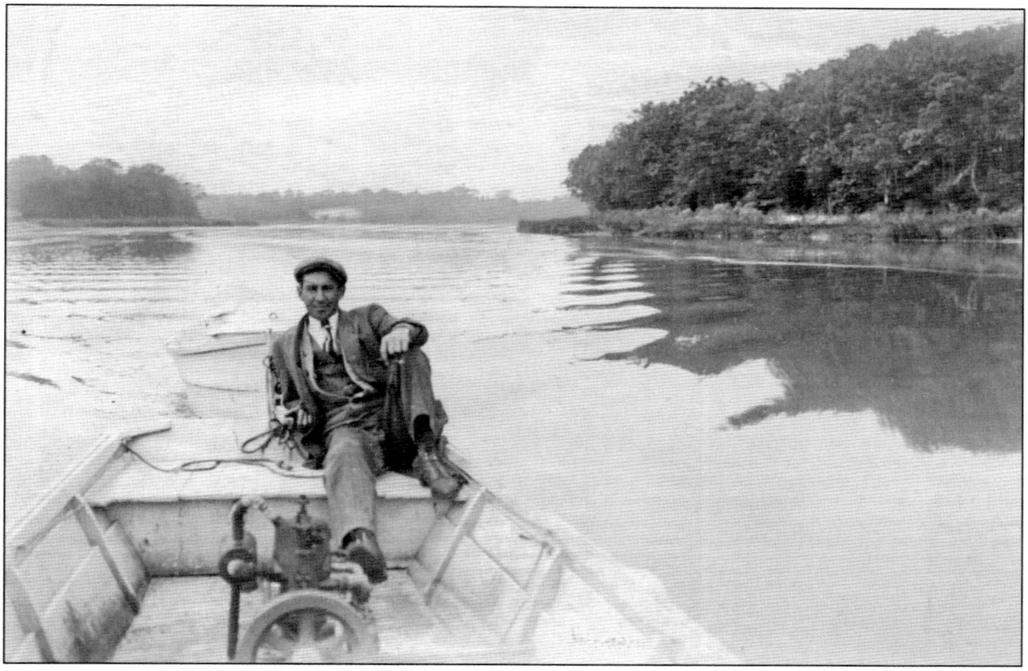

James A. Gildersleeve, c. 1910. Attracting summer boarders and bringing pleasure to local inhabitants were the resplendent waterways in and around Mattituck and Laurel: the Long Island Sound, with its lush wetlands, grassy dunes, and sandy beaches; and Mattituck Creek, with its peaceful ebb and flow of tidal waters. Here, James A. Gildersleeve leans back, cigar in hand, enjoying a cruise down Mattituck Creek with another boat in tow. Native American clans used the creek, with a brief canoe portage, as a passageway between the Long Island Sound and the Great Peconic Bay. Before the inlet was dredged, Mattituck Creek was also a winter wonderland, and taking a horse-drawn sled over the frozen creek from the foot of Love Lane to the picturesque Old Mill on a frigid winter's night was a pleasant and memorable trip. (MLL.)

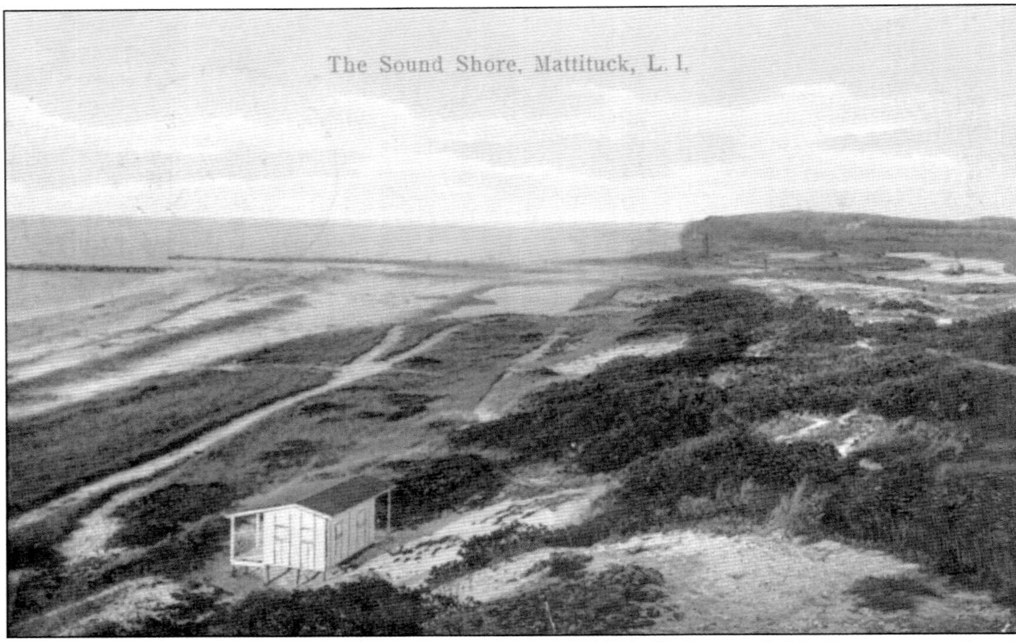

Sound Shore, c. 1910. Looking east from Captain Kidd's hill, the sandy bluffs are covered with vegetation. There were hundreds of beach plum bushes in this area at the time. In mid-August, people flocked here to pick beach plums, which they made into wonderful jam. A few local businessmen had cabins built on the sound shore for camping in the summer and hunting in the winter. (MLL.)

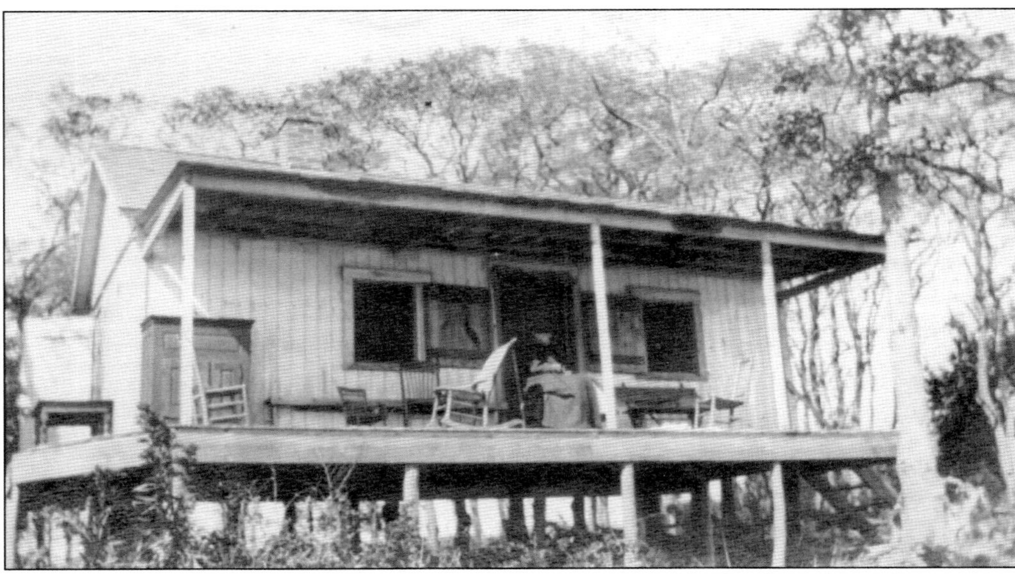

William V. Duryee's Cabin, 1916. The Duryee cabin was used by family and friends for outings on the beach in the spring and summer, and also as a hunting cabin in the winter duck season. Game was plentiful. In 1880, before there was any consciousness of conservation, Gilbert Howell of Mattituck reportedly shot 425 ducks in one winter season. (MLL.)

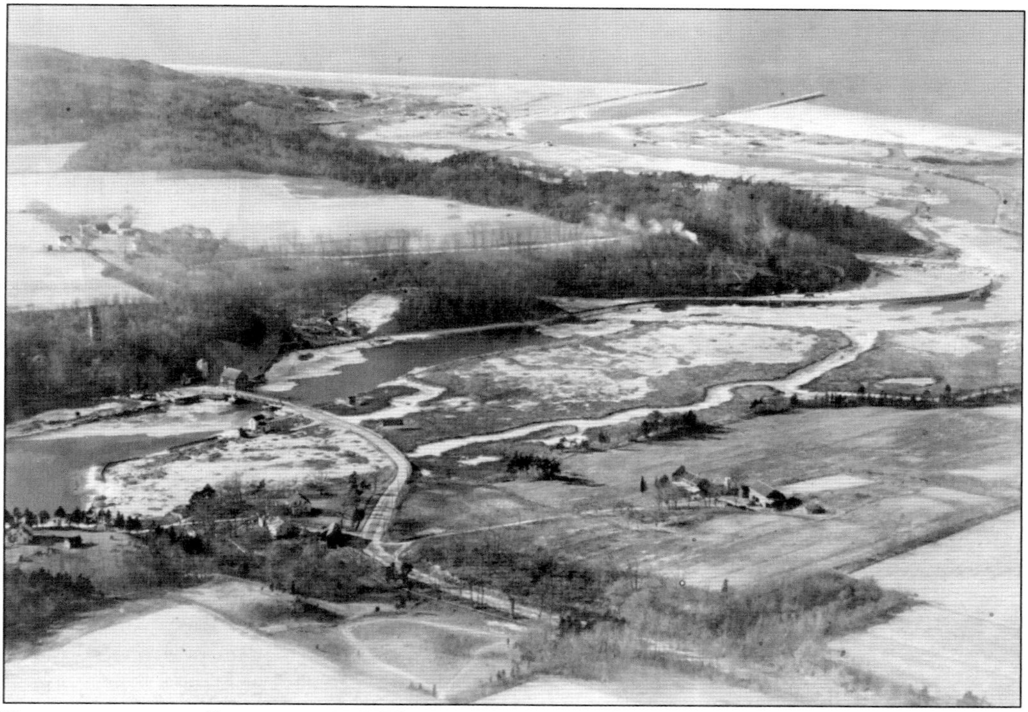

Breakwater and Creek, c. 1935. This view west towards the breakwater shows the iron bridge crossing Mattituck Creek from East Mill Road to the Old Mill tavern. The rotating iron bridge was demolished in April 1955 as part of a plan to have the creek dredged. (Courtesy of the Suffolk County Historical Society.)

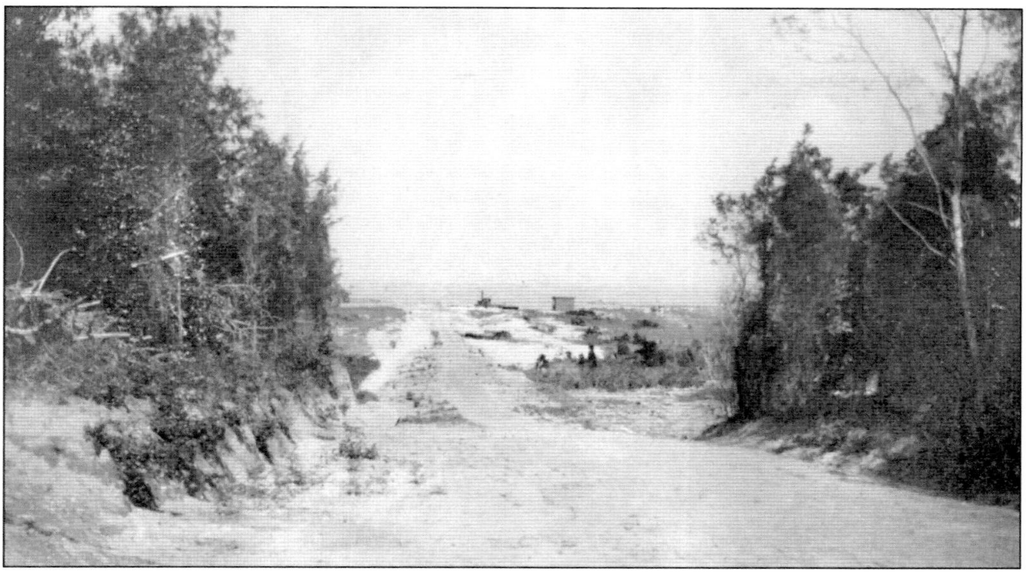

Breakwater Road, c. 1910. Breakwater Road was designated a public road on September 5, 1907. Andrew J. Cox requested a road be laid out through his property from Cox Neck Road to the west side of the Mattituck Creek Inlet at the Long Island Sound. Early roads were just dirt paths that cut through surrounding woods and farmland. (Courtesy of Michael J. Montgomery.)

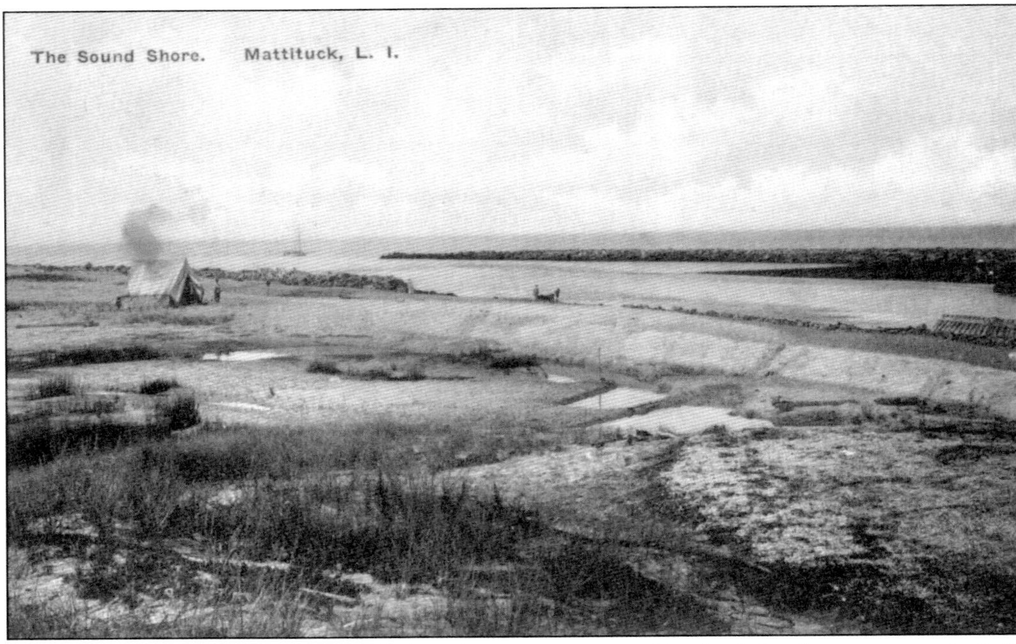

Mattituck Breakwater, 1910. The breakwater was created by the federal government in 1903 by building two stone jetties across the mouth of the inlet to prevent wind and tide from filling the entrance with sand, and to provide safe harbor for boats and pleasure craft. (Courtesy of the Cutchogue-New Suffolk Library.)

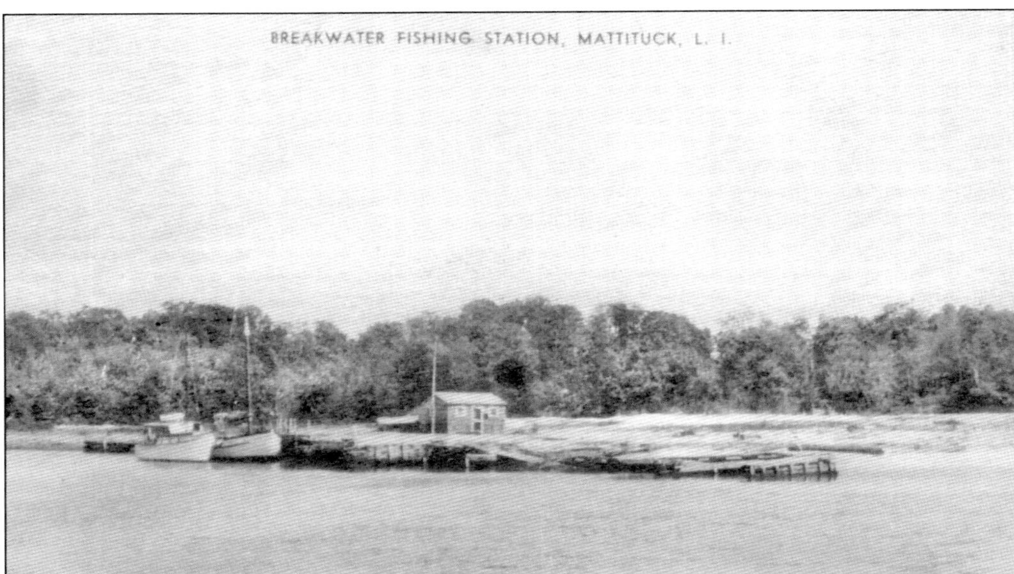

Breakwater Fishing Station, c. 1945. The breakwater was a prime location for bountiful fishing. This breakwater fishing station was owned by Frank Husak from about 1940 until 1962. All species of fish were plentiful: porgies, blackfish, and blowfish by the bushel at the inlet and flounder off the fishing station dock. (MLL.)

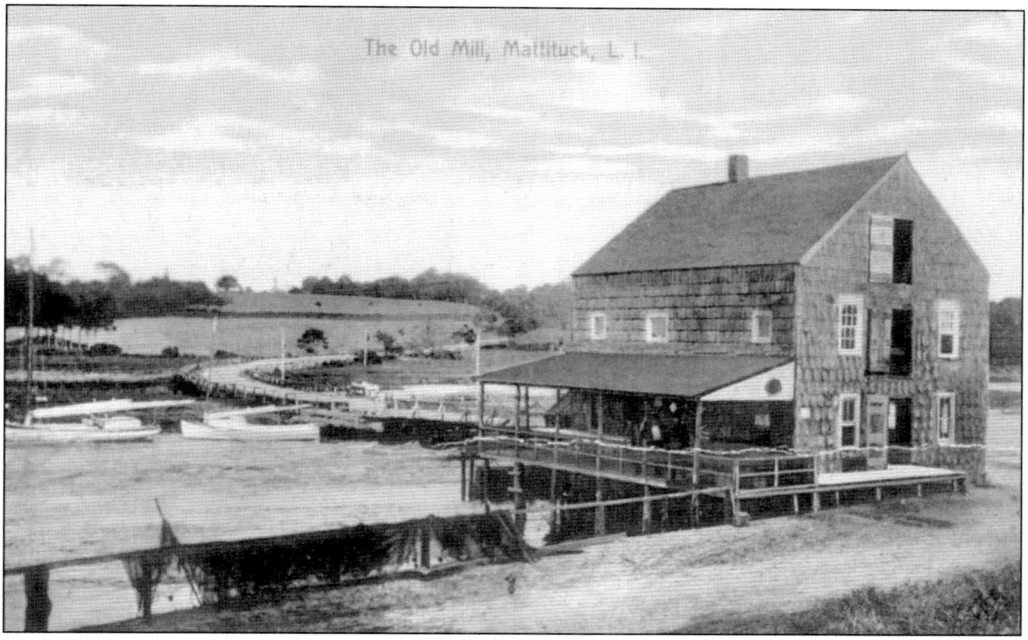

THE OLD MILL, c. 1900. The Old Mill on Mattituck Inlet was a gristmill that opened in 1821 and used the force of the tide as its power. A stone dam was built across the inlet to capture the incoming tide and channel it through huge gates to turn the mill wheel. The dam was later removed and replaced with the wooden bridge seen in this postcard. (MLL.)

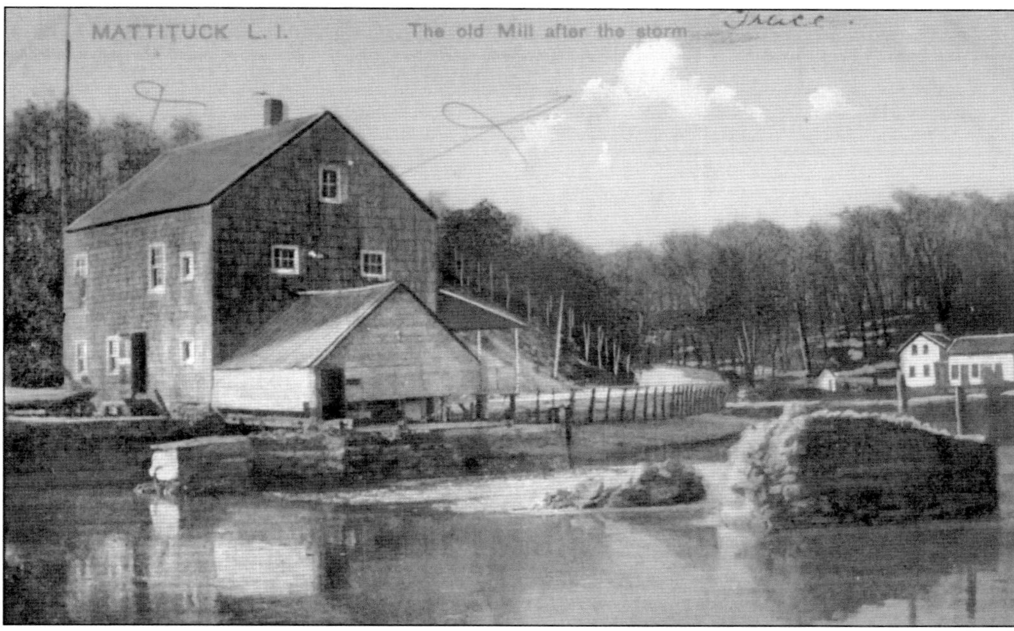

THE OLD MILL AFTER A STORM, 1906. In its peak period, around 1850, the mill worked all through the day and night. It was operated for 50 years by Joshua Terry, until his death in 1905. The farmer's grist was raised to the second floor and then fed into a hopper where two flat stones ground the grist into flour. A 1906 storm washed the wooden bridge from its foundations. (MLL.)

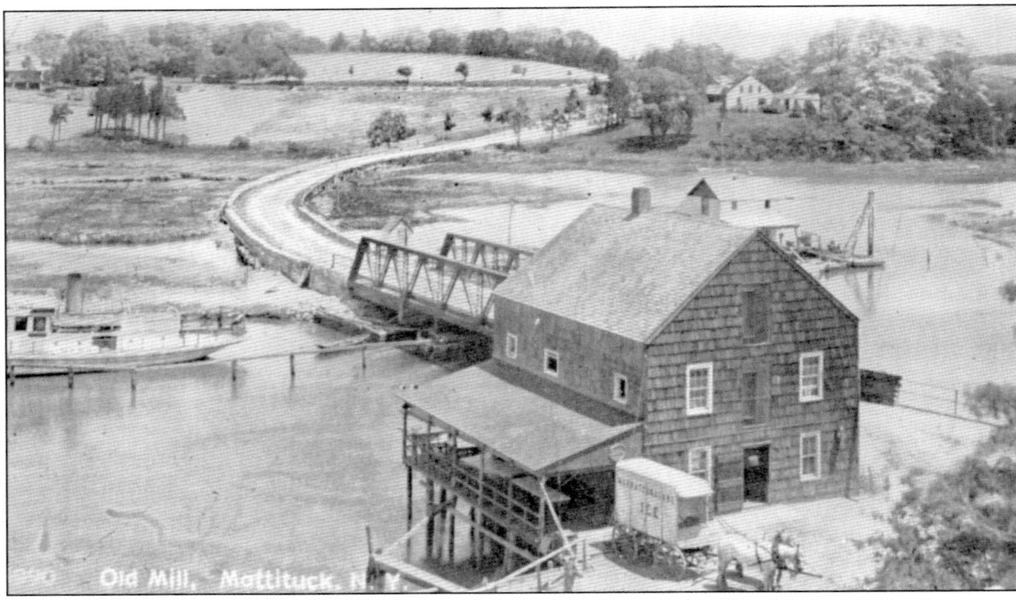

Swivel Bridge, c. 1910. The mill was sold to beverage wholesalers Yether and Moore and became a beer tavern. It was known to locals as the "grist mill that became a gin mill." About 1910, the town installed this iron bridge, which spanned the inlet and could swivel on a base in order to allow boats through. Charles Wickham's Marratooka Lake Ice wagon is pulled up in the foreground to make a delivery. (MLL.)

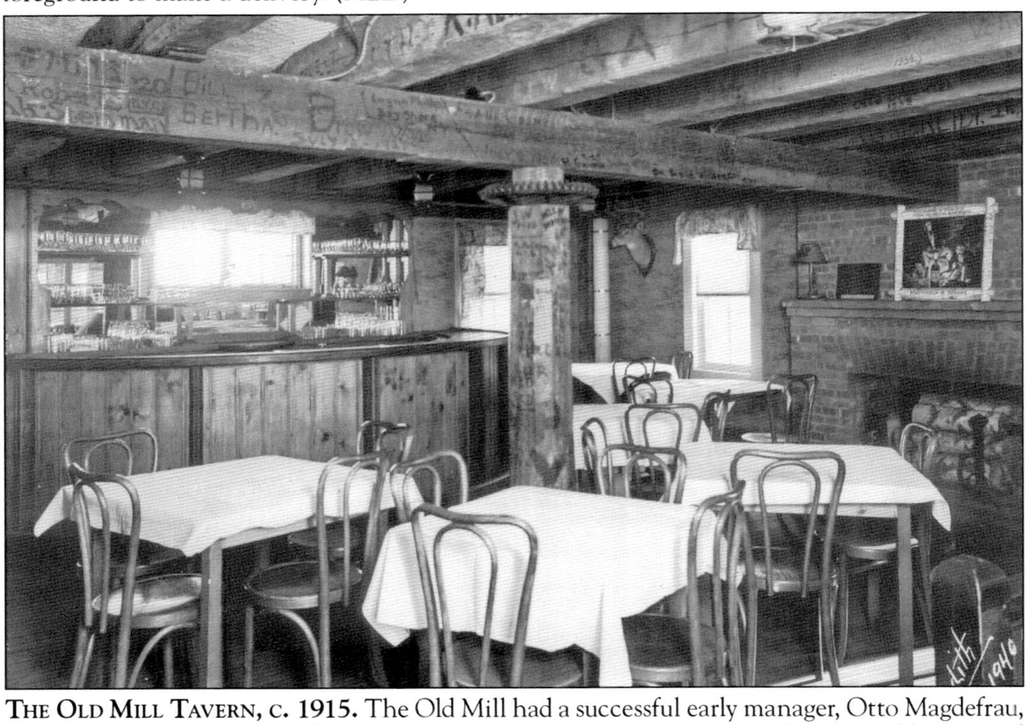

The Old Mill Tavern, c. 1915. The Old Mill had a successful early manager, Otto Magdefrau, who originated the custom of patrons signing their names in lipstick on the exposed beams and wooden shingles of the building. (Courtesy of Michael J. Montgomery.)

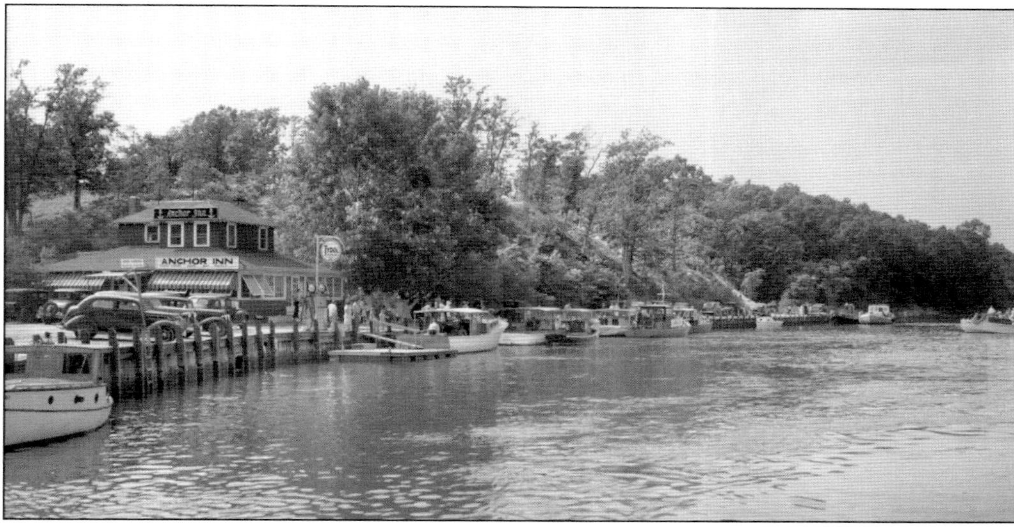

THE ANCHOR INN, c. 1945. When the Anchor Inn opened in 1938, boaters and fishermen anchored for a surf and turf meal and fine cocktails at the bar. Stephen Duke recalls pulling fresh oysters from the creek and bringing them to the Anchor Inn, where Chet, the bartender, opened them for Duke and Harold Wilsberg to enjoy with cold glasses of beer on tap. Unfortunately, a fire destroyed the popular restaurant in 1979. (Courtesy of the Queens Borough Public Library, Long Island Division, Postcard Collection.)

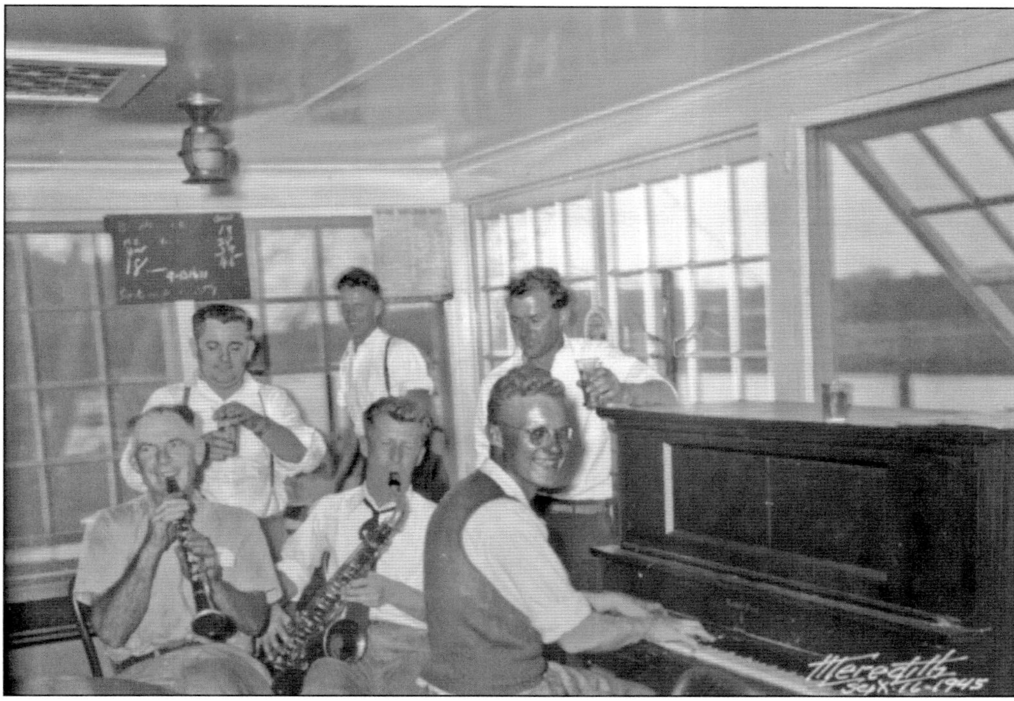

LOCAL ORCHESTRA, 1945. This local orchestra played Glenn Miller and Tommy Dorsey tunes for the pleasure of patrons at the Anchor Inn. Seated second from the left is "Ritz" Domalski, at the piano is Chester Swastinowicz, and standing behind him is John Elak. The Anchor Inn also provided entertainment on Saturday nights. (Courtesy of the Southold Historical Society.)

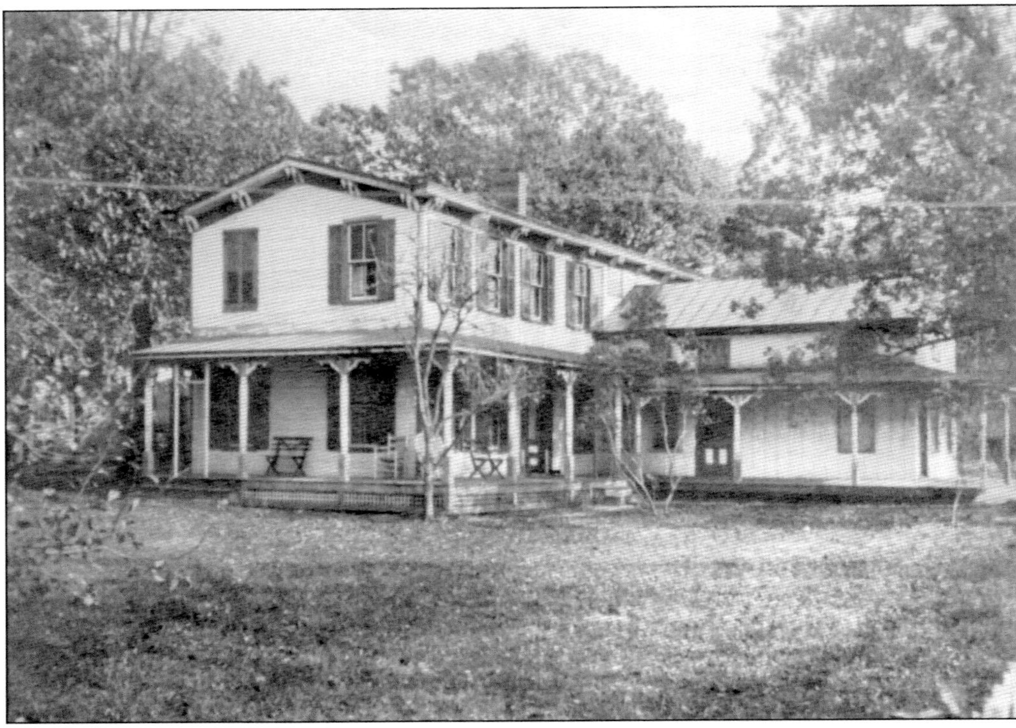

Old Colonial Inn, c. 1925. About 1920, Tyson L. and Arabella Hamilton purchased the Anniston and renamed it the Old Colonial Inn, making it a year-round boardinghouse that could accommodate 28 people. They served freshly caught fish, vegetables from their own garden, and fresh eggs, milk, and cream came from local farms. (Courtesy of Marilyn Gatz.)

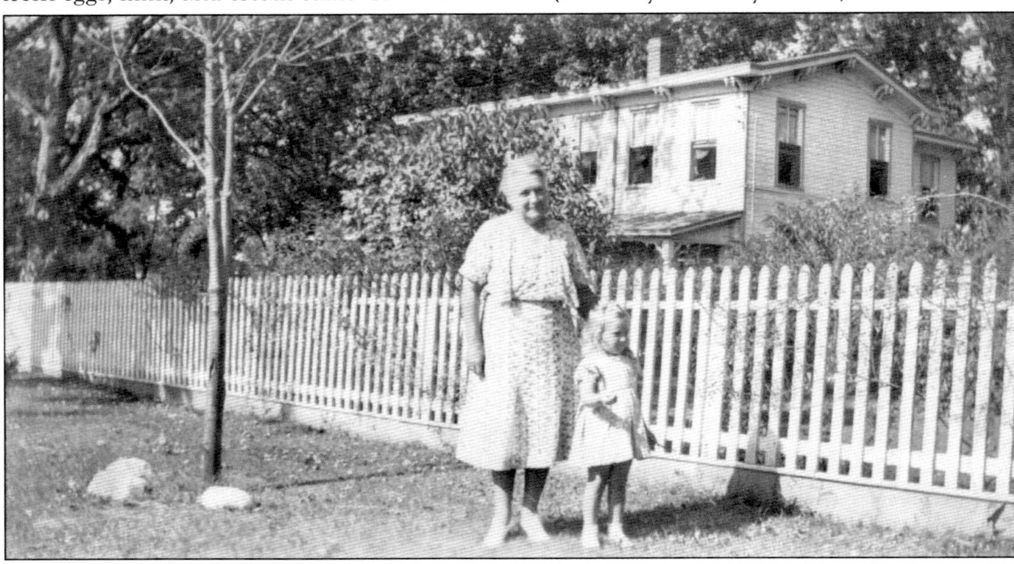

Arabella Hamilton. The Hamiltons ran the Old Colonial Inn on Mattituck Bay for many years. Arabella Wyckoff Hamilton was a descendent of Peter Wyckoff, one of the early Dutch settlers of Brooklyn. She is seen here in front of the inn with her granddaughter Marilyn (now Marilyn Gatz). (Courtesy of Marilyn Gatz.)

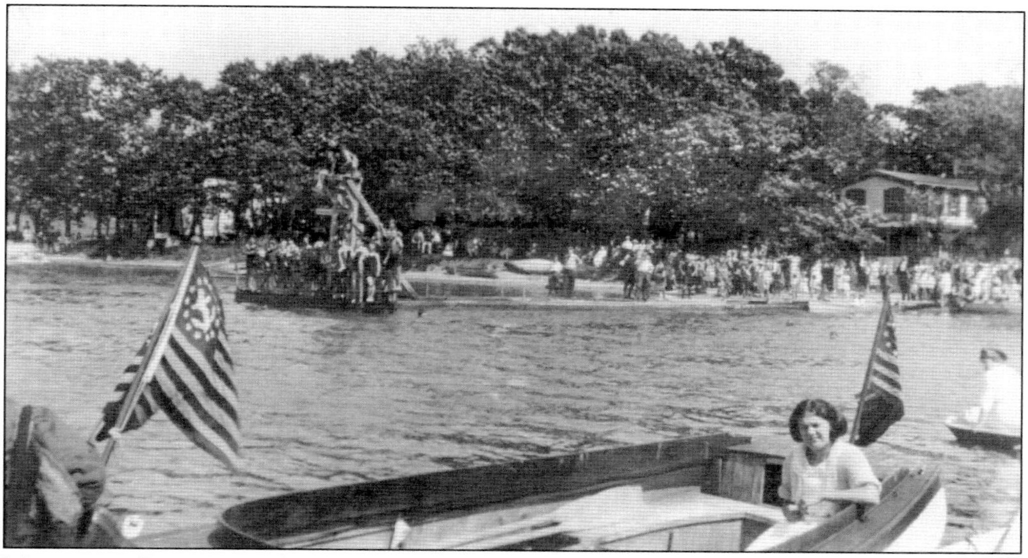

Mattituck Bay, 1921. The Old Colonial Inn (background, right) was at the end of Love Lane at the base of Mattituck Creek, which had been called Mattituck Bay, a popular site for swimming and boating events. The Mattituck Yacht Club Regatta took place there on August 19, 1921. Here, spectators crowd the floating dock and scale the diving pedestal to get a better view. (MLL.)

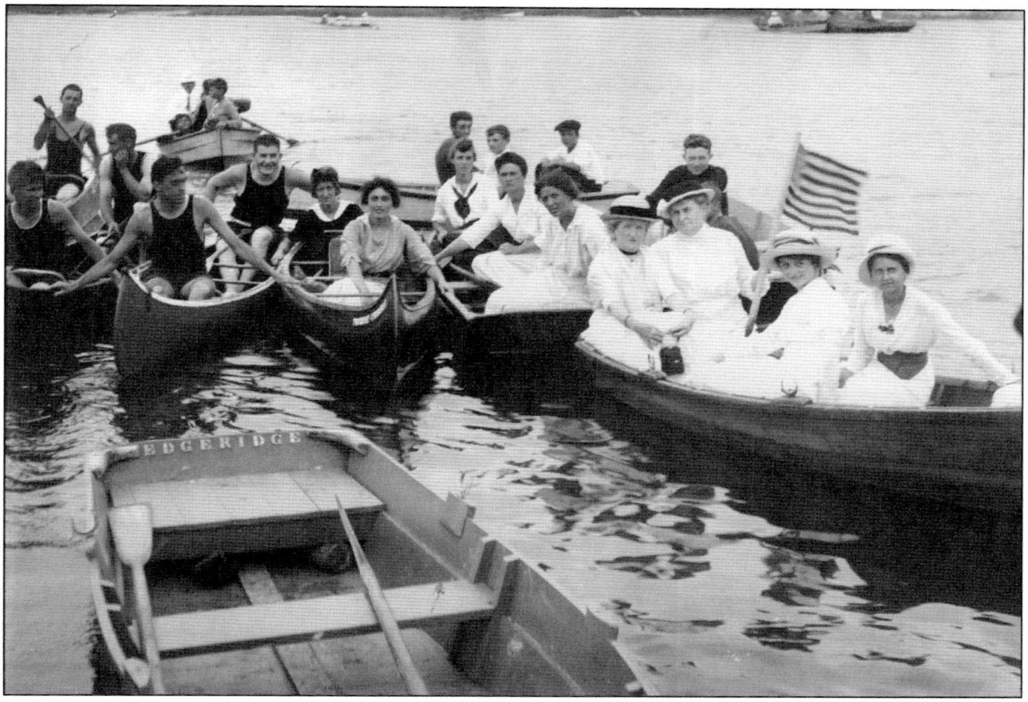

Contestants And Spectators, August 11, 1914. The Mattituck Yacht Club Regatta was a popular annual event. Most stores in town called it a holiday and closed for the afternoon. The young men on the left participated in the jousting contest. A crewman stood in the bow with a long punting pole while the other paddled. The object was to upset the opponent's canoe and crew in the joust. (Courtesy of Peter Kren.)

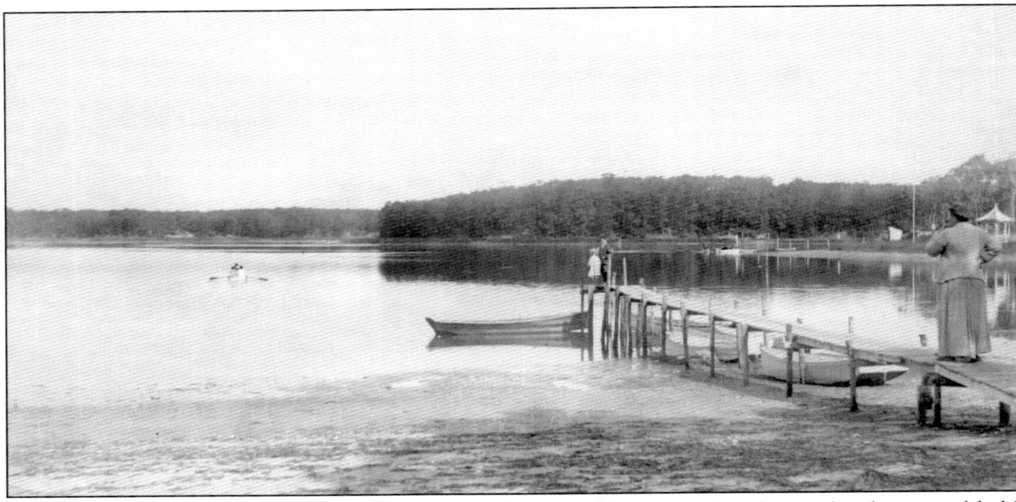

DOCK ON LOVE LANE, C. 1915. Before the creek was dredged to a significant depth, it would ebb and flow dramatically with the tide. This is the dock at the end of Love Lane on what was known as Mattituck Bay (Mattituck Creek) when the tide was low. When the tide rose, one could easily board the boats, which would then be at the level of the dock. (MLL.)

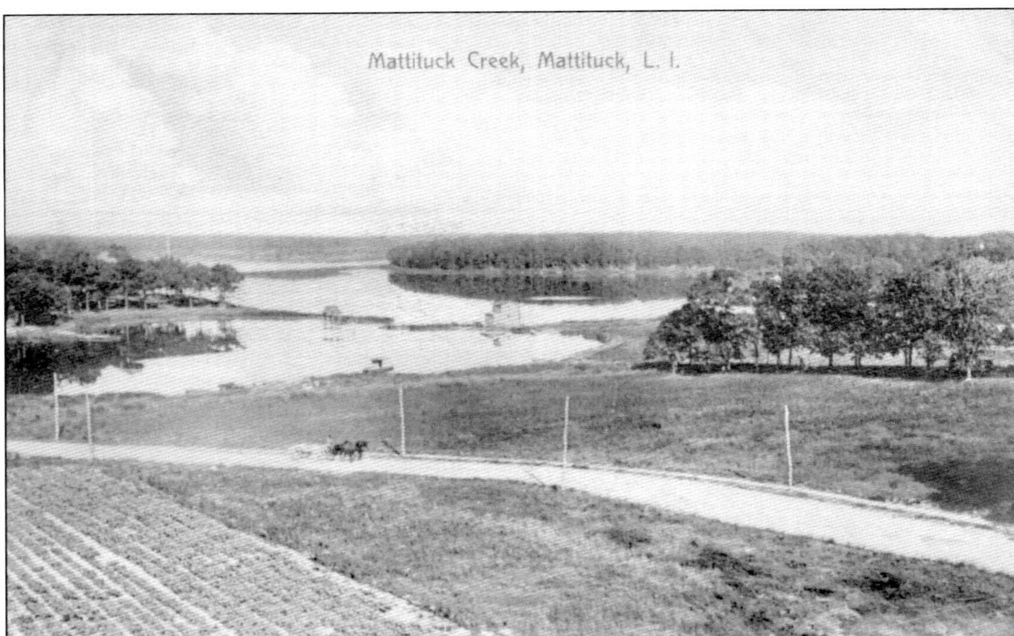

THE COVE, C. 1910. The southwest corner of Mattituck Creek, between the oyster house and the Westphalia Avenue Bridge, was known as the Cove. The Mattituck Oyster Company, which owned the white processing house seen here, had been formed to propagate the culture of oysters in Mattituck Creek. The removal of the tide gates from the Old Mill helped to make cultivation very successful. Oyster beds had been established as early as 1882. (MLL.)

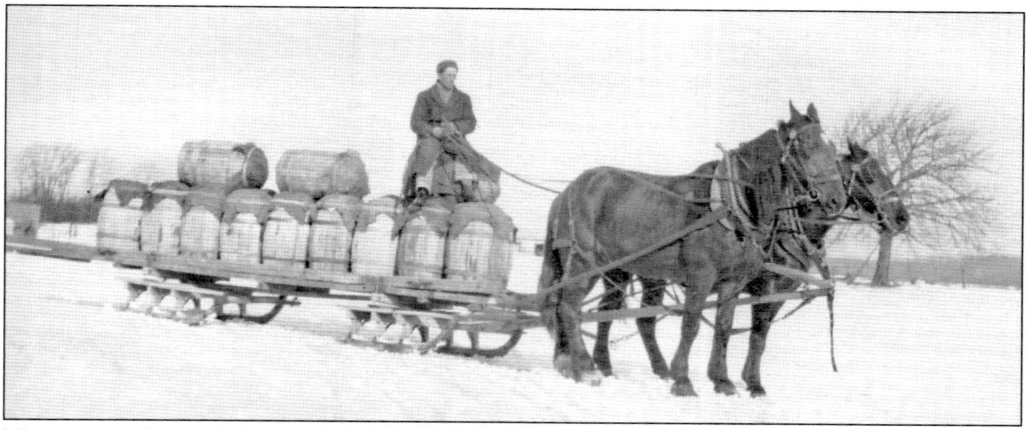

MATTITUCK CREEK OYSTERS, 1916. Mattituck Creek oysters had a well-established reputation for their superior quality and fine flavor. There was a large demand for them from the best restaurants and most famous hotels in New York City. Here, Henry Delaney, a driver for the Mattituck Oyster Company, transports barrels of oysters to the railroad depot for delivery to the city on March 2, 1916. (MLL.)

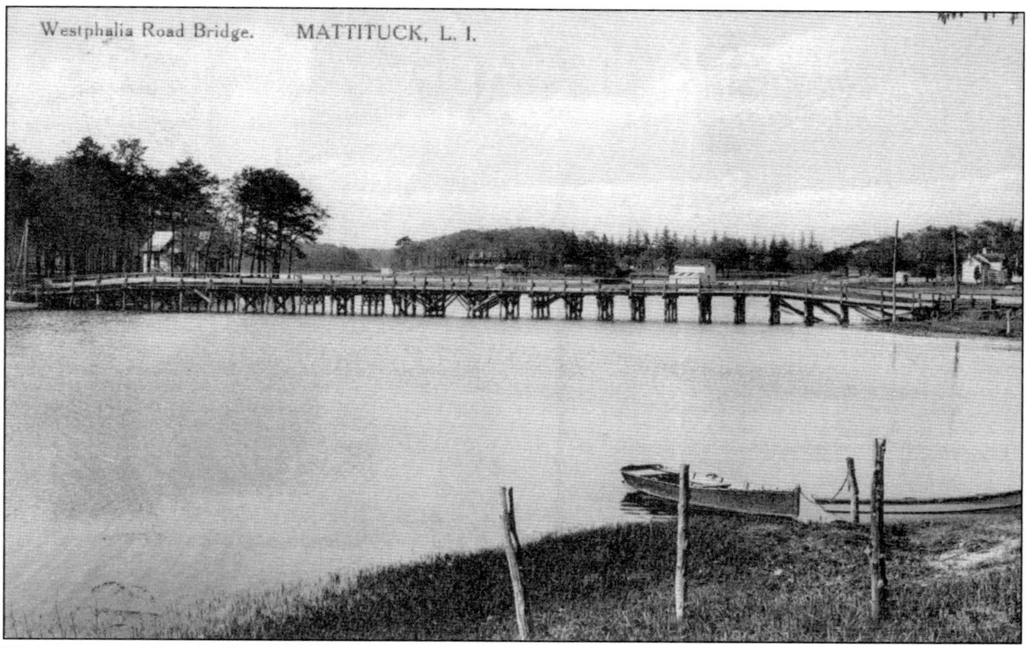

WESTPHALIA ROAD BRIDGE, C. 1910. In 1885, Frank Moore Lupton bought the property on the southwest portion of Mattituck Creek, known as Southard's Point, and built a grand home there. Lupton wanted a quicker route to his home from Mattituck village, so he had a wooden bridge built over the creek. The Town of Southold rebuilt the bridge in 1918, but the county demolished it in 1958 after filling in that part of the creek with dredged material. (Courtesy of the Cutchogue-New Suffolk Library.)

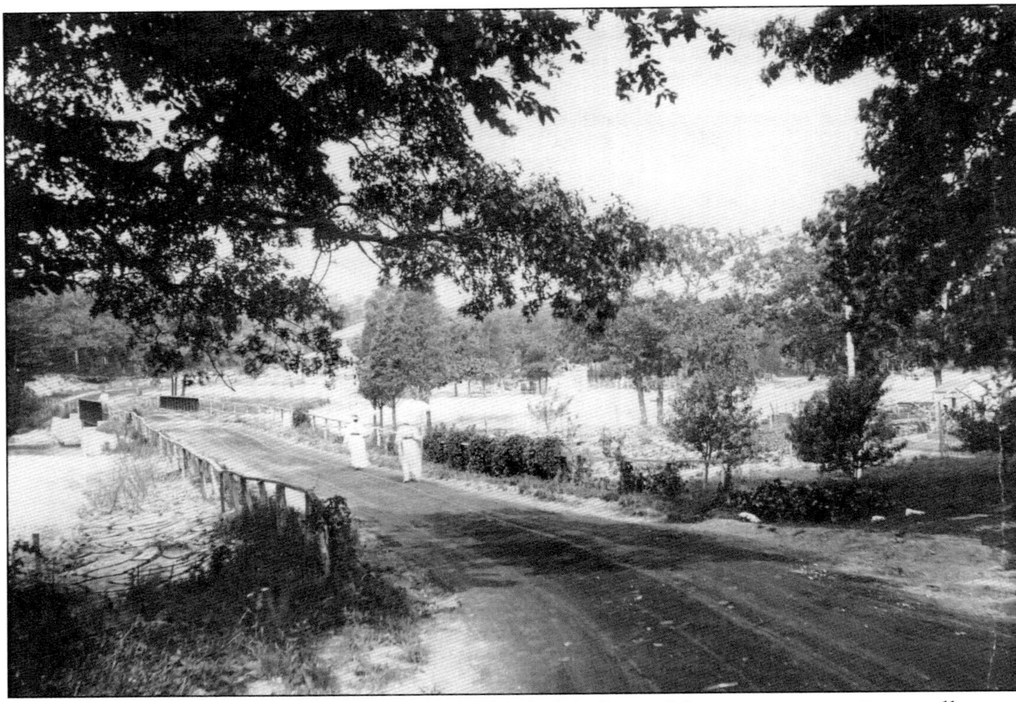

Entrance to Long Creek Bridge, 1913. Two ladies dressed for a summer outing stroll across the Long Creek Bridge. The road and bridge were opened in 1866 to connect with East Mill Road to the north. The road was originally called Howell Avenue because it ran through the property of Isaac Howell. (MLL.)

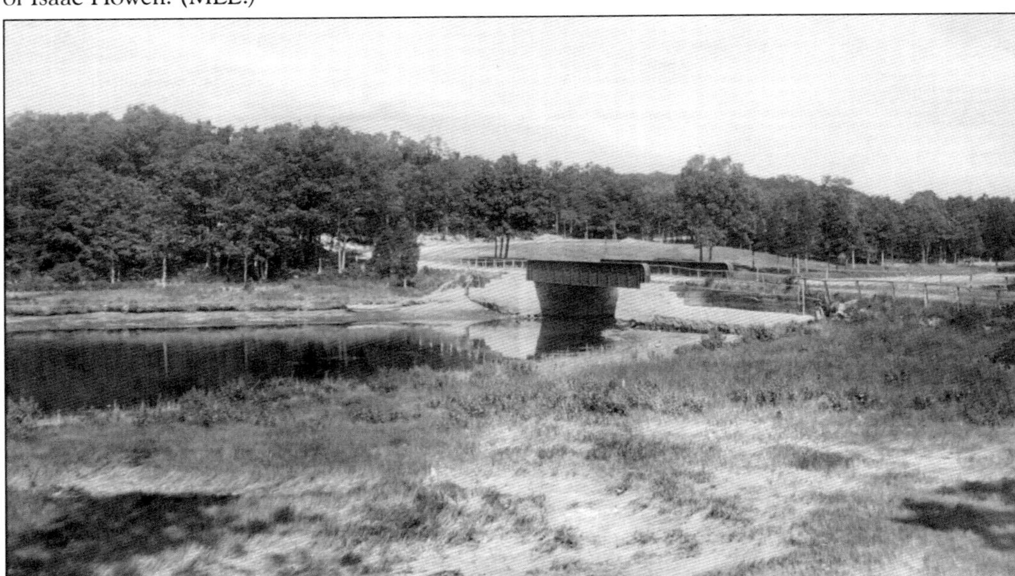

Long Creek Bridge, 1913. In 1884, the wooden bridge across Long Creek became unsafe after Patrick McNulty went through the deck with his horse and wagon. A proposal was made the following year to replace the old wooden bridge with a new iron bridge. The iron bridge lasted until 1973, when the new Grand Avenue Bridge was constructed. (MLL.)

Three

Lakes, Ponds, and Bay

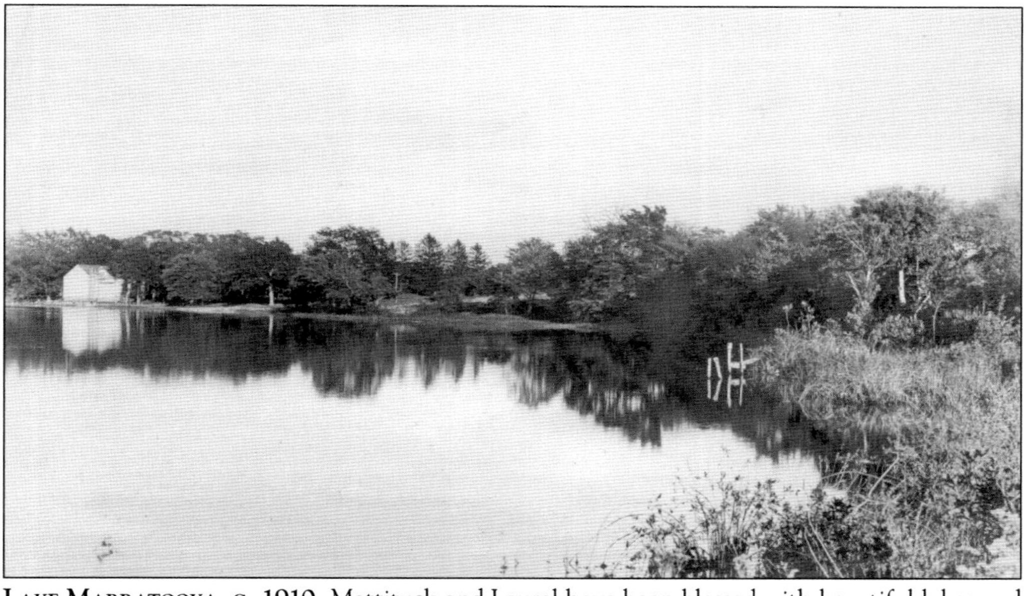

Lake Marratooka, c. 1910. Mattituck and Laurel have been blessed with beautiful lakes and ponds fed by underground water sources. Lake Marratooka has been a scenic location for boating and bird-watching, especially during winter migration, when flocks of geese descend upon the lake as well as species of ducks, including such regulars as the green-winged teal, American wigeon, bufflehead, and ring-necked duck. Laurel Lake, which holds some of the clearest pond water on Long Island, is stocked with trout for fine fishing. Wolf Pit Lake is a secluded pond in northern Mattituck on the road to Oregon, where one can enjoy tranquil communication with nature. On the south shore of the North Fork lies the glimmering tidal estuary of Great Peconic Bay, which Long Island poet Walt Whitman remembered for "the soothing rustle of the waves, and the saline smell—boyhood's times, the clam-digging, barefoot, and with trowsers roll'd up—hauling down the creek—the perfume of the sedge-meadows—the hay-boat, and the chowder and fishing excursions." (MLL.)

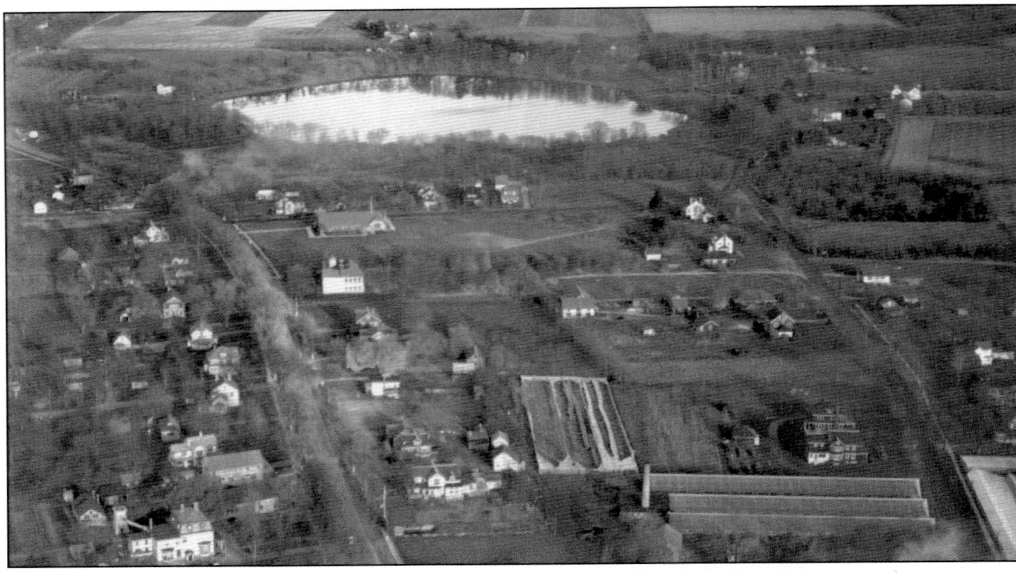

Lake Marratooka, 1938. The lake is formed from a glacial kettle hole of 24 acres, whose greatest depth is 20 feet. Originally known as Dekon Reves's pond during the Revolutionary War era, it later became known as Mattituck Lake. Charles W. Wickham gave the lake the euphonious name of Marratooka, at first a variation of Mattituck written as Marritook, and the name eventually settled into its current form. (Courtesy of Mike Richter Photography.)

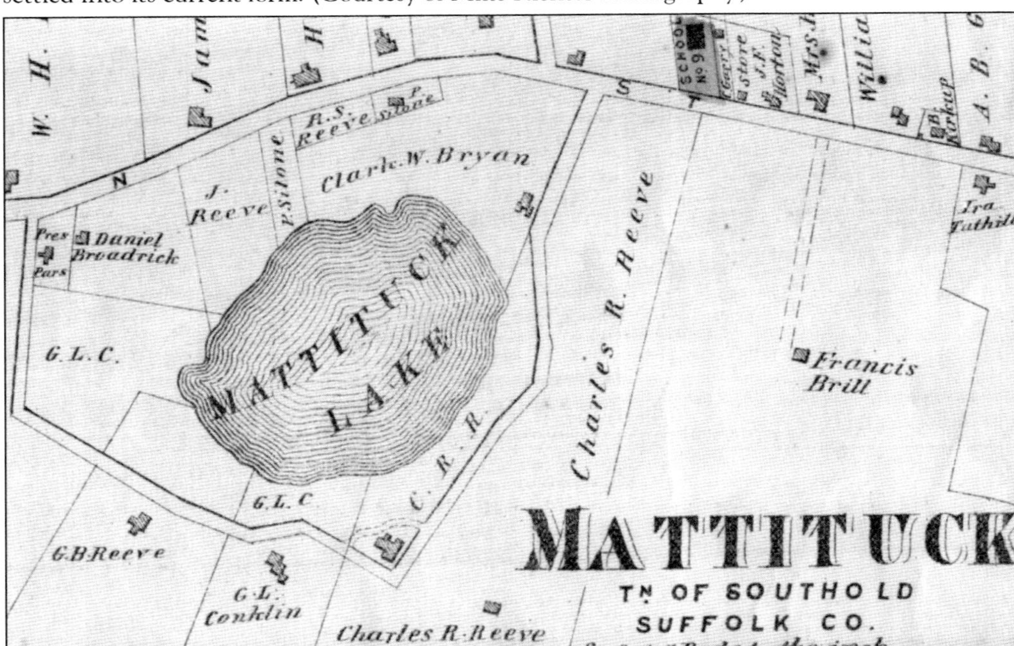

Beers Atlas, 1873. In 1778, about 1,000 British troops were encamped from the west shore of Marratooka Lake, then called Mattituck Lake, through the present library property of the Reeve farm. Officers were quartered on the north side of the lake. The invading troops were ordered to cease burning fences as firewood and prohibited from shooting firearms near the encampment. (MLL.)

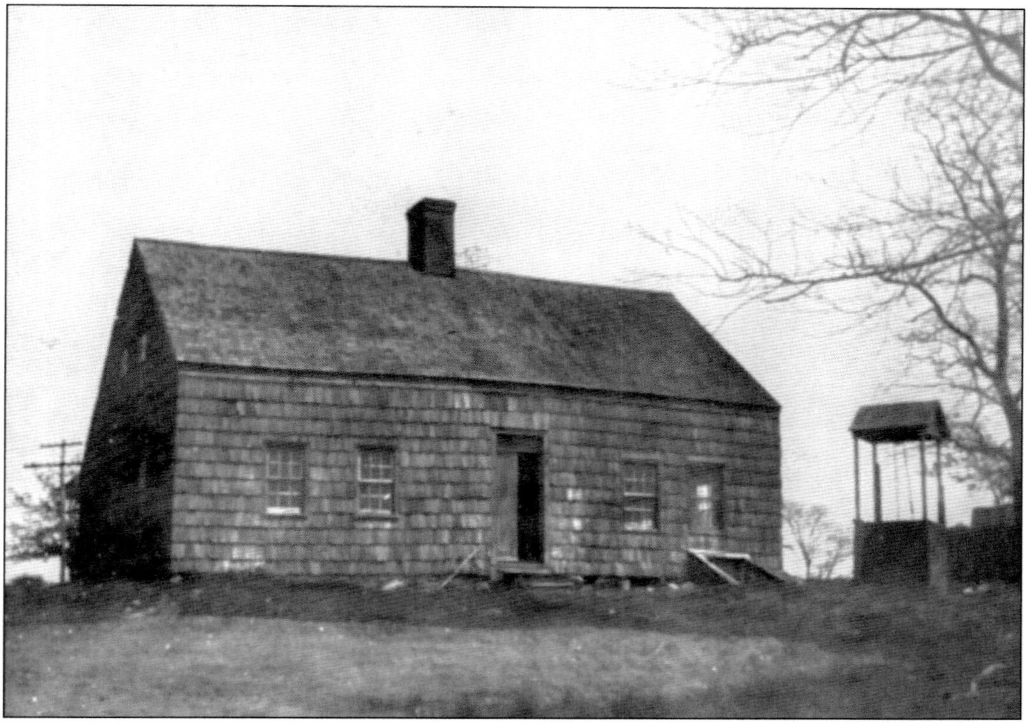

ELYMAS REEVE HOUSE, C. 1900. Elymas Reeve, a slave on the farm of James Wickham Reeve, became a free man in 1813 at the age of 29. He managed the Wickham farm and later became an official of the Cutchogue Presbyterian Church. In 1849, Elymas and his wife, Hagar, moved into their daughter Parthenia's house (pictured) on the north side of Marratooka Lake. (Courtesy of the Suffolk County Historical Society.)

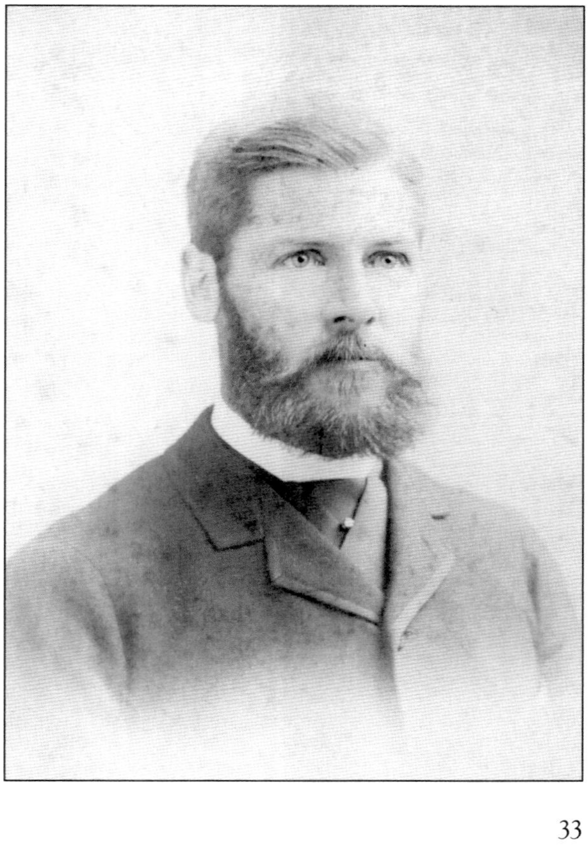

CHARLES WORTH WICKHAM, C. 1890. In 1876, Charles Wickham, a graduate of Cornell University, established the Marratooka Farm on 200 acres that extended from Marratooka Lake to the bay. The farm contained a herd of Jersey cows, Chester shoats, 25 Southdown ewes, 7 horses, and 300 chickens. The creamery, aided by a state-of-the-art steam engine, produced 500 pounds of Marratooka Butter, which was shipped to the finest metropolitan hotels. (MLHS.)

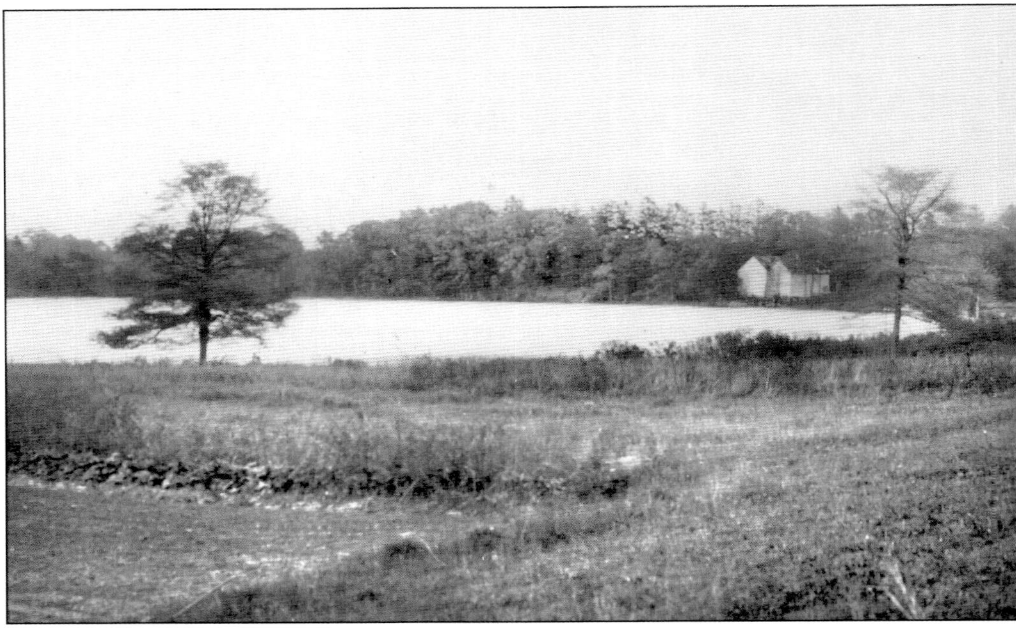

Wickham Icehouse, c. 1900. In 1878, Wickham built a large icehouse on the east side of Marratooka Lake. Blocks of ice were cut from the frozen lake, then floated into a cradle at the icehouse, lifted by horses, and slid into tiers in the house. Icehouses were insulated with sawdust and salt hay, a seashore grass good for insulation because it did not crumble or spoil if it became damp. George Fischer of Pike Street also had an icehouse on the north side of the lake. (MLL.)

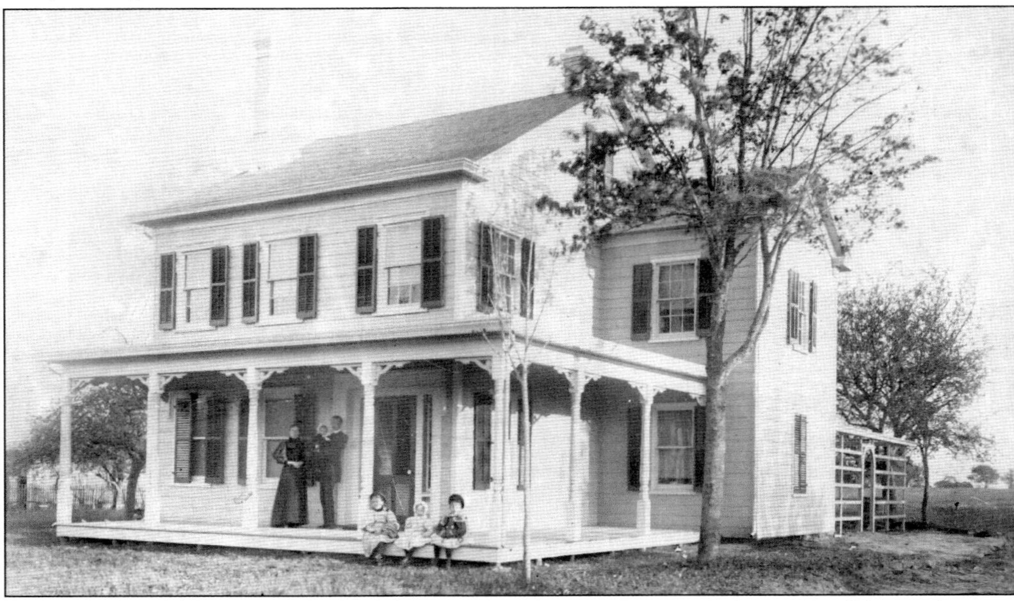

Presbyterian Parsonage, c. 1910. Rev. Charles E. Craven, DD, was the pastor of the Presbyterian church in Mattituck from 1895 to 1913. Reverend Craven lived with his family in the parsonage near Marratooka Lake. Elberta Hudson Reeve remembered, "Dr. Craven had a vegetable garden at the shore of Marratooka Lake. We always remarked that he said his prayers and got his sermon together on his knees in the garden." The house had been built by Andrew Gildersleeve. (MLL.)

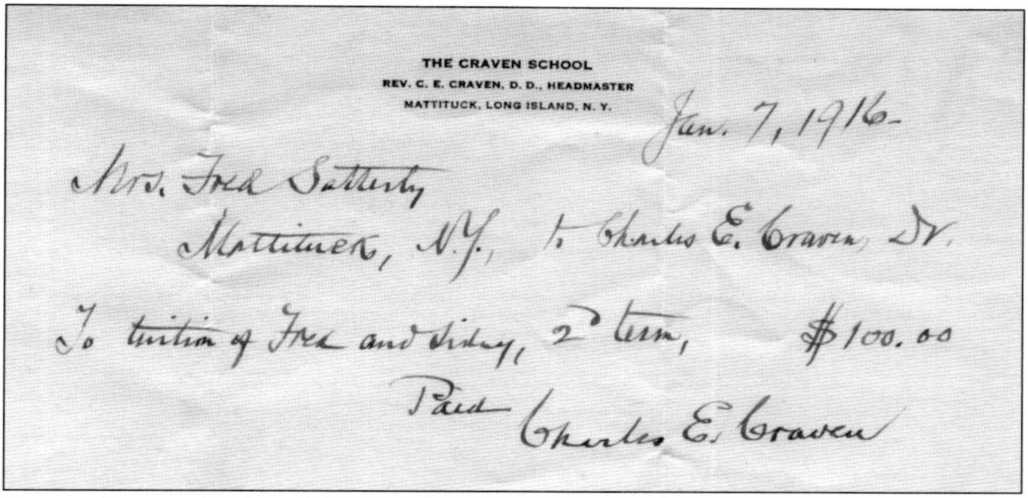

THE CRAVEN SCHOOL
REV. C. E. CRAVEN, D. D., HEADMASTER
MATTITUCK, LONG ISLAND, N. Y.

Jan. 7, 1916-

Mrs. Fred Satterly
Mattituck, N.Y., to Charles E. Craven, Dr.

To tuition of Fred and Sidney, 2d term, $100.00

Paid Charles E. Craven

CRAVEN SCHOOL, 1916. In 1913, Rev. Charles Craven opened a boarding school for boys across the lake, in the former residence of Charles W. Wickham. The Craven School, on four acres on Marratooka Lake, accepted boys from 12 years and upward, offering English, science, two languages, physical education (including boating and fishing on the lake), a darkroom for photography, and a wireless telegraph. (MLL.)

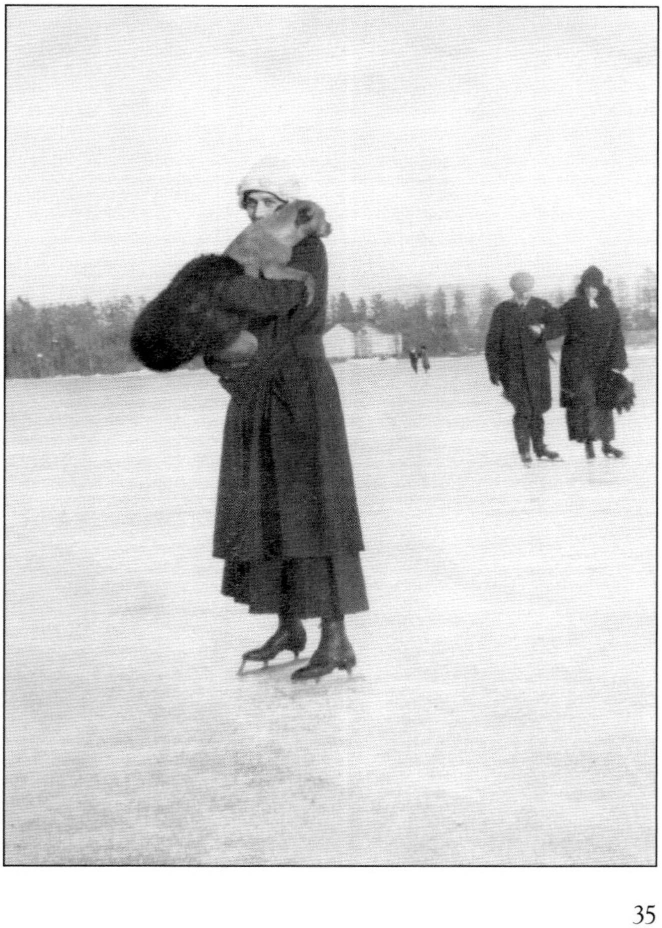

ICE-SKATING ON LAKE MARRATOOKA, 1917. An 87-year-old Gertrude Reeve Raynor reminisced: "Marratooka was the lake we wanted to skate on, but we couldn't go on that lake until Mr. Wickham said it was safe. When my father was a boy, the next door neighbor, the Brown boy, fell in. They got him out, but after that father always said, 'Not until Mr. Wickham says so.' " (MLL.)

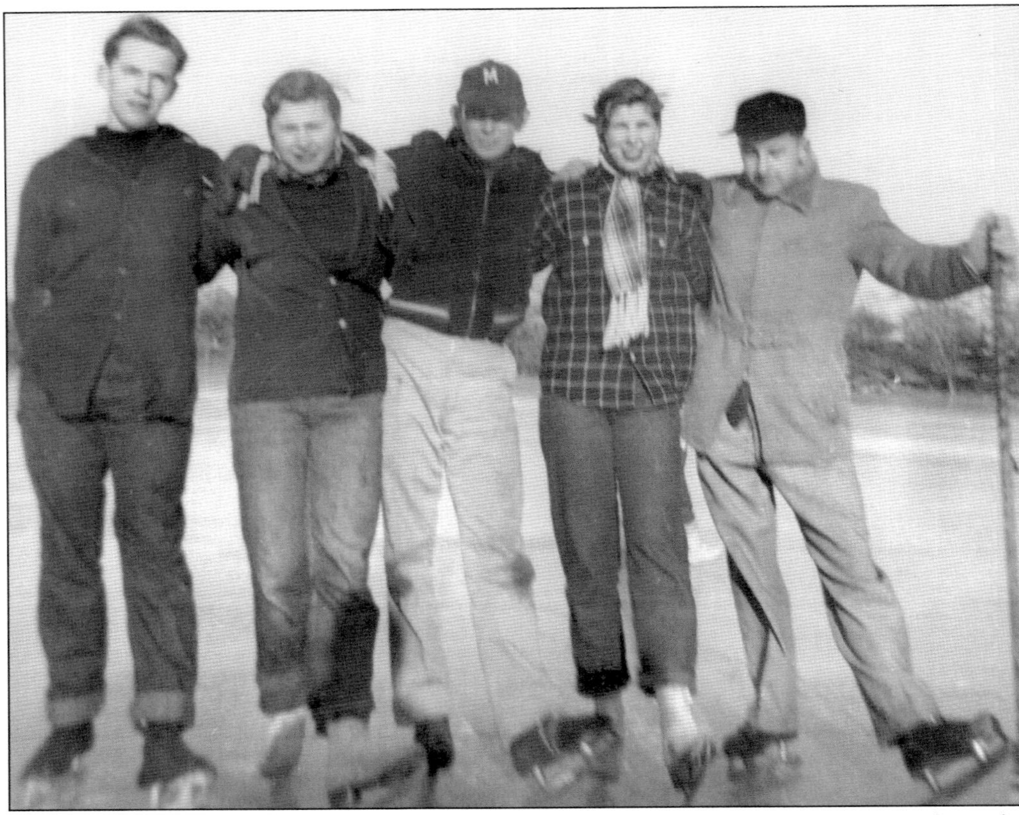

Ice-Skating on Lake Marratooka, 1954. Ice-skating on Marratooka Lake remained popular through the decades. Here, a spirited group of friends put their best feet forward while posing for the camera. From left to right, they are George Kaiser, Eleanor Wamback, Eddy Adams, Nancy Audioun, and Norman Wamback. (Courtesy of Norman Wamback.)

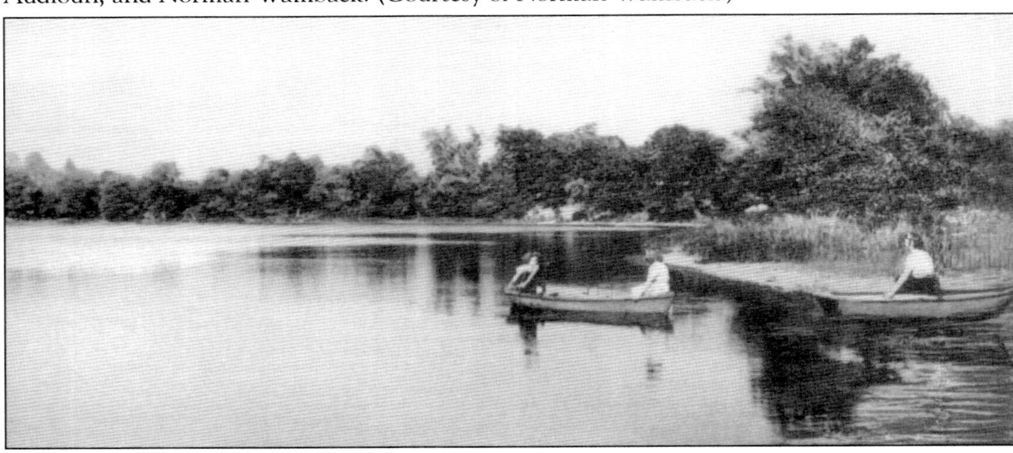

Boating on Lake Marratooka, c. 1920. The July 11, 1884, *Long Island Traveler* reports: "Miss Mamie Hayes, while rowing on Lake Marratooka, asked permission of one of the gentlemen to try her luck at angling. They gave her the poorest line 'to amuse and keep her quiet,' but great was their chagrin when at the first haul she landed a black bass that weighed four pounds. The average size for the Lake weigh two pounds." (MLL.)

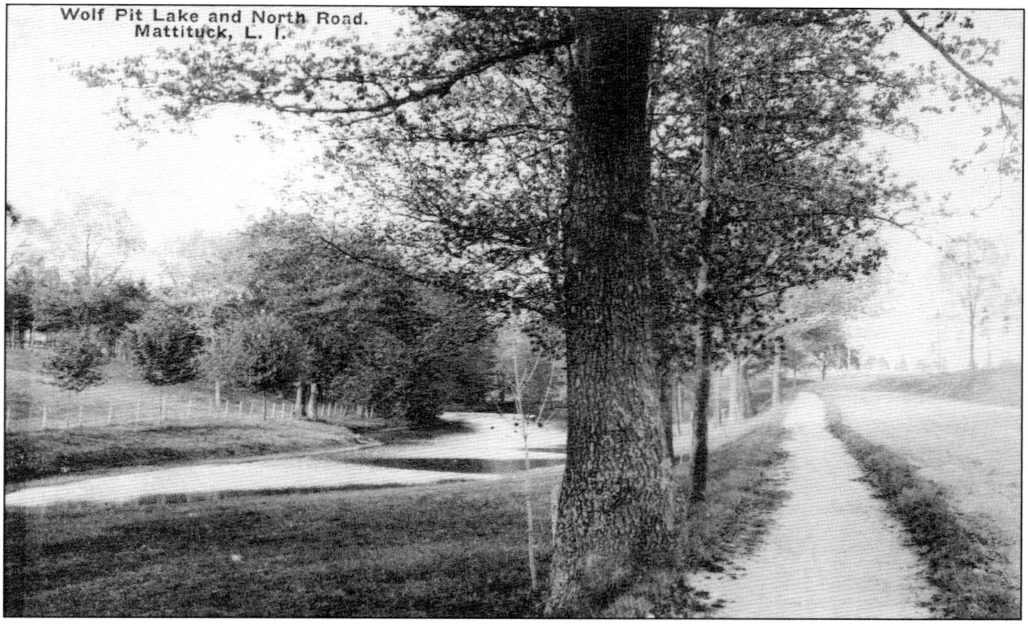

Wolf Pit Lake, 1900. The April 22, 1887, *Long Island Traveler* reports: "Capt. Ellsworth Tuthill has a large force of German laborers employed cleaning and digging out the pretty pond in front of his house. This pond and its adjacent swamp were always known as 'Wolf Pit Hollow' as it was a great place for wolves to make their lairs, and many have been killed there. The pond was full of gold and silver carp." (MLL.)

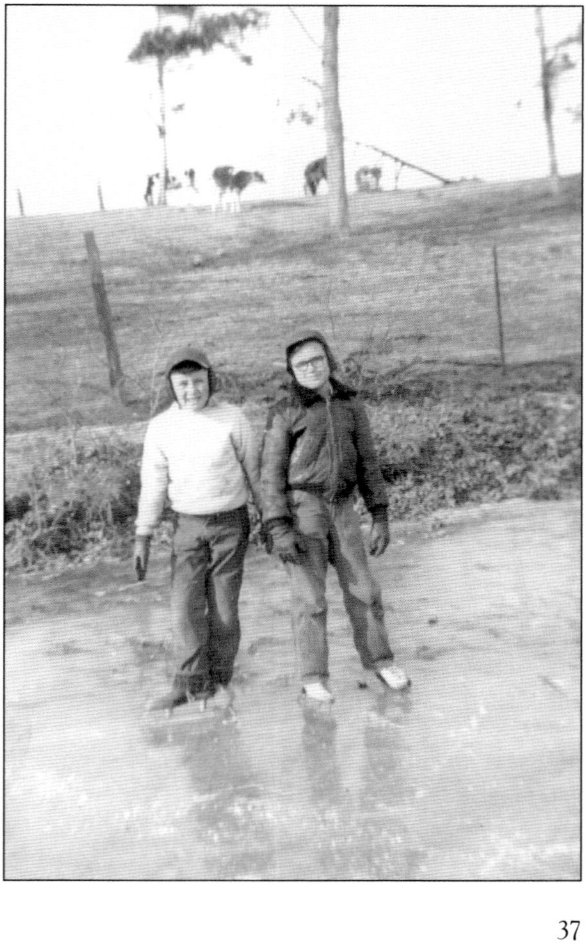

Skating on Wolf Pit Lake, 1952. Lloyd Stanley (left) and Jimmy McCarthy ice-skate on Wolf Pit Lake, with cows meandering on the hill behind. Judge Ralph W. Tuthill and his wife, Laura, donated the pond and the surrounding land to the Mattituck Park District in 1968. (Courtesy of Norman Wamback.)

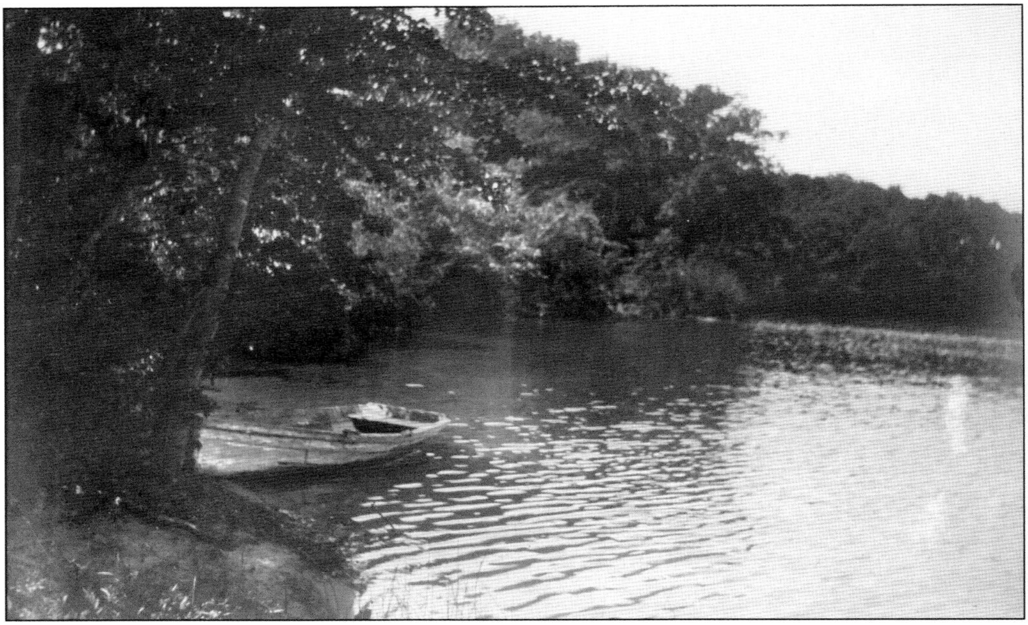

LAUREL LAKE, C. 1910. Laurel Lake is a freshwater lake formed by a glacier that once crept across Long Island. The 26-acre lake is 47 feet deep in the middle, stratifying in cold water from 13 to 18 feet down in summer, making it a favorable trout-fishing spot. With no inlet or outlet stream and almost no storm water runoff, Laurel Lake is one of the clearest freshwater bodies in the state. (MLL.)

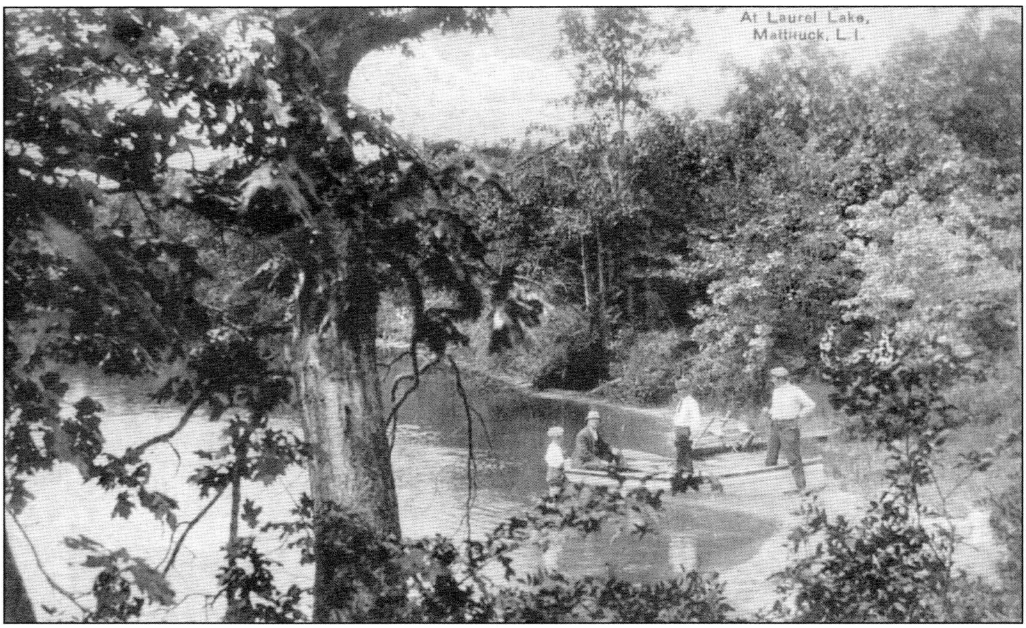

BOATING AT LAUREL LAKE, C. 1900. Laurel Lake contains pickerel, white and yellow perch, large- and smallmouth bass, sunfish, and brown bullheads. It is one of the few places on Long Island that has freshwater jellyfish. In July 1895, F. Vernon Corwin, L.C. Austin, Charles Longett, and Charles Nesbitt from Riverhead caught a black bass weighing five pounds. (MLL.)

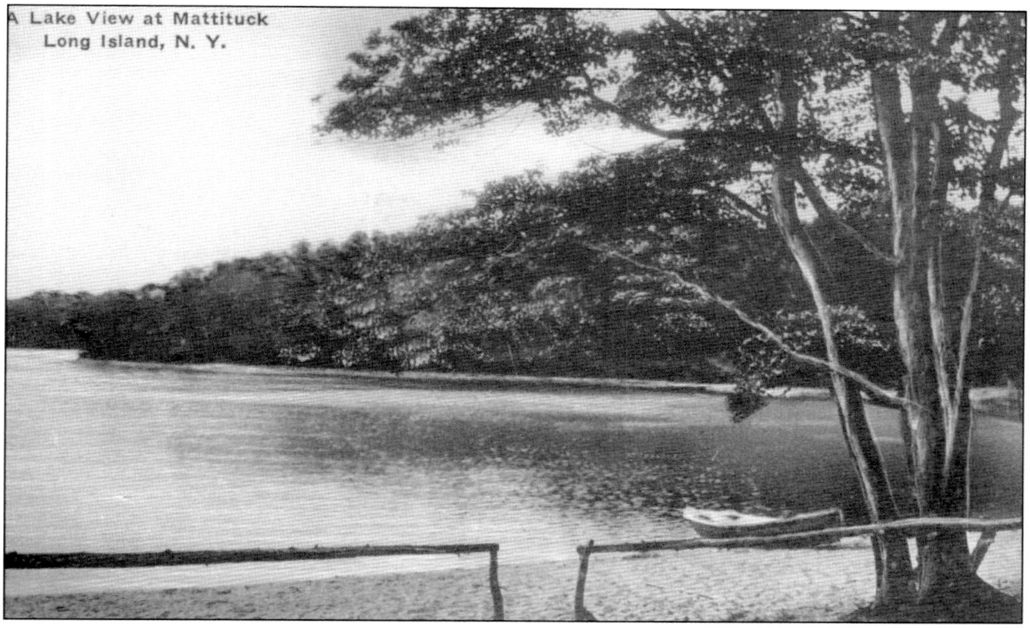

Laurel Lake View, c. 1930. Myron Young, a lifelong resident of Laurel whose father owned a farm on Laurel Lake, has fond memories of the lake as an adolescent in 1946. After a long day of work, his father would take him and the laborers to the lake, where they would take off their work clothes and go for a dip. There was not any thought of bathing suits, just intentions for a refreshing swim in cold, clear water. (MLL.)

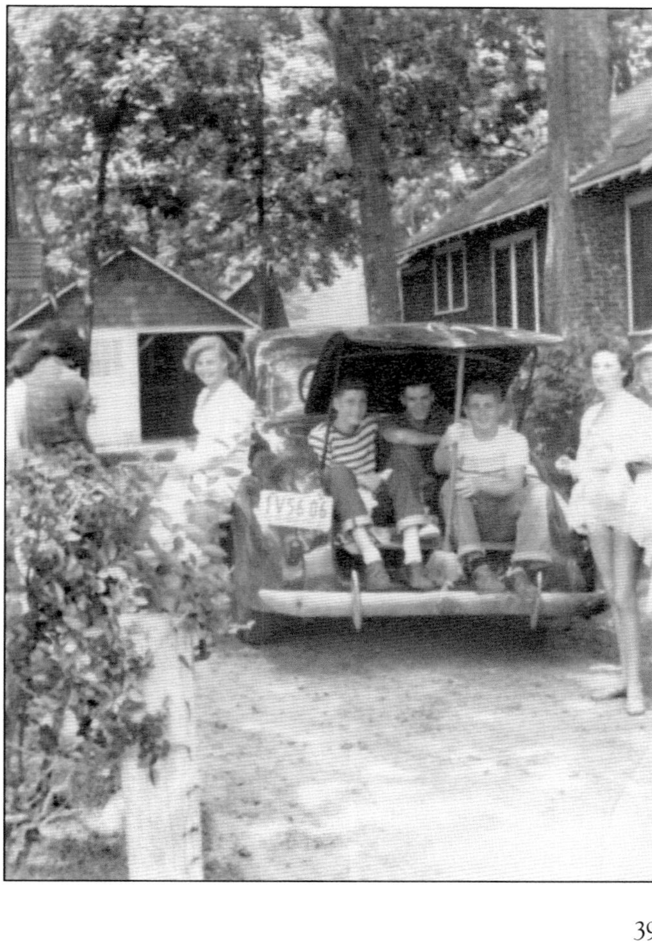

On the Way to Laurel Lake, 1951. Local families had to improvise ways to transport their young people for an enjoyable day at Laurel Lake. Here, from left to right, Eleanor Wamback, Patty Pierce, and Beverly Young stand to the left of the car; Donald VanCott, Anthony Mendo, and John McGarry are ready to ride in the trunk; and Mrs. Pierce and her daughter stand on the right. (Courtesy of Norman Wamback.)

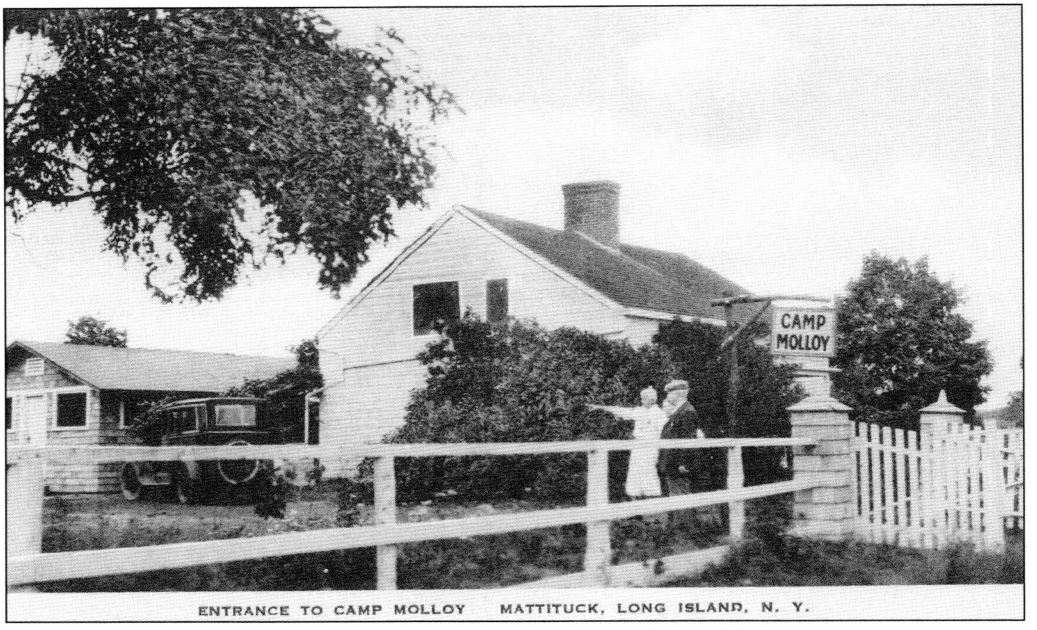

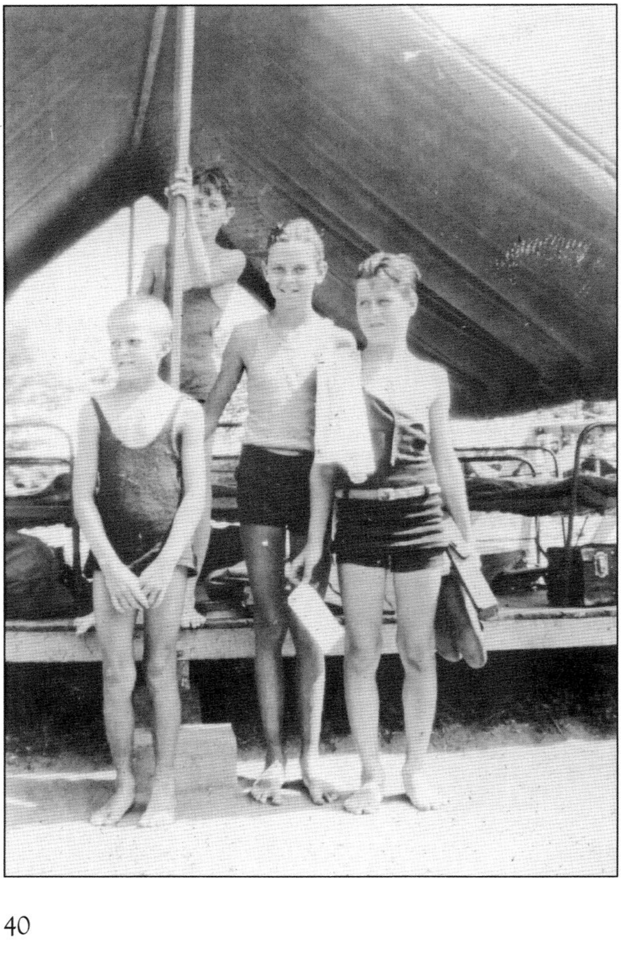

CAMP MOLLOY ENTRANCE, C. 1930. Camp Molloy was founded by the Catholic Diocese of Brooklyn in 1926 for children from the city to enjoy part of their summer in the country. Annie Silkworth sold her property on Main Road to the diocese so it could be developed into a camp. The camp entrance (pictured) was on Main Road and ran down to scenic Laurel Lake. (MLL.)

CAMP TENT, 1931. In 1931, there were no cabins in the camp. Instead, campers slept in tents mounted on wooden platforms that were built along a line known as Camp Street. After a few years, the tents were replaced by small wooden cabins. Swimming, basketball, and horseback riding were popular activities in the camp. (MLL.)

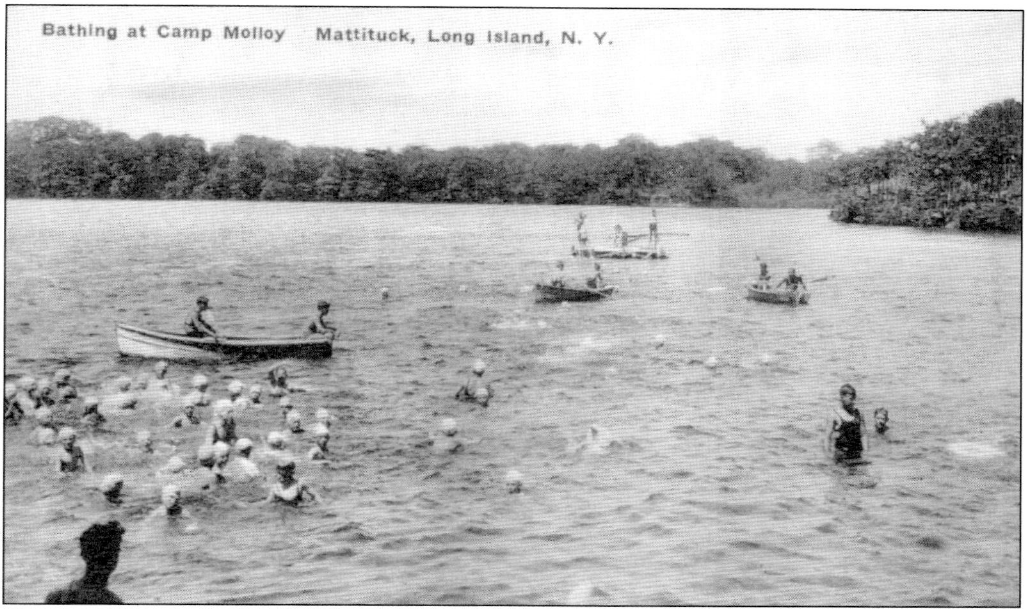

BATHING AT CAMP MOLLOY, C. 1935. At the center of camp activities was swimming in Laurel Lake, as there was nothing more refreshing than swimming in the clear, cold lake in the middle of summer. Camp Molloy maintained a dock and a raft on the lake. Excursions in rowboats and canoes led to sights of lake trout, herons, and perhaps an old snapper turtle. (MLL.)

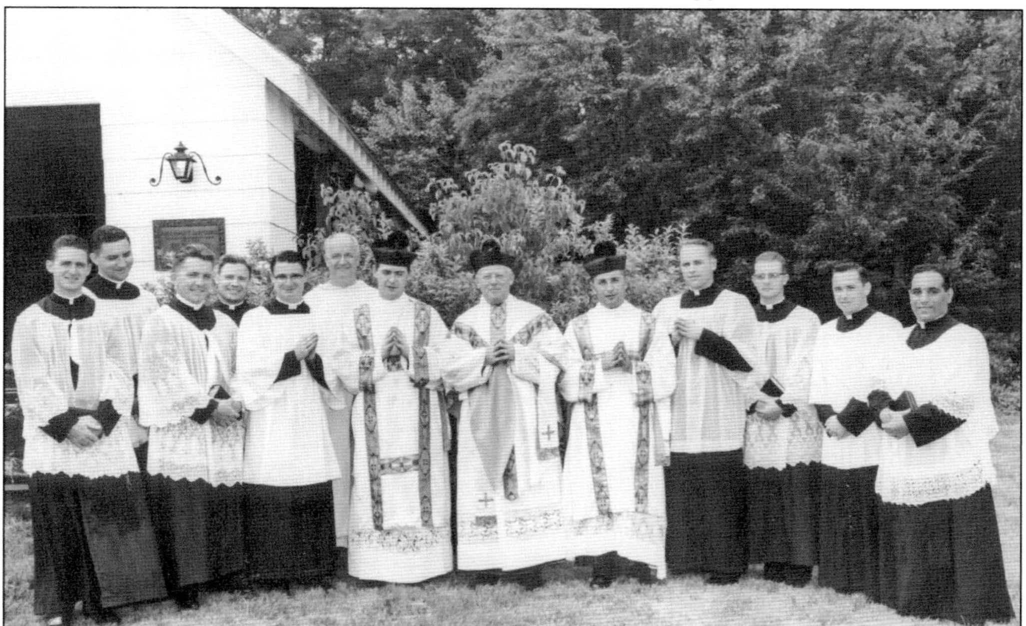

CAMP CHAPLAINS AND COUNSELORS, 1959. At the heart of camp life were the religious services provided by visiting Catholic priests. Seminarians were part of the counselor staff. Mass was celebrated in the open-air chapel. Seen here are, from left to right, unidentified, Rev. George Deas, Rev. Ken Nee, Rev. Jim McMahon, T. Peter Ryan, unidentified, Rev. Bill McLaughlin, unidentified, Bob Saccacio, Frank Gillen, and three unidentified men. (Courtesy of Donald Russo.)

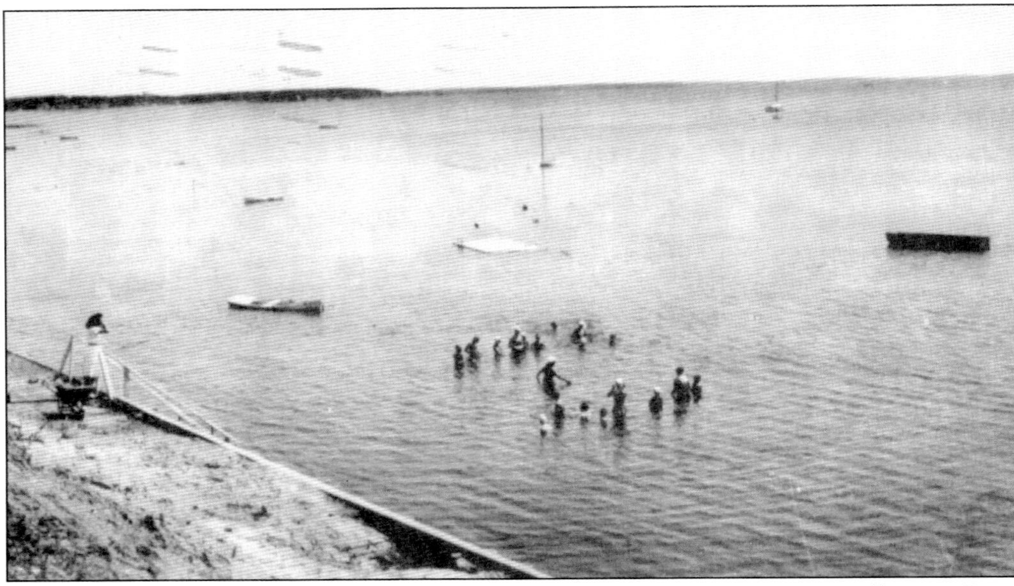

CAMP CATHOLIC DAUGHTERS OF AMERICA, C. 1935. The sister camp to Camp Molloy was Camp Catholic Daughters of America, which was also founded by the Catholic Diocese of Brooklyn in 1926. The camp, later renamed Camp Immaculata, was located on the Peconic Bay off of Peconic Bay Boulevard. This is a view of the bay from the camp in 1948. Swimming meets took place each week, and certification in lifesaving was offered by the American Red Cross. (MLL.)

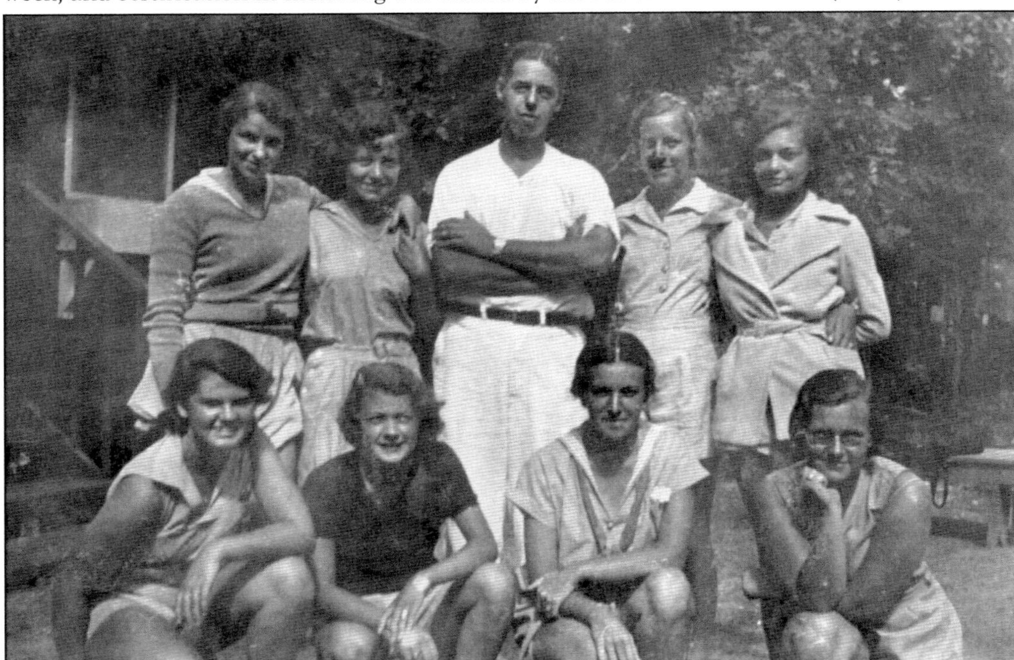

CHAPLAIN AND CAMPERS, 1932. The chaplain, Rev. Frederick Boschert (second row, center), stands with a group of campers. At his right is Elizabeth Sweeney, whose best friend, Eleanor "Fuzzy" Hynes, is on the far right of the second row. When both Catholic camps were eventually closed, the bungalows and cabins were sold to local residents and can still be seen around town. (MLL.)

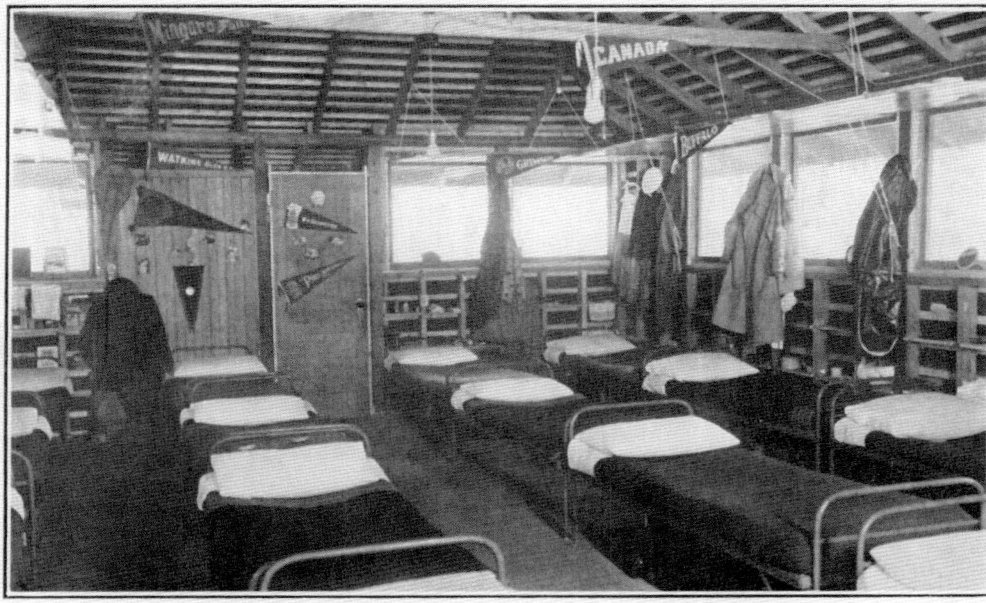

Interior of a Bungalow - Camp C. D. A., Mattituck, L. I.

INTERIOR OF A BUNGALOW, C. 1940. This is the interior of one of the large, airy bungalows, perhaps the Eagle cabin. Here, the girls could rest after long days that included archery, arts and crafts, hiking, dramatics, and music. A branch of the Brooklyn Public Library at the camp provided campers with books to read in their free time. (MLL.)

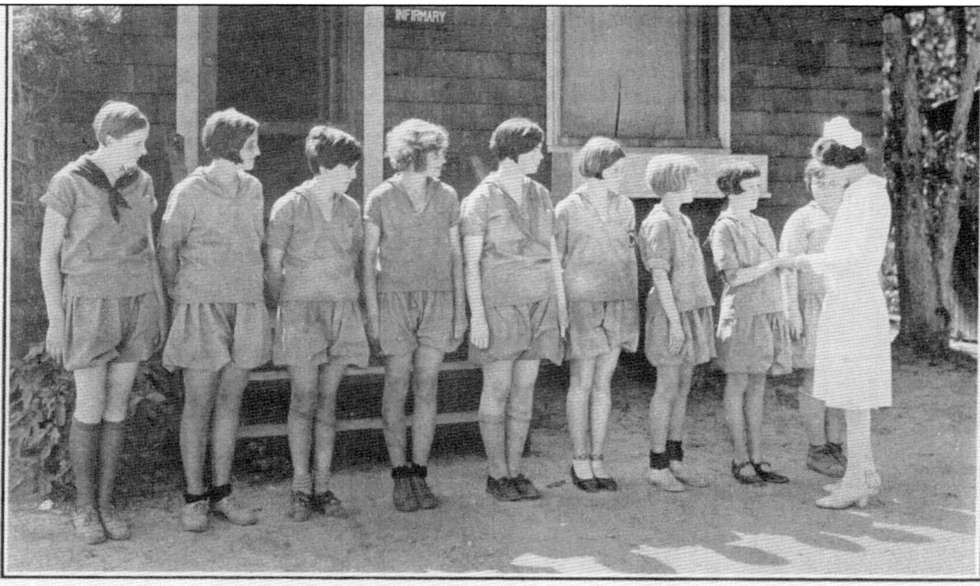

Daily Inspection—Camp C. D. A., Mattituck, L. I.

DAILY INSPECTION, C. 1950. The daily inspection, following the Holy Sacrifice of the Mass, started every day at Camp Immaculata. In the 1950s, the camp was operated by the Catholic Youth Organization (CYO) and the Diocese of Rockville Centre, and was staffed by the Sisters of St. Dominic and a professional lay staff. (MLL.)

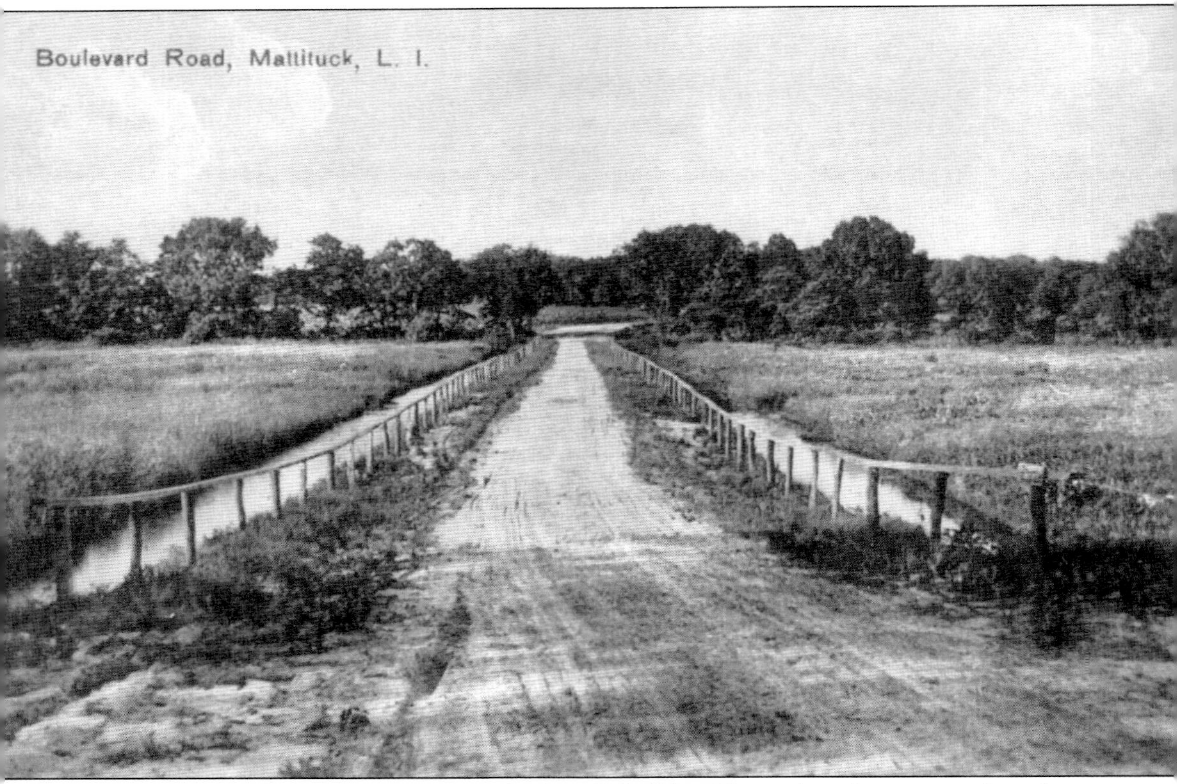

Peconic Bay Boulevard, c. 1895. In the 1870s, John Husing bought property for a farm on Peconic Bay that included a salt marsh and a creek, with a dirt boulevard running through it. The site was gradually turned into a freshwater pond after the construction of a dam in connection with the building of Peconic Bay Boulevard, which opened from Jamesport to Bay Avenue in Mattituck between 1893 and 1895. In 1972, Martha Husing and her brother George donated the pond and the property to the Long Island Nature Conservancy to become a nature preserve, now known as Husing Pond. (Courtesy of the Queens Borough Public Library, Long Island Division, Postcard Collection.)

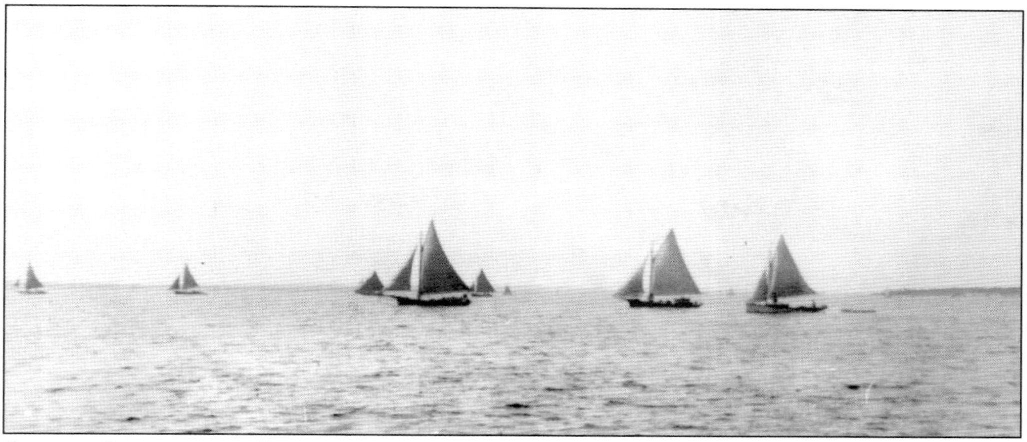

Scallop Boats, 1923. Great Peconic Bay, with its shallow, calm waters and fresh sou'westers in late afternoons, has always been alluring to boaters, bathers, sun-worshippers, and fisherman. Fed on its western end by the Peconic River, this tidal estuary with brackish water once supported large numbers of clams, oysters, and succulent bay scallops. Here, a fleet of scallop boats rides the wind on Great Peconic Bay to harvest sweet catches. (MLL.).

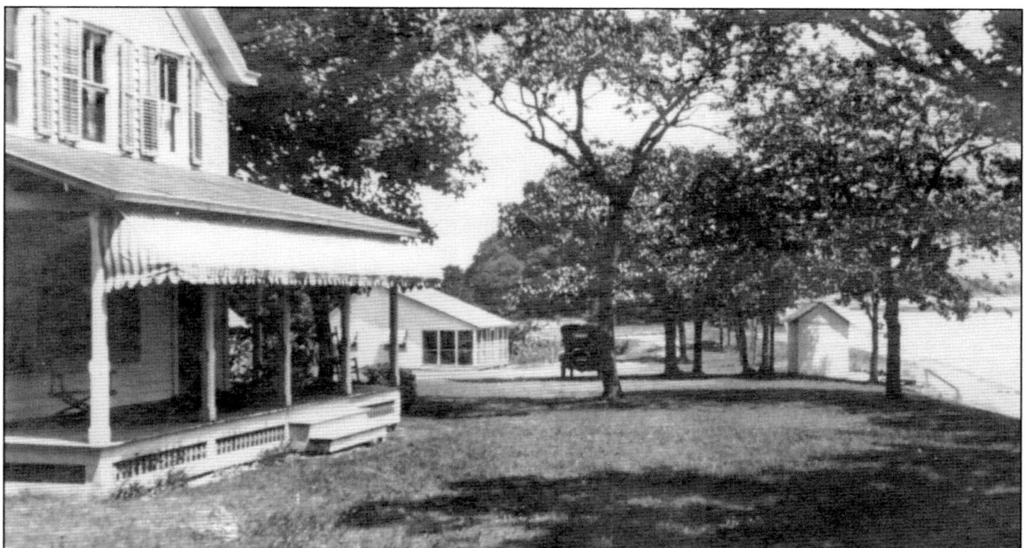

Wickham Gildersleeve House, c. 1930. Wickham Gildersleeve inherited his grandfather Andrew's carpentry skills, building many homes on Great Peconic Bay in Mattituck and Laurel. After his death in 1956, his heir and cousin, Sidney Gildersleeve, sold the property to the Mattituck Park District. This property, with 350 feet of frontage on Great Peconic Bay, is now Veterans Memorial Park. (MLL.)

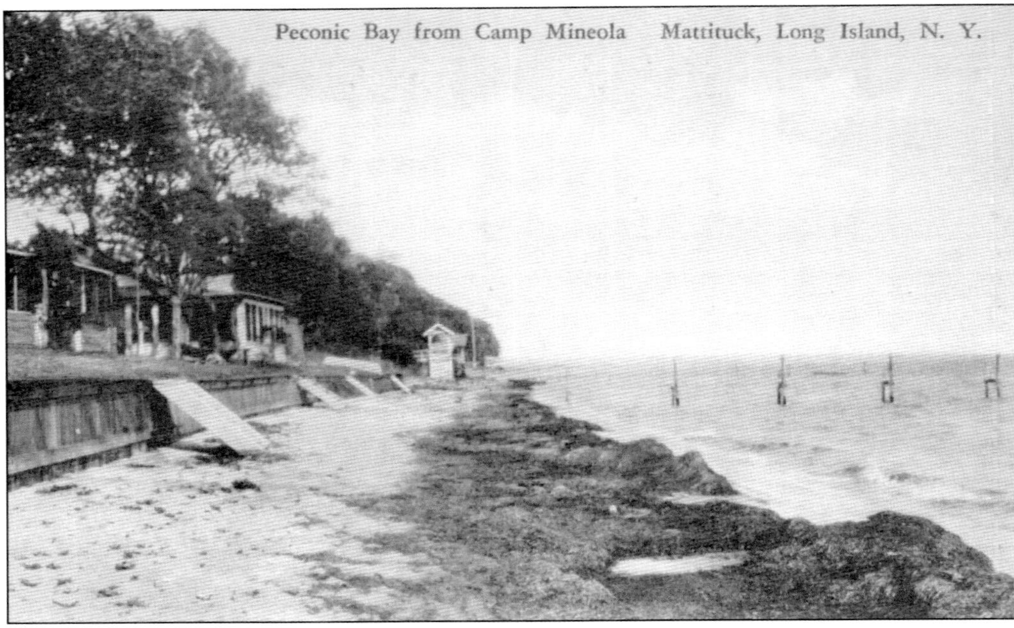

GREAT PECONIC BAY FROM CAMP MINEOLA, C. 1925. By the 1920s, many people were coming to Mattituck by automobile. Farmers began selling their bay front lots for vacation homes. Surrogate judge Leone D. Howell of Nassau County interested nine friends connected to the Nassau County Courthouse to buy bay front lots from Laetitia Reeve, the widow of George B. Reeve. As their common bond was Mineola, they named their private enclave Camp Mineola. (Courtesy of Norman Wamback.)

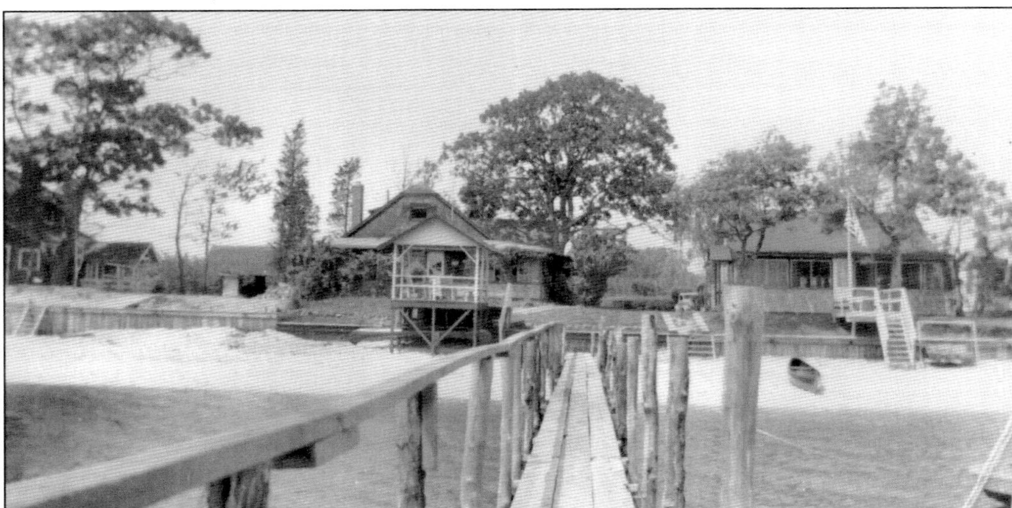

DOCK AT WILMOT Y. HALLOCK'S BEACH HOUSE, C. 1935. Judge Howell bought 16.8 acres of bay front property west of Camp Mineola and began selling building lots. He named this area Bay Aire. The lots were sold to people affiliated with Nassau County government, most of whom lived in Mineola. Soon, they dropped the name Bay Aire and used Camp Mineola. The additional lots were all sold to the Republican political elite of Nassau County; by 1940, there were 27 homes there. (Courtesy of Norman Wamback.)

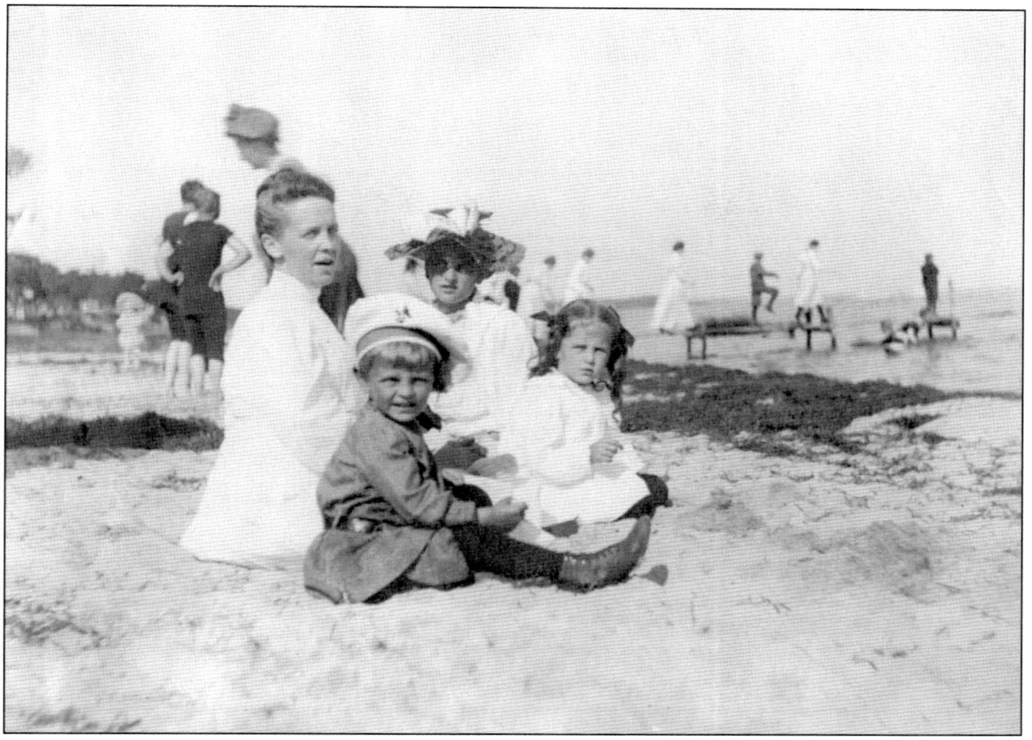

Great Peconic Bay, c. 1905. Beulah Duryee sits in the sand with her children on a lovely summer day. The sunshine shimmers from white dresses and makes the steps of Sunday strollers a little lighter on the boardwalk out into Great Peconic Bay. Windrows of eel grass dry in the sun as gentle bay waters lap the shore. (Courtesy of Michael J. Montgomery.)

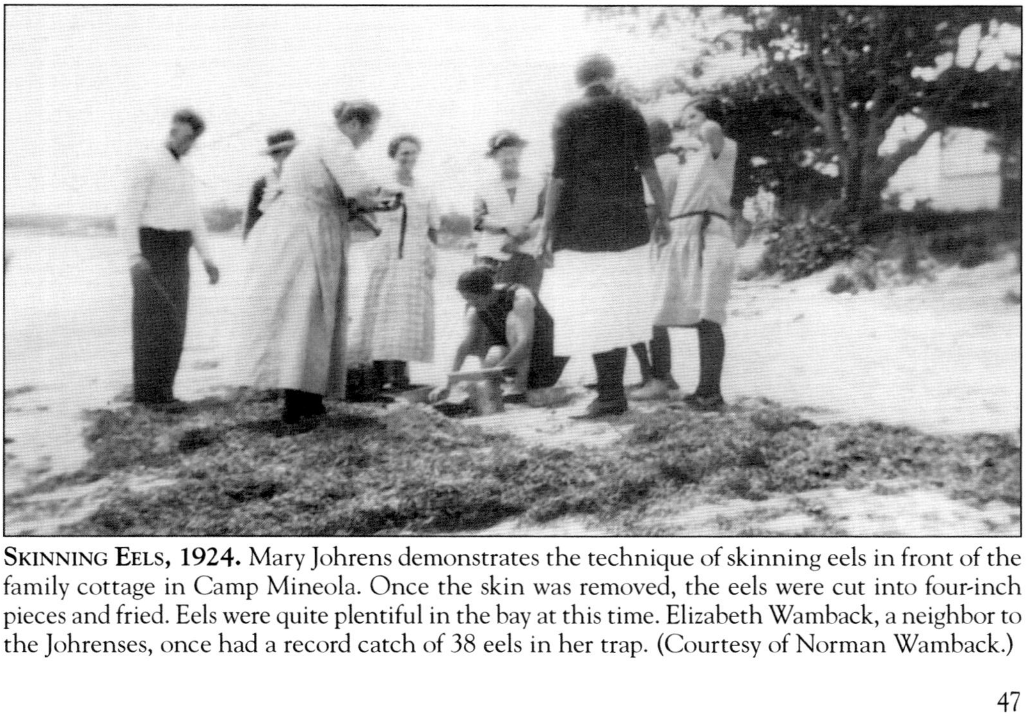

Skinning Eels, 1924. Mary Johrens demonstrates the technique of skinning eels in front of the family cottage in Camp Mineola. Once the skin was removed, the eels were cut into four-inch pieces and fried. Eels were quite plentiful in the bay at this time. Elizabeth Wamback, a neighbor to the Johrenses, once had a record catch of 38 eels in her trap. (Courtesy of Norman Wamback.)

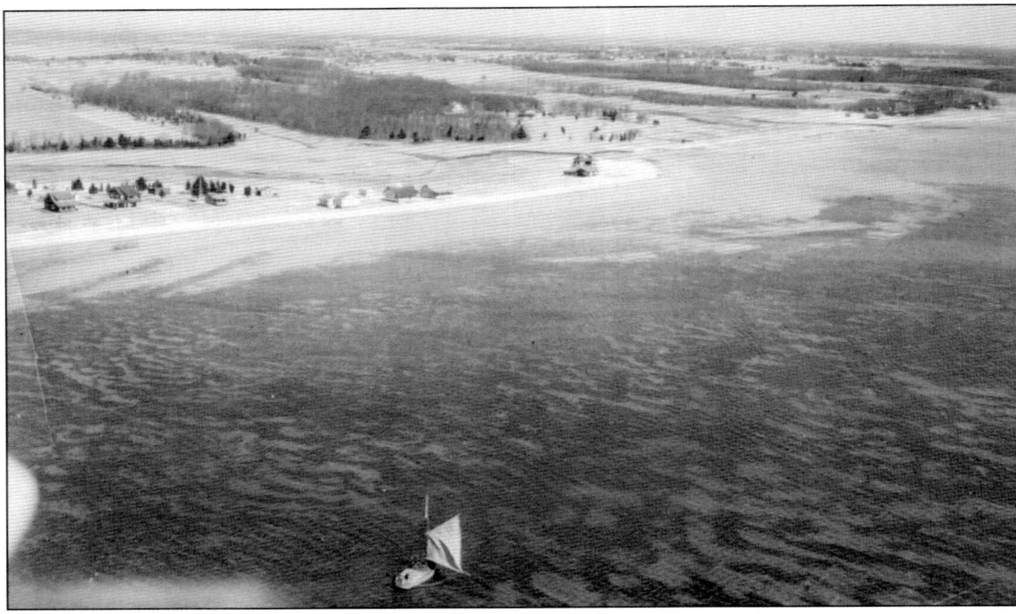

Marratooka Point, c. 1930. This aerial view of Marratooka Point looks east, with the entrance to Deep Hole Creek seen behind the last house on the point. This small strip of land was owned by Charles W. Wickham, whose son, Cedric Hull Wickham, was the first to build on the point, erecting a small honeymoon cottage in 1910. Several more cottages were built on the point by 1930. (MLL.)

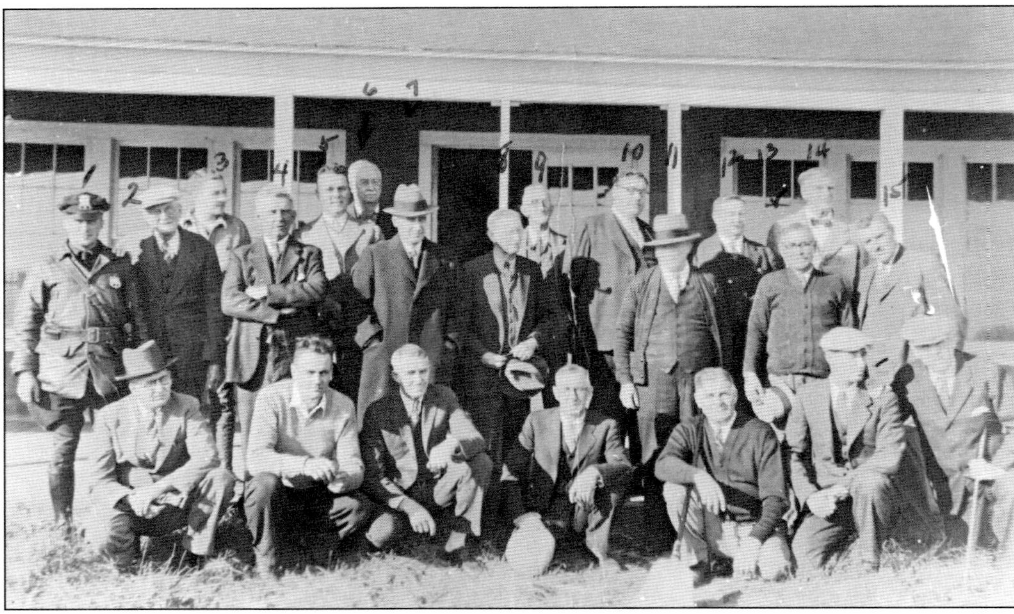

Marratooka Club, c. 1925. By the early 1920s, large sections of Great Peconic Bay waterfront were being sold to nonresidents for the construction of summer homes. A group of local men decided to buy a piece of bay front property and erect a clubhouse, guaranteeing them access to the bay. In 1921, the Maratooka Club was formed with 30 members, all of whom could trace their ancestry to an original North Fork family. (Courtesy of Norman Wamback.)

Four

Mattituck 100 Years Ago

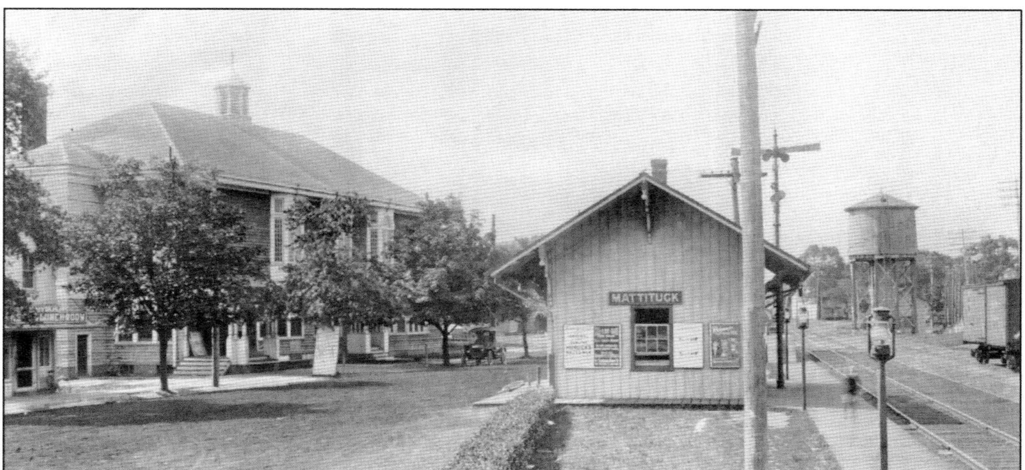

Mattituck Station, c. 1910. The commercial part of town developed on Love Lane and Pike Street, near the railroad station. During this era, the establishment of a new business in town was an occasion for celebration. In 1888, Harvey P. Duryee and Otto Hallock opened their new fertilizer factory. The *Mattituck Traveler* describes the event: "The jollification at Hallock & Duryee's new factory Wednesday evening was a grand success. About sixty couples were present. The music was fine, the floors were in capital shape for dancing and everyone stayed until a late hour in the morning. This is a very fine building for manufacturing. Three stories in height with cupola, fitted up with the latest steam apparatus, new steam pumps, elevator, and with a handy side track of their own, which the Railroad company had installed." (MLL.)

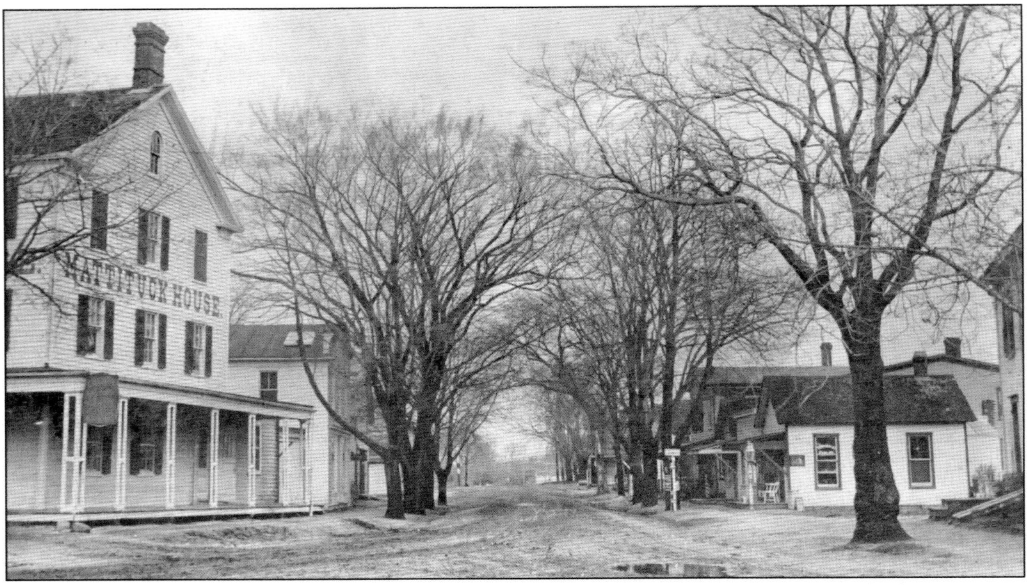

LOVE LANE, 1910. In 1910, Love Lane was called Railroad Avenue, while north of Pike Street up to Mattituck Creek it was called Lover's Lane. Walking up Railroad Avenue—the present Love Lane—one would pass the Mattituck House Hotel on the left and then reach Harry DePetris's fruit and stationery store. (MLHS.)

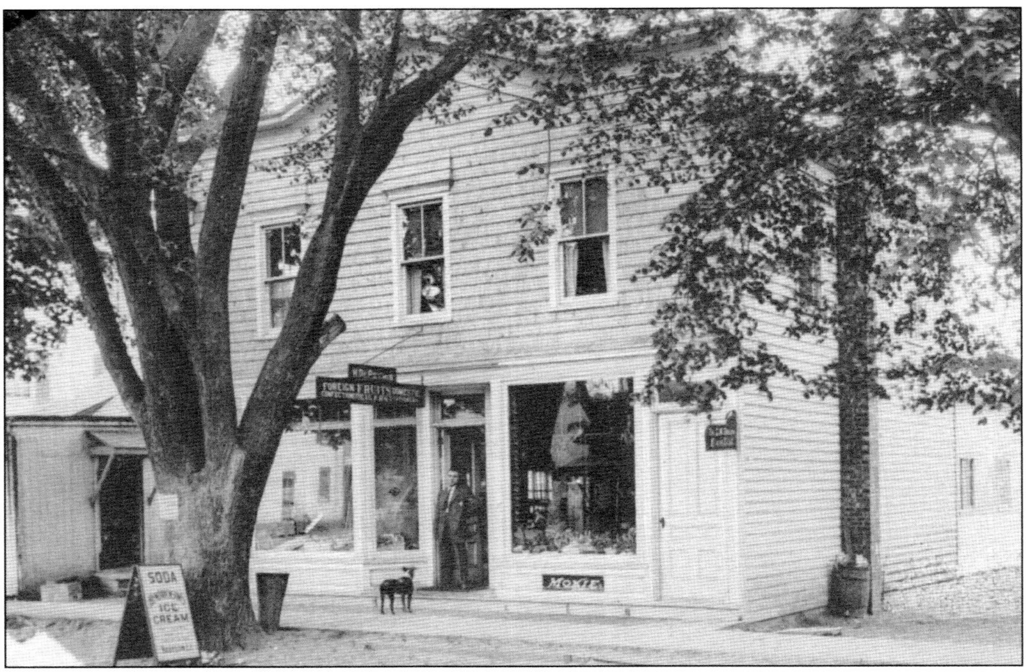

HARRY DEPETRIS FRUIT MARKET, 1910. Italian immigrants Harry and Jennie DePetris opened a fruit store and ice cream parlor on the west side of Love Lane in 1910. People flocked there for refreshments after entertainments and dances. Harry was one of Mattituck's leading entrepreneurs, whose enterprises included a restaurant, trucking company, gas station, and real estate interests. (MLHS.)

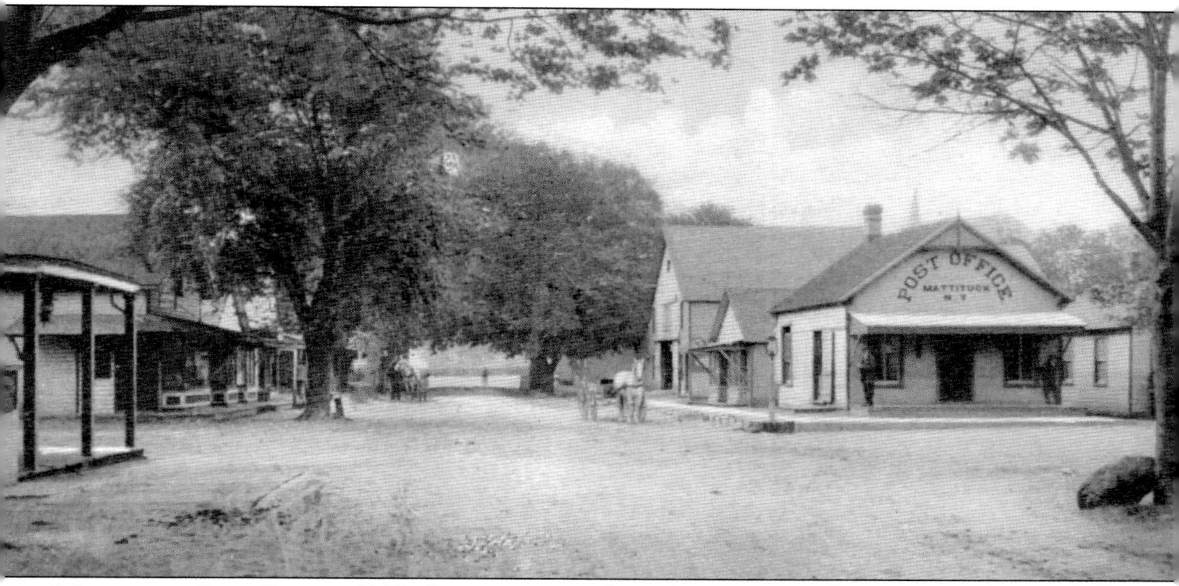

Mattituck Post Office, 1910. Continuing north on Love Lane, pedestrians saw the large livery stable of George and William Riley. The Riley Brothers livery rented rigs to locals and visitors, including drummers, traveling salesmen who came by train to Mattituck to make the rounds of their customers. The Rileys boarded other people's horses and, once a year, brought in two train carloads of hayburners (horses) for sale. Jack Zenzius had a competing livery business on Pike Street. North of the livery stables was the shop for the Mattituck House. This was later divided into the harness shop of E.P. Reeve and a barbershop. In 1892, the post office was on the southwest corner of Pike Street and Love Lane, where the Capital One Bank is today. In those early days, mailboxes had glass fronts so people could see if they had any mail. If they did, they still had to go to the window to ask for it. (MLHS.)

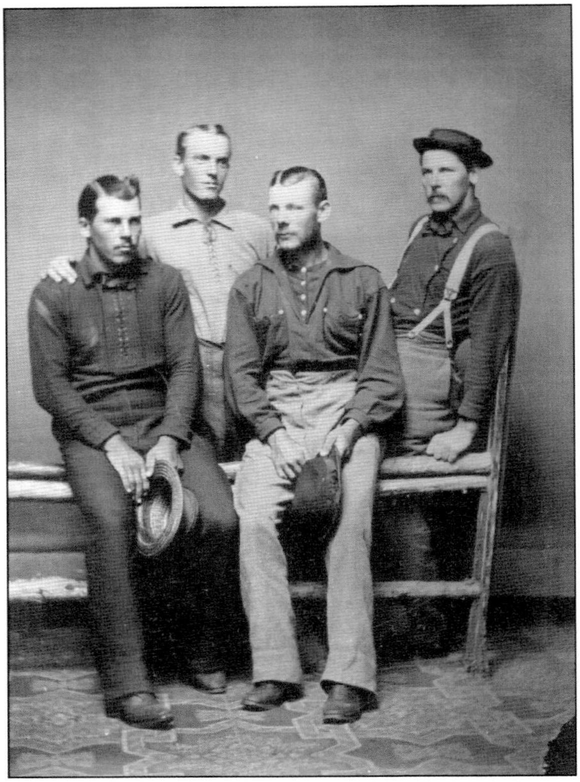

Rising Mattituck Entrepreneurs, c. 1885. These young men, (from left to right) W.H. Reeve, J. Wood Wickham, Leon Hall, and Herbert Conklin, were the rising entrepreneurs of Mattituck in their time. Conklin is remembered as the man who made Mattituck Creek oysters more sought-after than the widely advertised South Bay "Blue Points." Reeve and Hall were butchers whose renowned sausage meat was in demand on the island and in New York City. Wickham owned the tinsmith and plumbing shop on Pike Street. (MLL.)

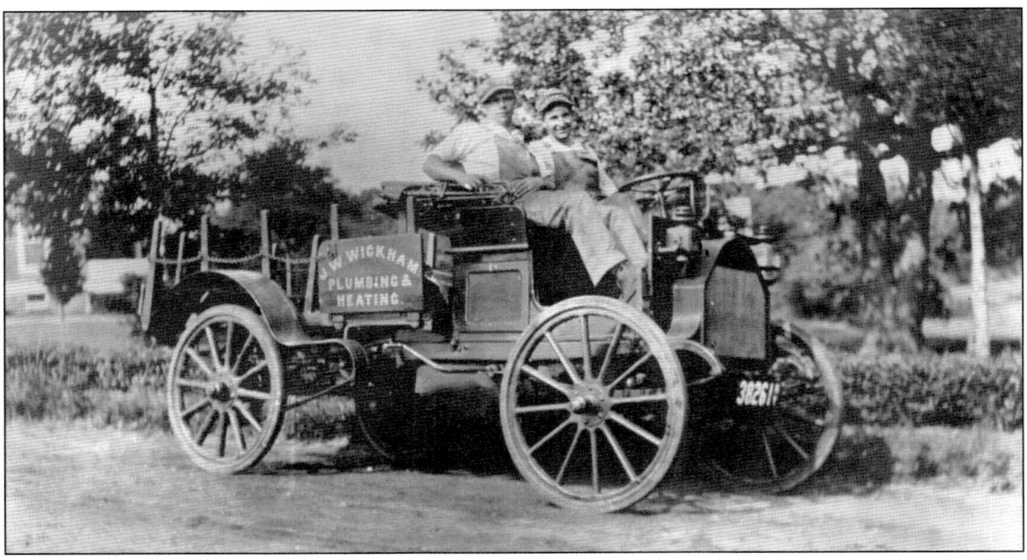

J.W. Wickham Delivery Truck, c. 1915. J. Wood Wickham, the Mattituck tinsmith and plumber, was the first local owner of a delivery truck, which he used for his business. He had handled his truck very well the first day he used it, but when he steered through the barn door to park it, he neglected to stop, and the truck went through the other end. The next day, he stopped before the door and told his son Carleton, "We'll push it in this time." (Courtesy of the Suffolk County Historical Society.)

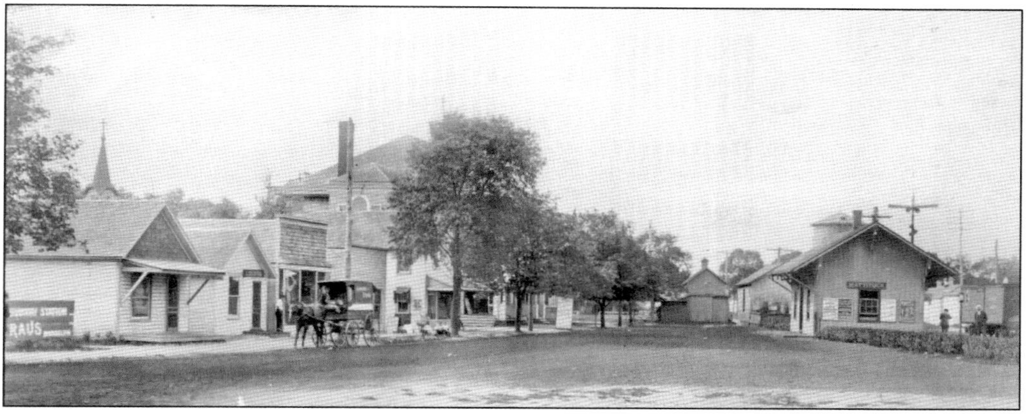

Station Square, c. 1910. This view looking west on Pike Street shows the Abraham & Straus Agency (far left) and Frederick Bicking's barbershop next door. Here, the driver of the A&S wagon is seen leaning in his seat. The Woolworth 5 and 10 cent store and Emil Myrus's bakery are next, and then Library Hall. The train depot is on the right, with the water tower in the distance behind it. (MLL.)

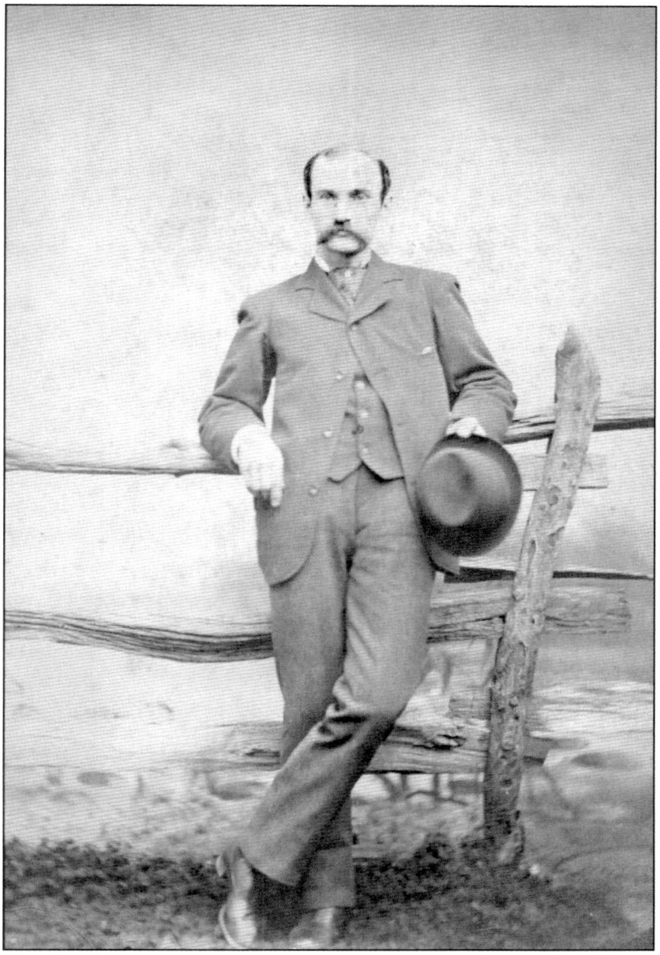

Charles Gildersleeve, c. 1885. For more than 50 years, Charles Gildersleeve strengthened the social fabric of the Mattituck community as the local correspondent for the *Long Island Traveler* and as a charter member and organizer of the Mattituck Literary Society, the Mattituck Grange, and the Mattituck Bank. He also acted as the station agent for the railroad at Mattituck for 40 years, receiving a certificate of honor for his loyal service. (Courtesy of Jim and Pauline Gildersleeve.)

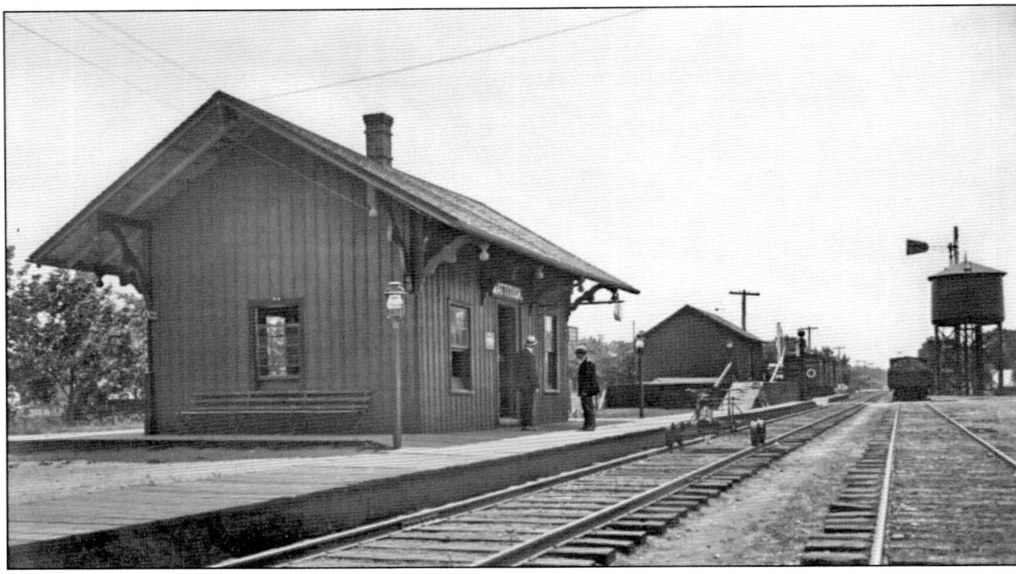

Mattituck Station, 1905. The Mattituck railroad station had sidetracks to serve the various businesses, as well as a water tower. In 1905, the same year this photograph was taken, Ernest Corwin resigned as stationmaster after many years of faithful service to accept a position as a cashier at the new Mattituck Bank. (Courtesy of Ron Ziel.)

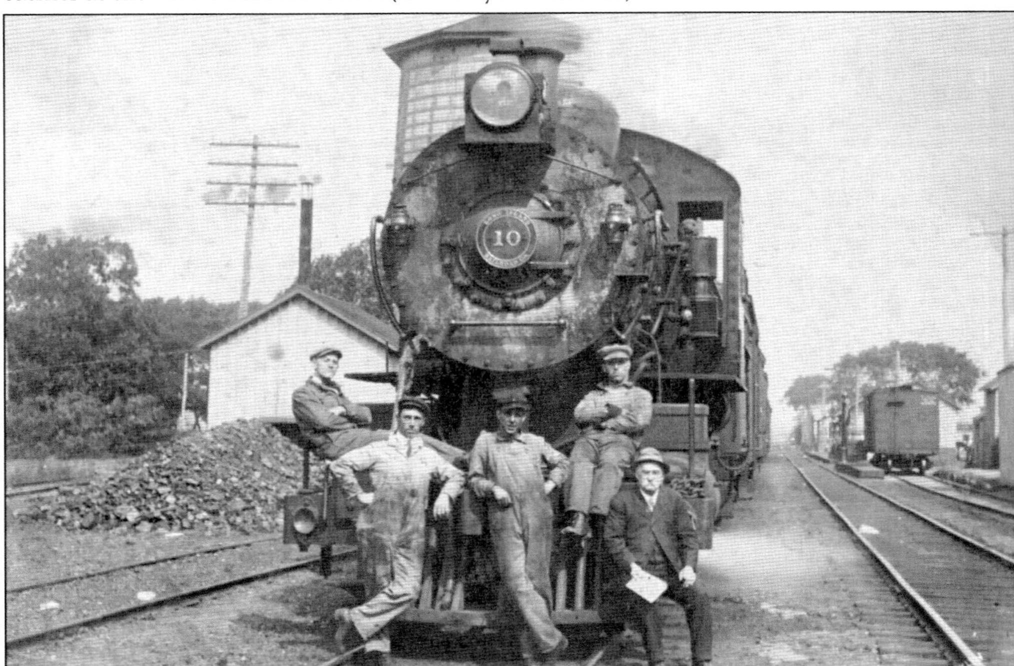

Railroad Engine No. 10, c. 1915. The crew of the train poses for a photograph at the Mattituck station. Both the conductor and the fireman are covered in coal dust because the conductor helped shovel coal into the fire. Mattituck had as many as four sidetracks built near the station to accommodate the many businesses shipping and receiving goods from New York City. (MLHS.)

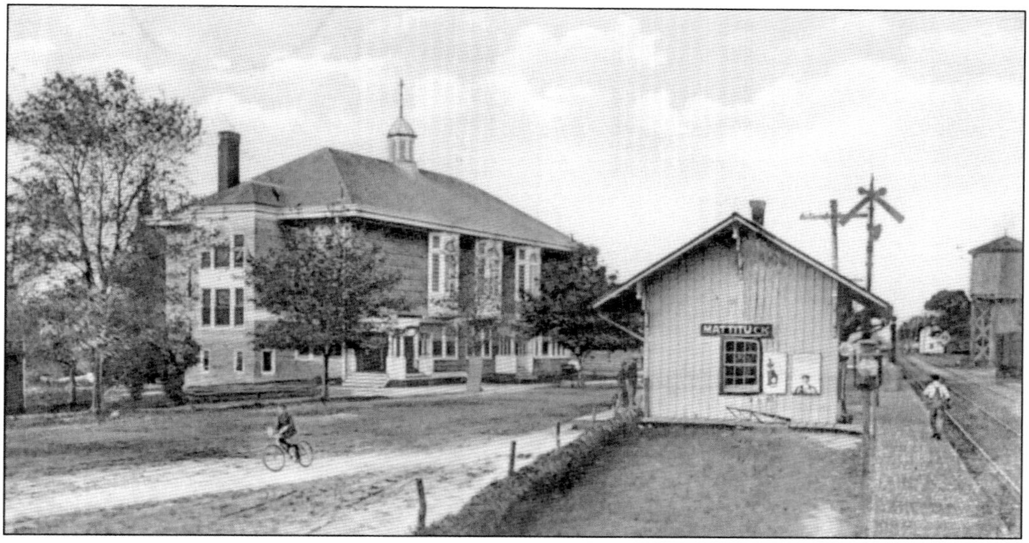

DEPOT AND LIBRARY HALL, c. 1905. Library Hall, on the corner of Westphalia Avenue and Pike Street, was Mattituck's great hall, donated to the people of Mattituck in 1905 by Frank Moore Lupton, a native son who found success in New York City publishing. On the main floor were the library rooms, the Mattituck National Bank and Trust, and Dr. Lahy's pharmacy. (MLL.)

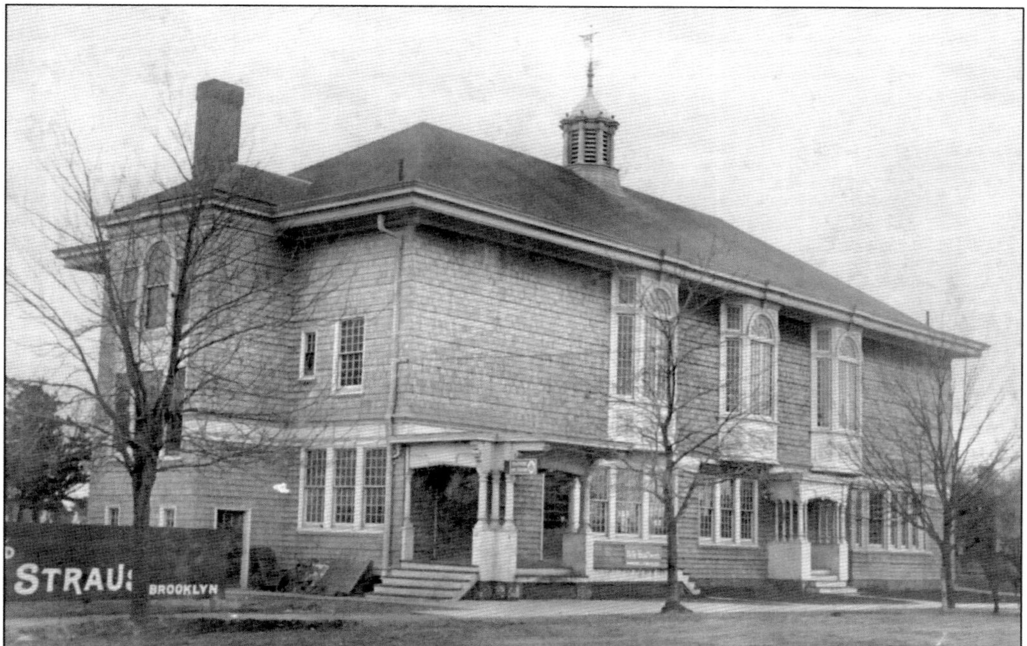

LIBRARY HALL, c. 1905. On the second floor of Library Hall was the assembly hall, which could accommodate 800 people and had a stage on one end. The seats were moved for dances and basketball games. As the home of the Mattituck Literary Society, the Mattituck Lecture Association, and the Dramatic Association, the hall provided the venue for entertainment, education, and self-expression. The Order of United American Mechanics held annual meetings here as well. (MLL.)

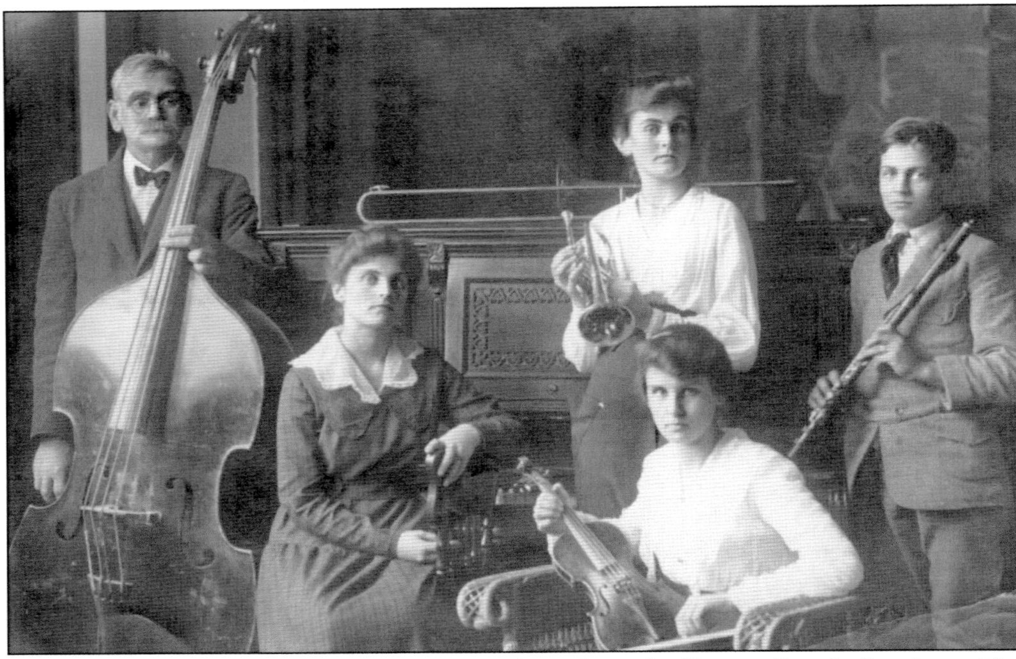

Duryee Family Band, c. 1910. Townspeople such as the Duryee Family Band provided entertainment at Library Hall. The Mattituck Lecture Association also hired outside performers. The 1909 season featured several artists from the Eastern Lyceum Bureau of Boston: the College Singing Girls, the Katherine Ridgeway Readings, Victor's Venetian Band of 26 Pieces, Roland Dwight Grant's lecture "Rome with Michael Angelo," and the musical comedy *Her American Husband*, which was presented by the Walter Cluxton Company. (MLHS.)

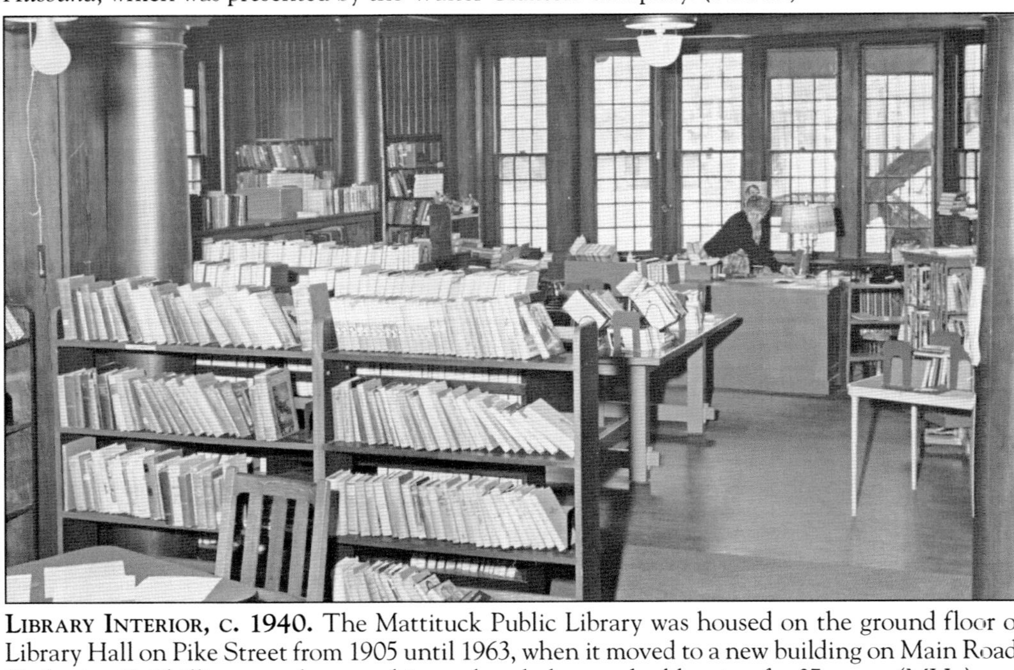

Library Interior, c. 1940. The Mattituck Public Library was housed on the ground floor of Library Hall on Pike Street from 1905 until 1963, when it moved to a new building on Main Road. Catherine K. Phillips, seen here working at her desk, was the librarian for 37 years. (MLL.)

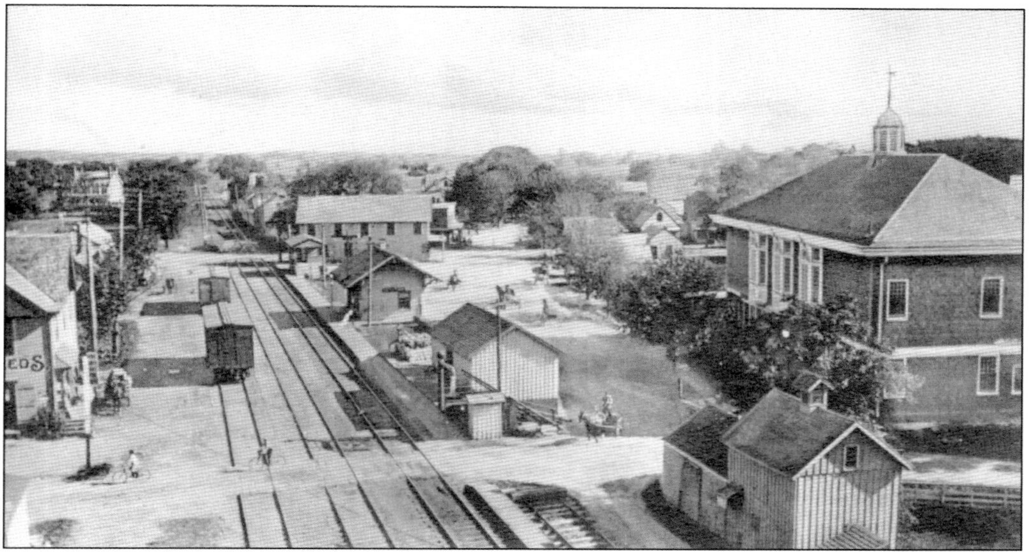

Pike Street and Westphalia Avenue, 1906. In this bird's-eye view, townspeople travel by horse and buggy or bicycle on Station Square, with its main rail line and side rail lines. On the left, on Westphalia Avenue, is the corner of W.V. Duryee's Long Island Seeds and Hardware building. (MLL.)

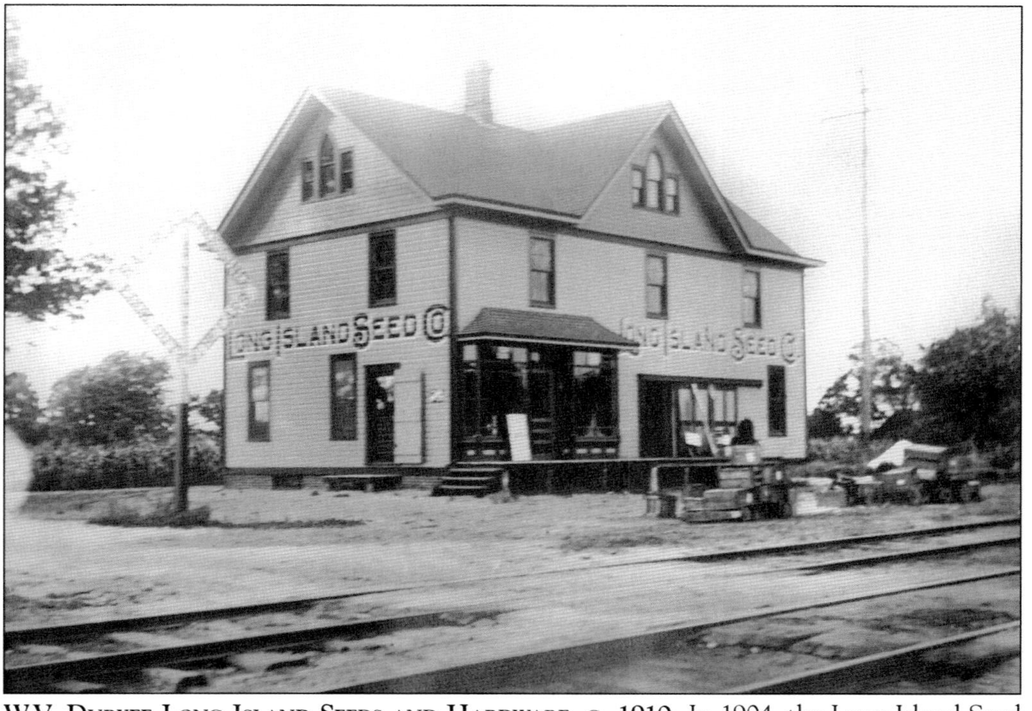

W.V. Duryee Long Island Seeds and Hardware, c. 1910. In 1904, the Long Island Seed Company was organized by John M. Lupton, Robert M. Lupton, W.V. Duryee, and F.B. Garvey. Later, Duryee specialized in seeds and hardware. His building stood on the east corner of Westphalia Avenue, north of the railroad track. John Lupton also had his own seed business, one of the most important cabbage seed producers in the country. (Courtesy of Michael J. Montgomery.)

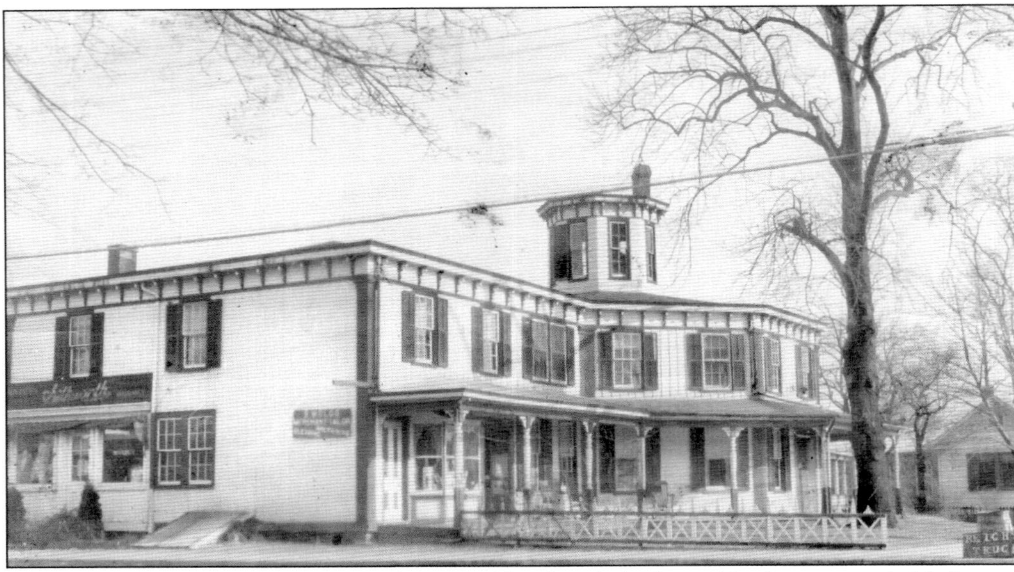

Octagon House, c. 1900. This architectural landmark, built in 1854, has a remarkable history as an important locale for businesses in the community. Through the years, the building has been used as a post office, a barbershop, a tailor shop, a paint store, a dentist's office, and real estate offices. (MLHS.)

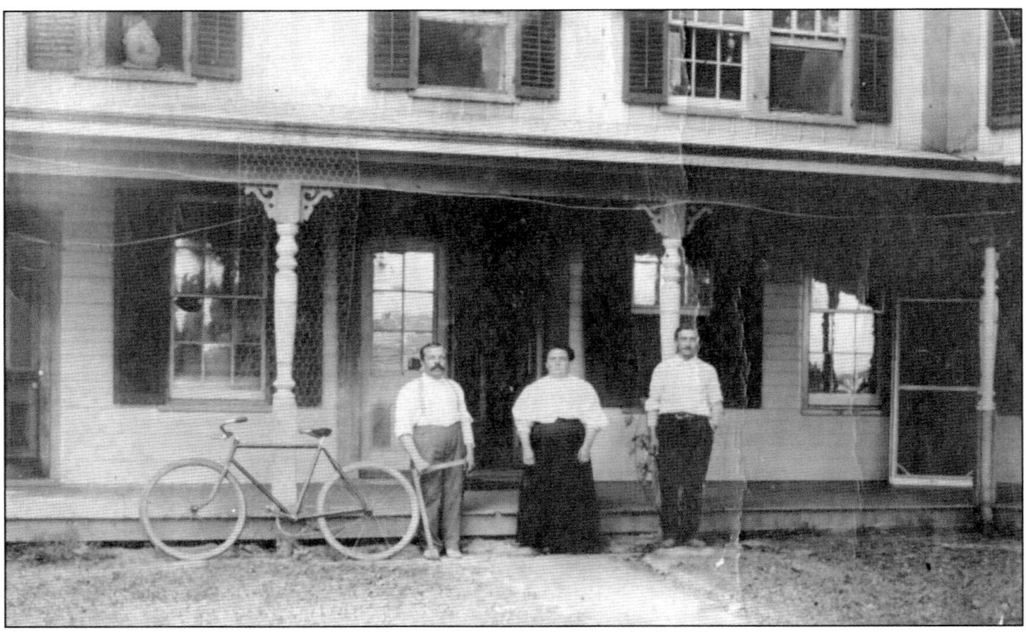

Stanley Wolgo, c. 1910. Holding a tailor's diagram square, Stanislaw "Stanley" Wolgo stands on the left in front of his shop in the Well's Corner of the Octagon Building. Wolgo was a Polish immigrant who came to Mattituck from Brooklyn in 1903 to set up a tailor shop. He worked at his trade until his retirement in 1950. (Courtesy of Charlotte Dickerson.)

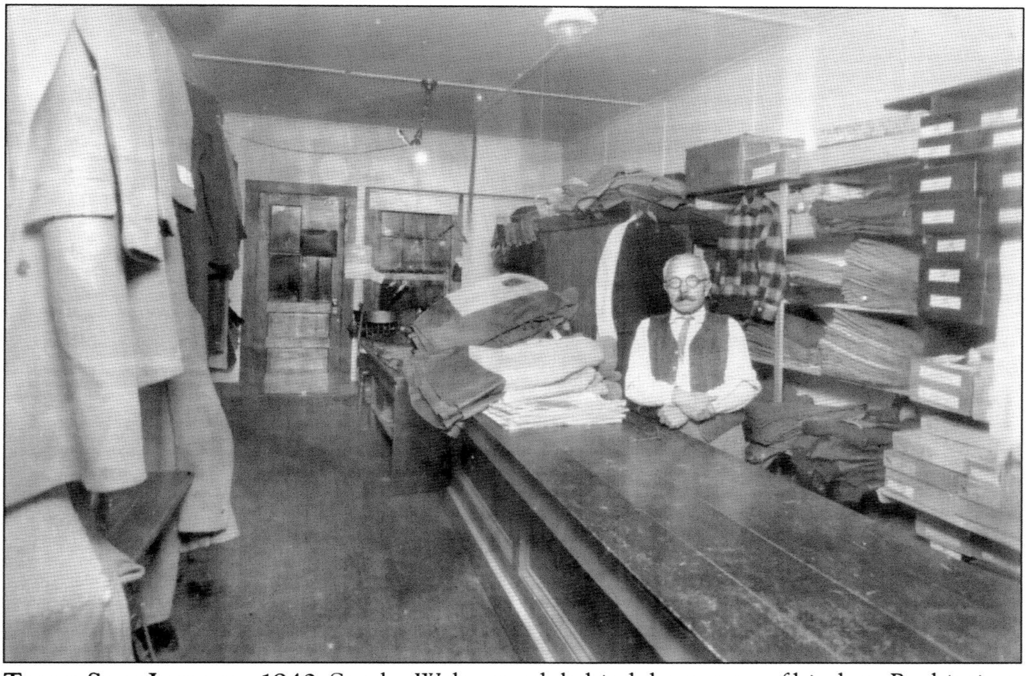

TAILOR SHOP INTERIOR, 1940. Stanley Wolgo stands behind the counter of his shop. By this time, he had been a tailor for more than 68 years, and Mattituckians found him a skilled workman, friendly, and obliging. He often worked late at night to accommodate his customers. He lived on Old Sound Avenue and walked to work each day. (Courtesy of Charlotte Dickerson.)

LOVE LANE, NORTHEAST TO PIKE STREET, C. 1910. On the east side of Love Lane just north of the Octagon House was the barbershop of P.V. Butler. Behind that was Tom McGuire's white barn and shop, which upholstered carriages, sleighs, and, later on, automobiles. On Pike Street are John Zenzius's livery and barns in dark wood. East of that is the firehouse. (MLL.)

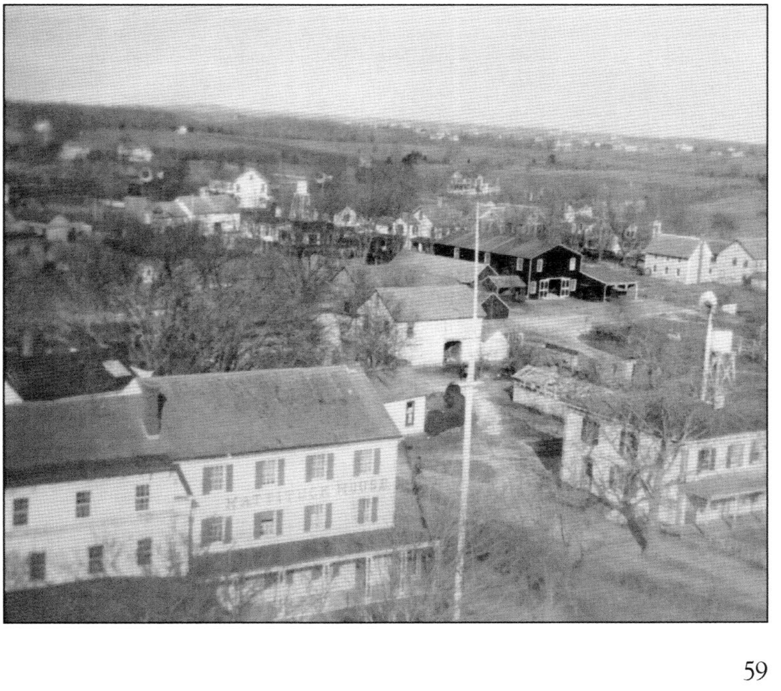

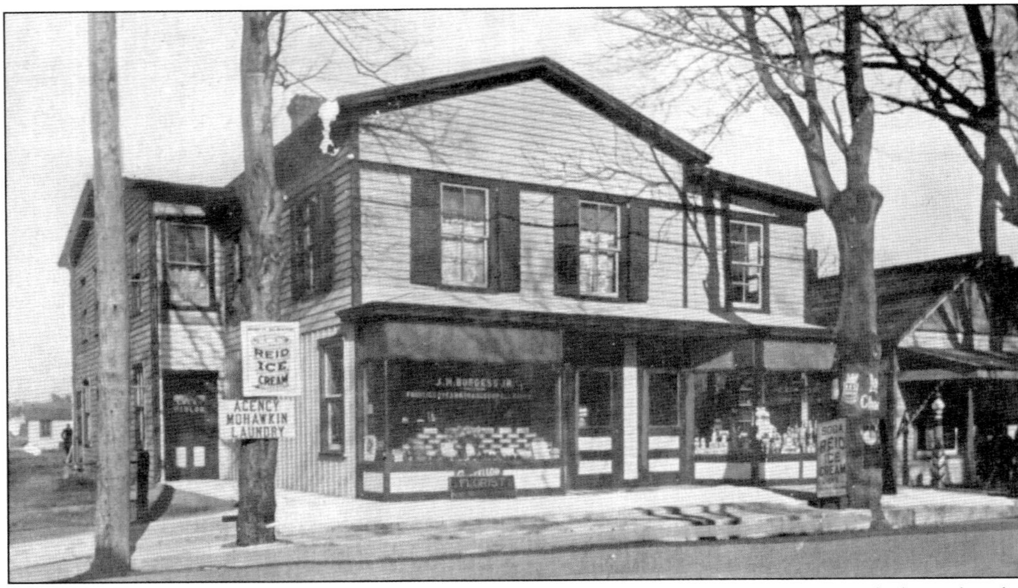

Dick Cox's Ice Cream Parlor, c. 1910. In 1887, Cox started his business as a bakery, but he made the change because ice cream, candy, and soda had a greater public appeal, and he ran a successful business as long as he lived. The second floor was a tenement house prior to 1883, owned by Thomas B. Reeve. The store was later owned J.M. Burgess Jr. (Courtesy of the Louis "Chub" Gildersleeve family.)

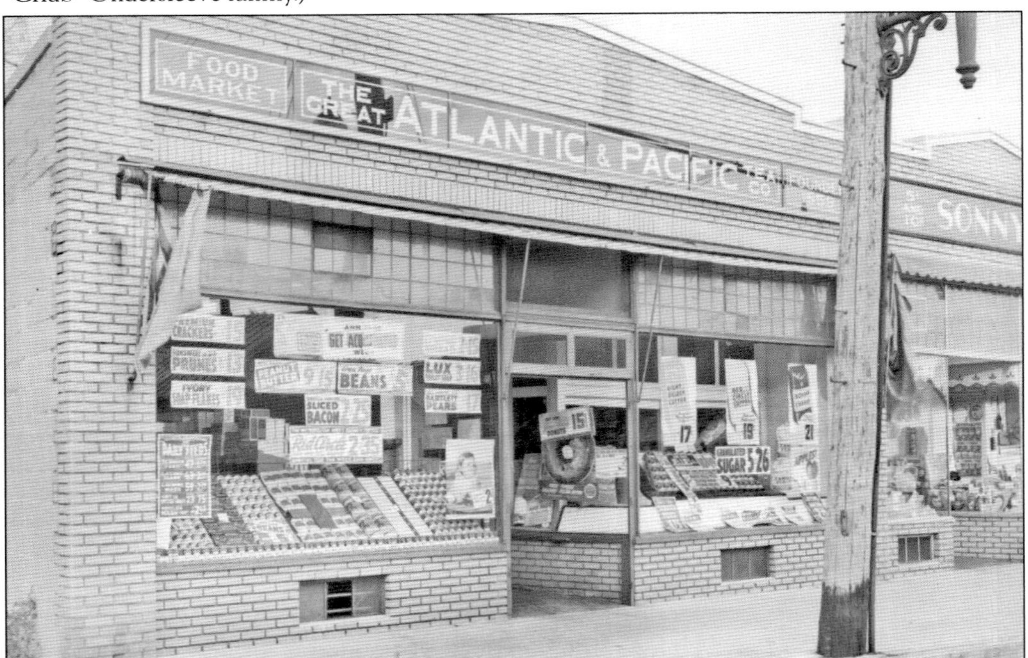

A&P, 1938. Dick Cox's ice cream parlor became the Great Atlantic & Pacific Tea Company (A&P) food market in 1916. In 1929, Melvin Kelsey renovated a block of stores on Love Lane, including the A&P, which then became this brick structure. At the time, coffee was 19¢ a pound and donuts were 15¢ a dozen. (Courtesy of the Southold Historical Society.)

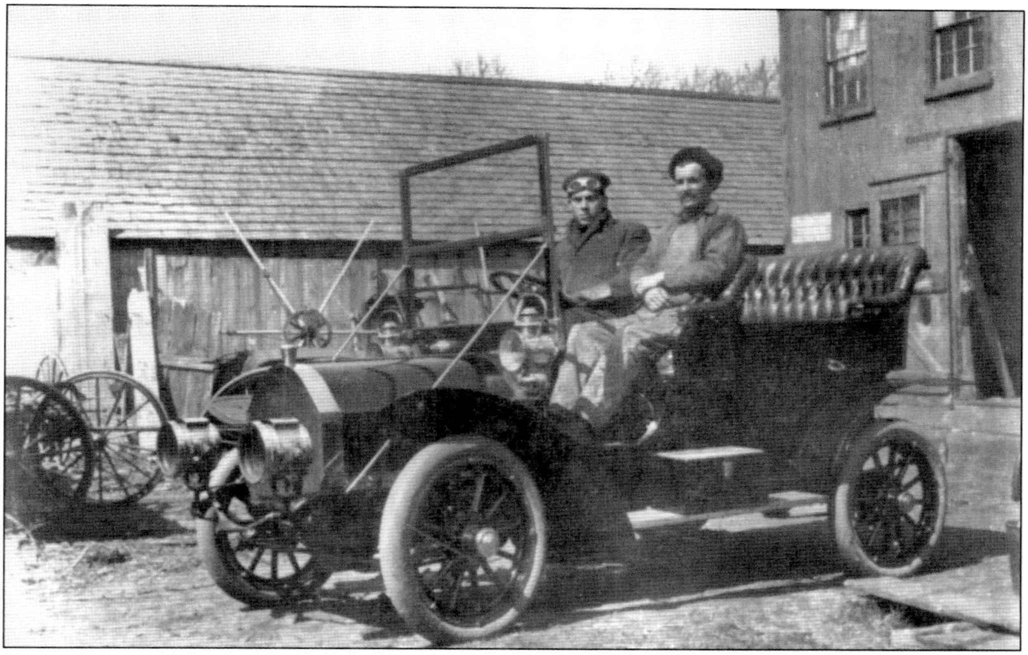

CONRAD AND ARTHUR GRABIE, 1907. Conrad Grabie, the village blacksmith, had his shop adjacent to Reeve and Hall's butcher shop. Everyone brought horses to Grabie to be shod, and if there was a piece of farm machinery to be repaired, Grabie did it. Here, Conrad is on the right, with his son, Arthur, in the driver's seat. An expert mechanic, Arthur Grabie was the first person to own an automobile, a Cadillac, in Mattituck. (MLHS.)

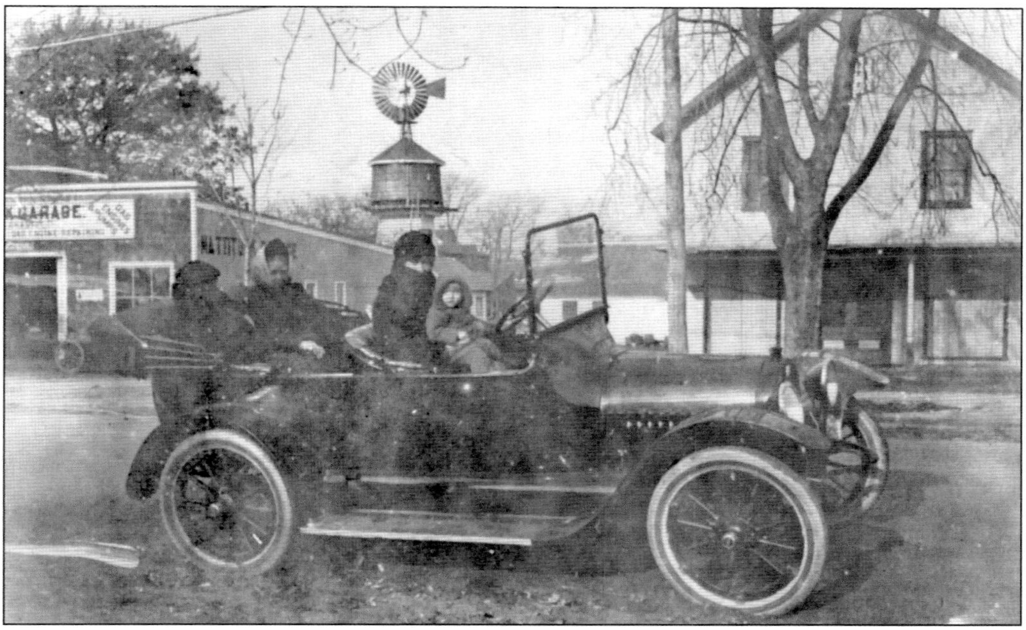

MATTITUCK GARAGE, 1918. Conrad Grabie's other son, Walter "Buck" Grabie, opened Mattituck Garage in 1909 on Main Road. The Grabie family is seen here in one of their cars. In the background is the water tower, which was used to provide acetylene gas to residents of Mattituck. (MLHS.)

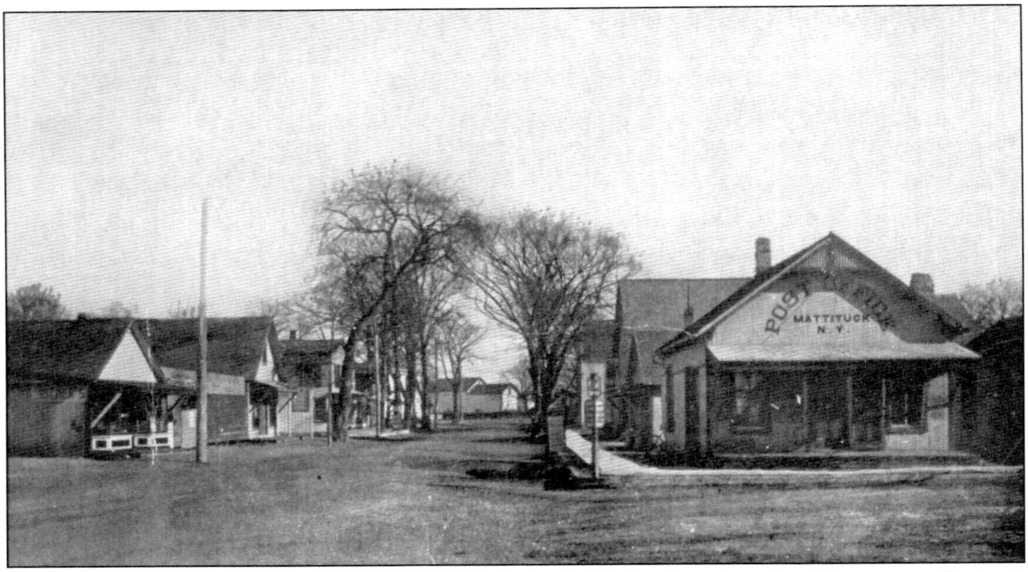

Love Lane's East Side, c. 1915. On the east side (left), the first three buildings were Fischer's meat market, Frank Wong's laundry, and the Reeve and Hall butcher shop. William Reeve and Leon Hall opened the butcher shop in 1878 adjacent to Grabie's blacksmith shop. They won fame for their sausage locally as well as in New York City. Frank Wong's Chinese laundry opened in 1878, providing expertly washed and pressed laundry. (MLL.)

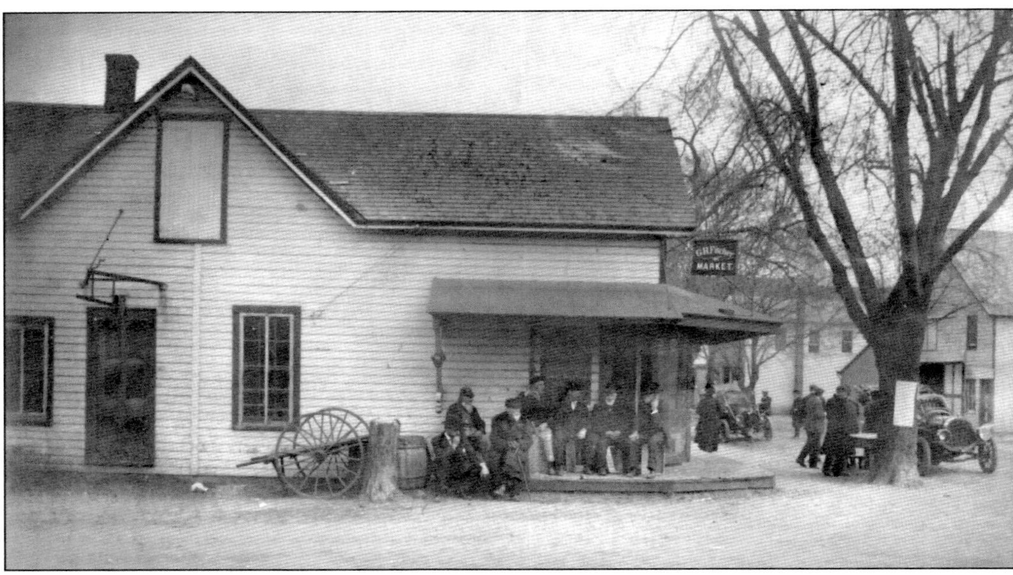

George H. Fischer's Market, 1910. In 1892, George H. Fischer opened his meat market on the southeast corner of Love Lane and Pike Street. "Economy" was his motto. At Fischer's market, fresh lamb, veal, pork, and poultry could be purchased. He also sold vegetables, pickles, canned goods, and fresh- and saltwater fish. This photograph was taken on Election Day in 1910. (Courtesy of the Louis "Chub" Gildersleeve family.)

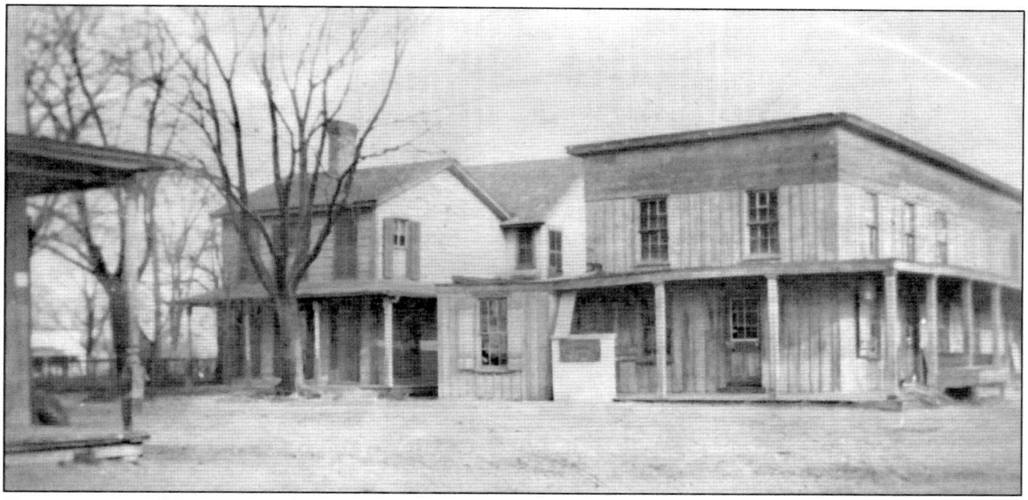

GILDERSLEEVE HOME AND STORE, C. 1900. Located on the northeast corner of Love Lane and Pike Street, this store, built around 1850, offered many items, including freshly ground coffee and famous cheddar cheese in 30-pound wheels. Customers could get a brown jug filled with New Orleans molasses from a barrel, and also bought kerosene lanterns, candles, foot warmers, and even coal for their stoves. (MLL.)

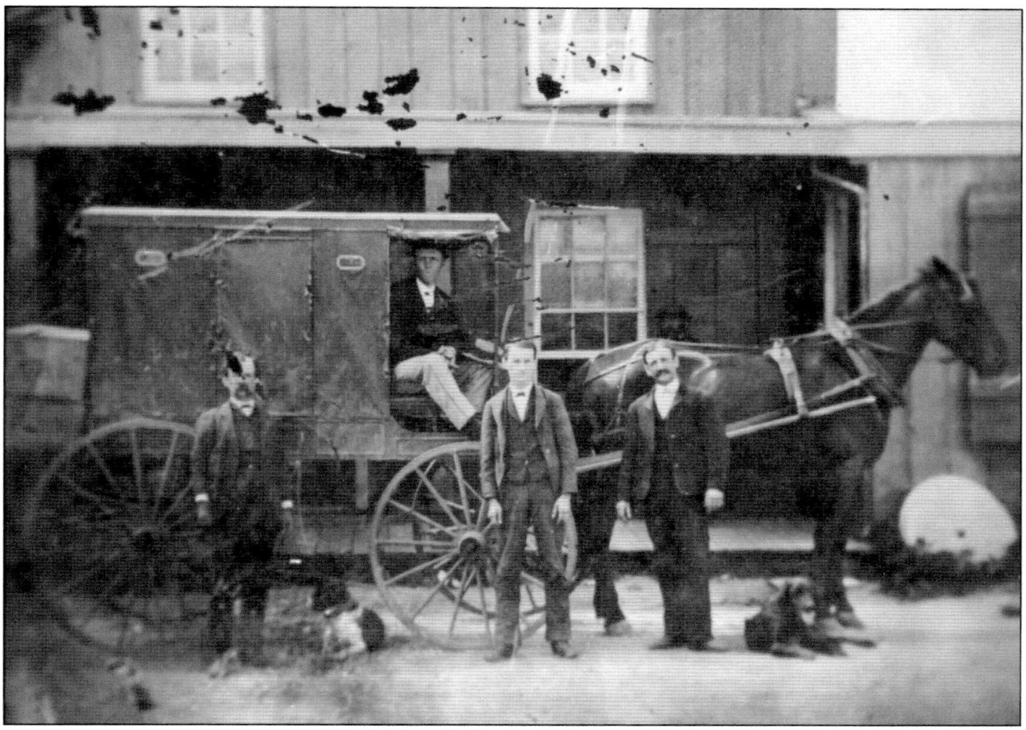

IN FRONT OF GILDERSLEEVE'S, C. 1900. Deliveries were a necessity for farm families, especially in outlying areas. The Gildersleeve horse and wagon made the rounds, dropping off goods at customers' doorsteps. The goods on the second floor included a pretty assortment of percale fabric, as well as groceries, medicines, notions, hats, shoes, and ladies' wear, even corsets. Standing here from left to right are Irad, Charles, and James Gildersleeve. Sidney P. Tuthill is in the wagon. (MLL.)

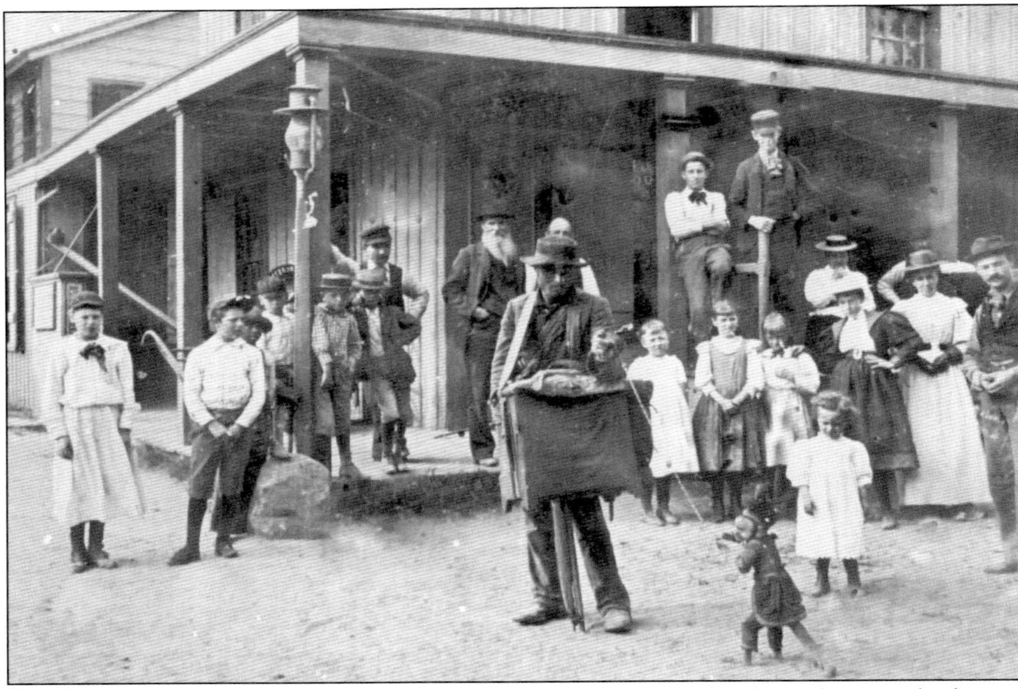

Hurdy-Gurdy Man at the Gildersleeve Store, c. 1900. The hurdy-gurdy man, also known as the organ grinder, traveled around with a hand-operated organ, or hurdy-gurdy, playing tunes and hoping that his grateful audience would drop a coin into his tin cup. A pet monkey, often dressed in a cute little costume, would dance for the audience and sometimes perform simple tricks, like doffing his little cap, or "playing dead for the Queen." (MLL.)

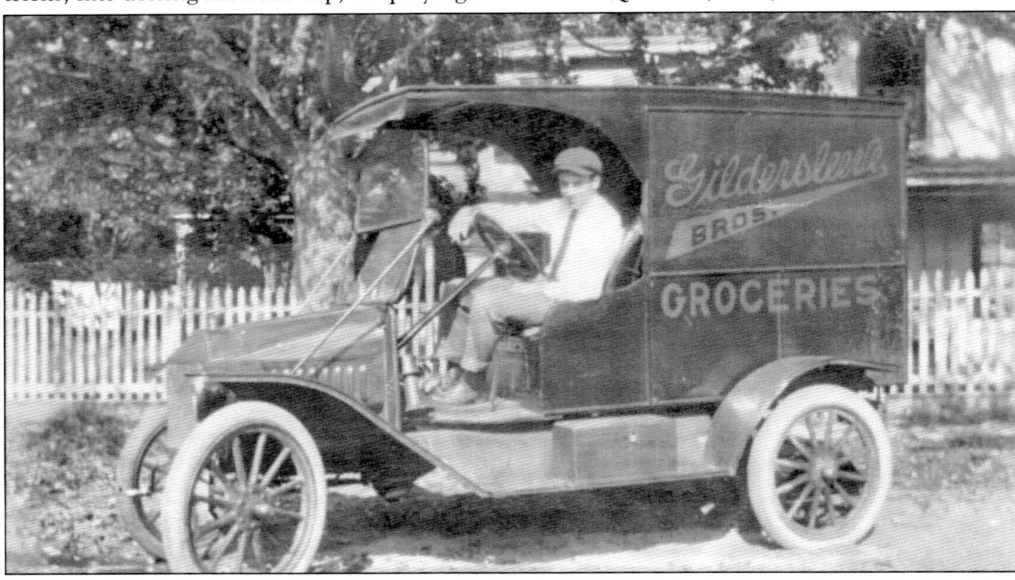

Gildersleeve Brothers Delivery Truck, c. 1915. When automobiles arrived on the scene, the Gildersleeve brothers purchased a fine truck to deliver groceries and supplies to farmers and residents. They had three main delivery routes before adding the summer colony of Camp Mineola as the fourth in 1923. (MLL.)

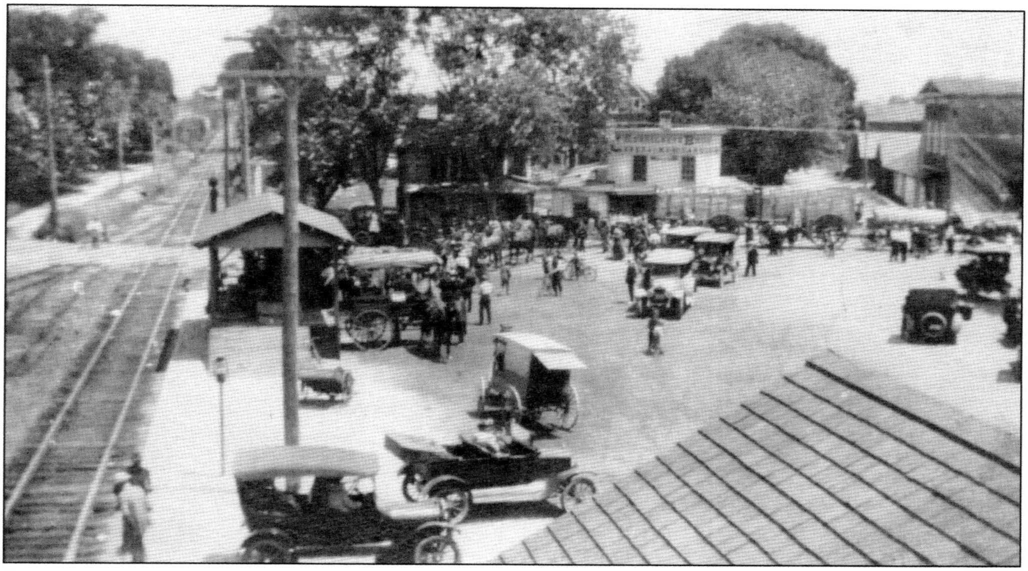

STATION SQUARE, 1918. In June 1918, the soap known as 20 Mule Team Borax was delivered to the Gildersleeve store. Borax was first manufactured by the Dial corporation in 1894. It was named after the 20-mule team that was used to move the borax out of Death Valley, California, to the nearest rail spur. Consumers used borax to aid digestion, keep milk sweet, improve their complexion, and remove dandruff. (MLL.)

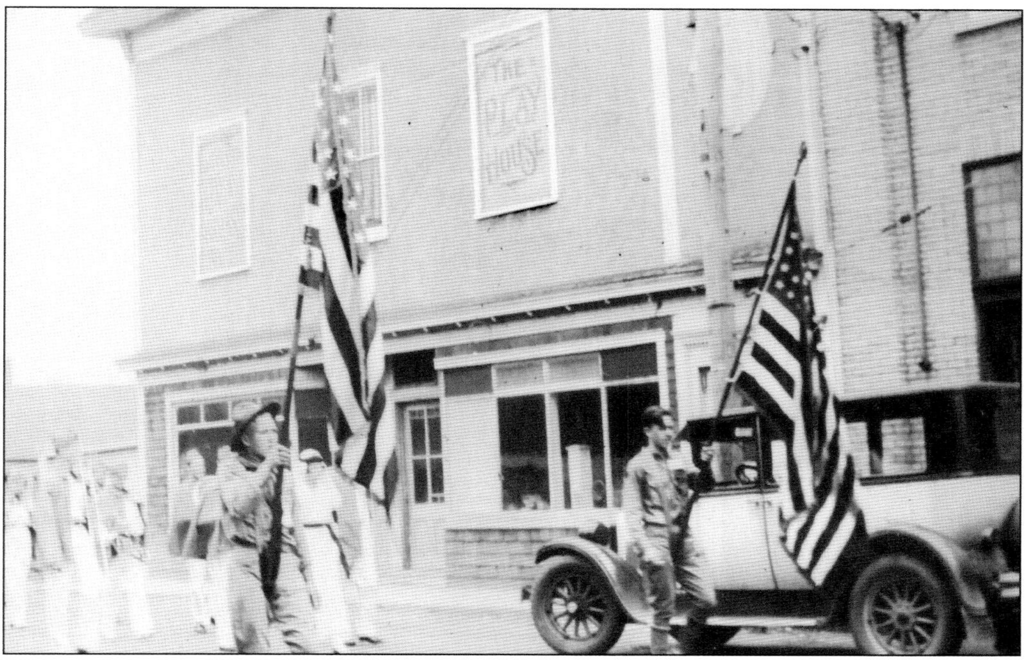

PARADE BY FISCHER'S HALL c. 1920. George H. Fischer built a two-story building east of his market on Pike Street in 1913. The second floor contained Fischer's Playhouse, which was used as a movie house, dance hall, and basketball court. At one time, both the Catholic and African American communities utilized the space for church services. The ground floor had a lunchroom and billiard parlor. (Courtesy of the Louis "Chub" Gildersleeve family.)

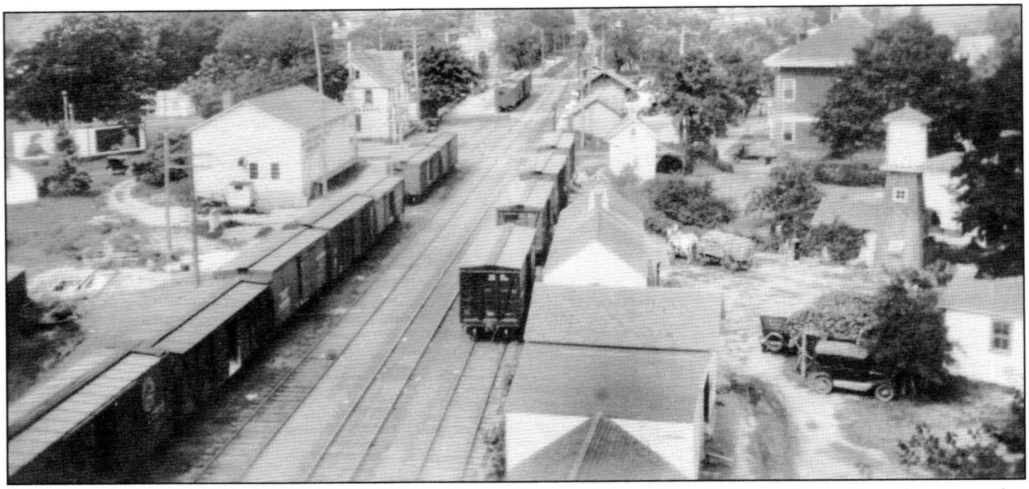

SIDETRACKS IN MATTITUCK, 1923. The sidetracks on either side of the main rail underscore the importance of the railroad to commerce in Mattituck and Laurel. By 1900, freight trains were taking out nine carloads of produce per day. The horse and wagon on the right carrying sacks of potatoes is a remnant of an earlier age, while the automobiles, truck, and billboards presage the modern era of transportation. (Courtesy of the Louis "Chub" Gildersleeve family.)

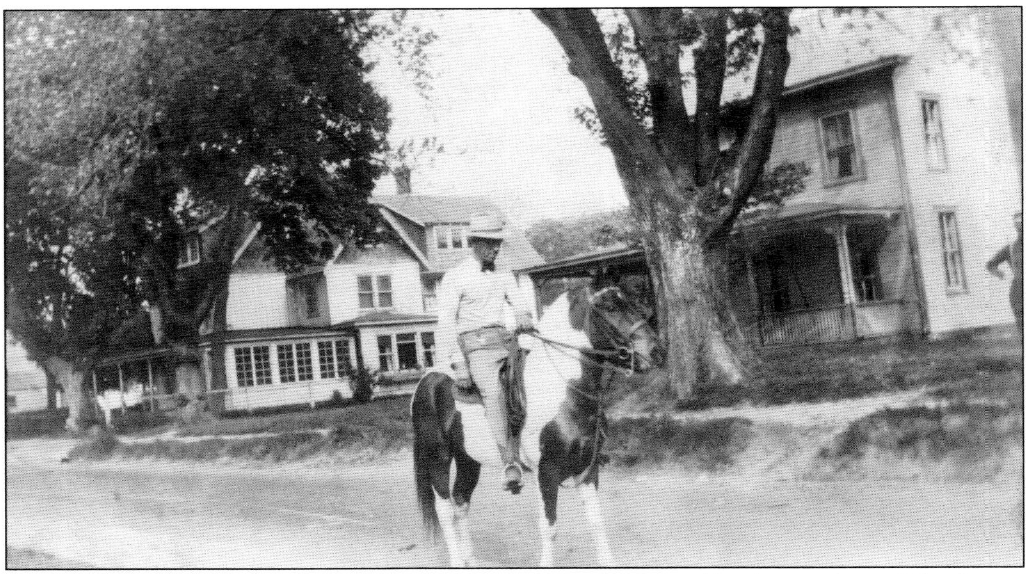

JOHN H. ZENZIUS, C. 1920. John H. "Jack" Zenzius rides one of his horses down Pike Street. In the background on the left is the home of George Fischer, and the Gildersleeve house is on the right. Jack's livery stables and barn were east of Duryee's hardware store. His livery business included service for the Glenwood Hotel, where his father, John P. Zenzius, was the proprietor in 1910. (Courtesy of Anne and Joseph Traynor.)

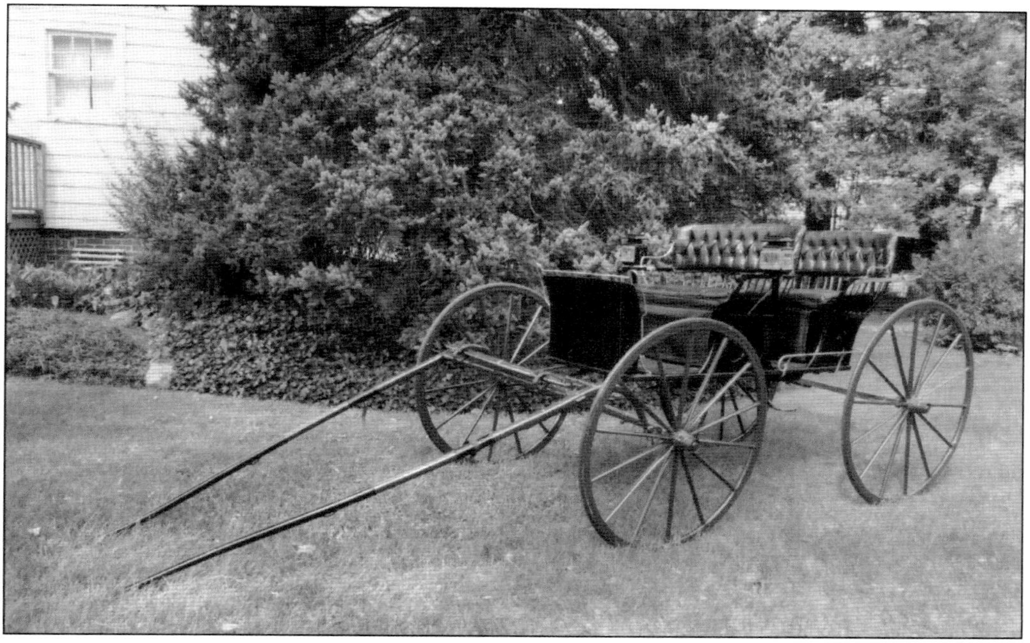

E.V. Knipe's Carriage, c. 1910. On the south side of Pike Street, near Wickham Avenue, were the fire department, Knipe's wheelwright and harness shop, and Dohm's blacksmith shop. Knipe was known for his fine carriage-making. This Knipe carriage is presently owned by the Mattituck-Laurel Historical Society. (MLL.)

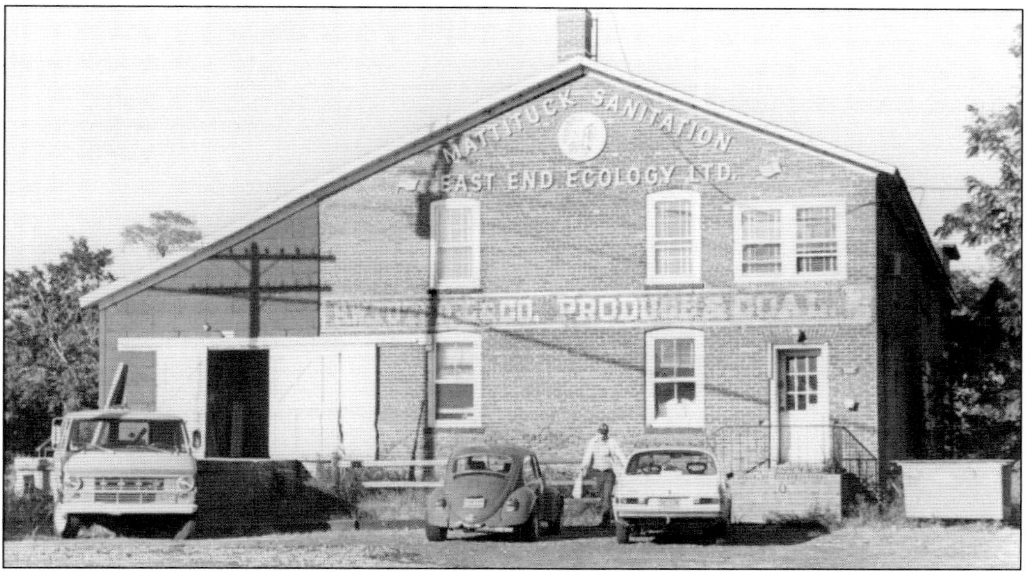

Mattituck Sanitation Building, c. 1960. In 1885, the Alart and Maguire pickling factory opened on the railroad tracks and Wickham Avenue with 12 great pickling vats, shipping pickled cauliflower and cucumbers as far as Iowa. A 1900 blizzard blew off the east end of it. What remained of the building became S.W. Tuthill & Co. Produce and Coal, then C.H. Wickham Coal and Produce, and finally Mattituck Sanitation. (MLL.)

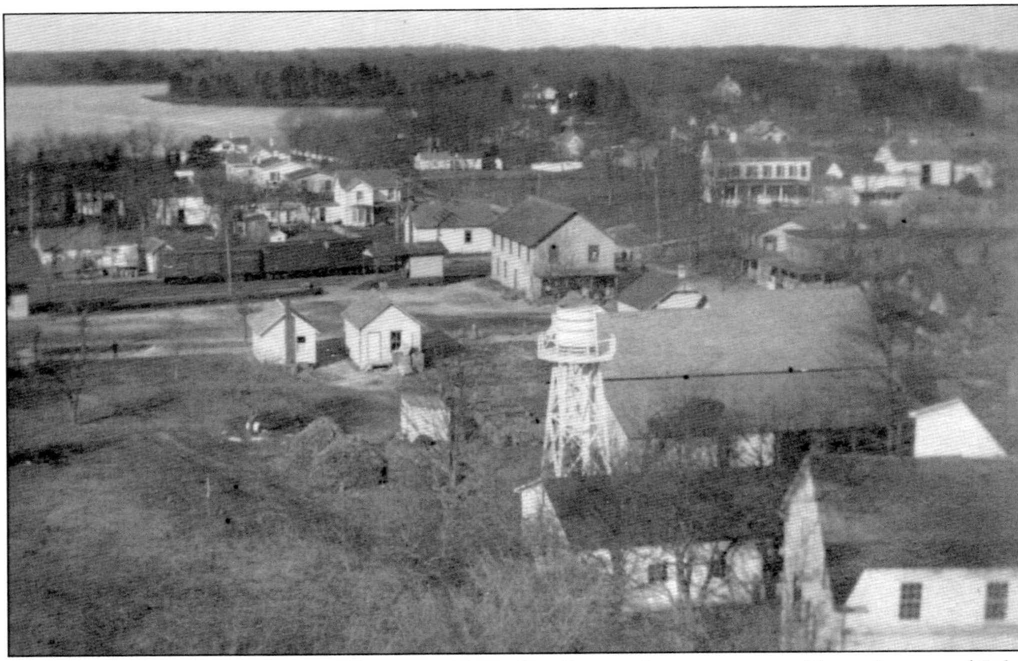

Reeve and Tuthill's Apollo Hall, c. 1910. On the northwest corner of Love Lane and Pike Street stood the Reeve and Tuthill building, seen in the middle of this photograph just above the water tower. Opened in 1878, Reeve and Tuthill sold general merchandise. In 1879, they opened an upstairs hall called Apollo Hall, a place for dances and plays, meetings of the Mattituck Literary Society, and political rallies. (MLHS.)

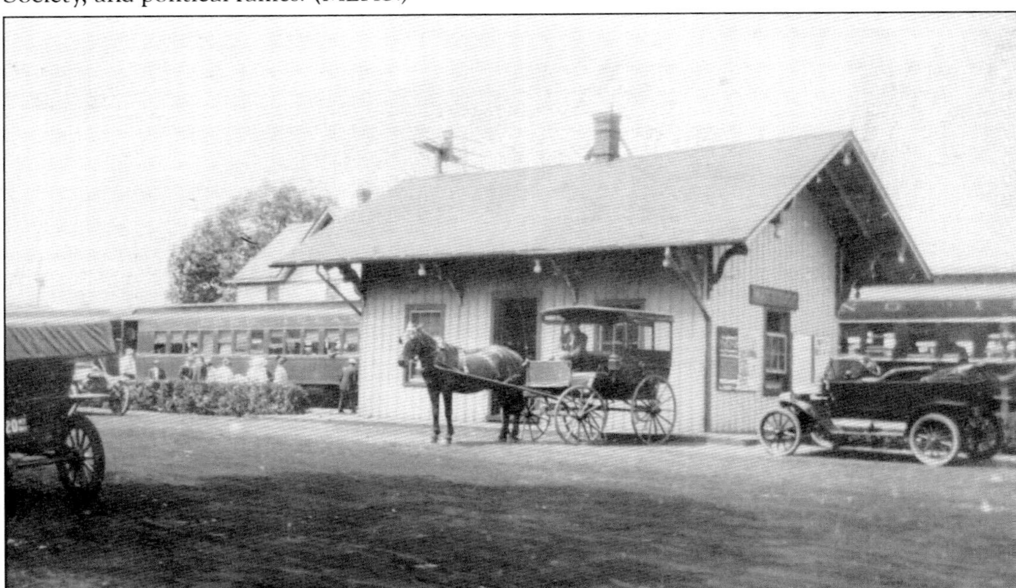

Mattituck Station, c. 1910. This photograph records the transition to a new era in transportation, as a horse-drawn omnibus sits surrounded by parked automobiles at the Mattituck depot. Passengers depart from or board the train as it pauses at the station. (Courtesy of the Louis "Chub" Gildersleeve family.)

LOUIS "CHUB" GILDERSLEEVE, C. 1905. Louis C. Gildersleeve worked for the Long Island Rail Road for more than 40 years. He began in 1900 as an assistant to his uncle, Charles Gildersleeve, and succeeded him in the position of stationmaster in 1929. Chub, liked by all for his never-failing cheerfulness, handled passenger, freight, and express traffic, as well as mail and the telegraph, all without the services of an assistant. (Courtesy of the Louis "Chub" Gildersleeve family.)

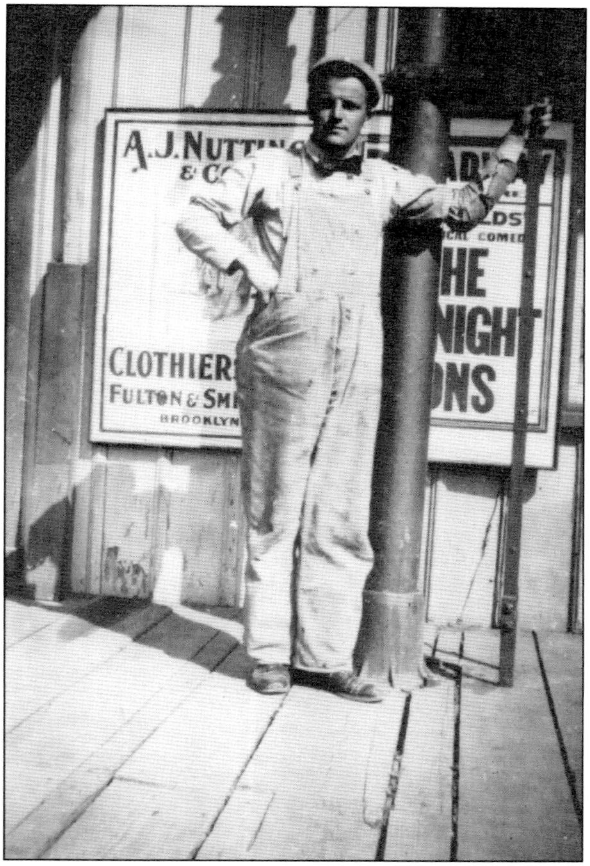

PEDDLE WAGON IN STATION SQUARE, C. 1905. In 1881, Abe and George Brown opened a grocery store on Hamilton Avenue. Abe did the greater part of the business by loading up his peddle wagon (pictured) and selling from house to house, often accepting eggs in trade, as did other grocery stores of the period. (Courtesy of the Louis "Chub" Gildersleeve family.)

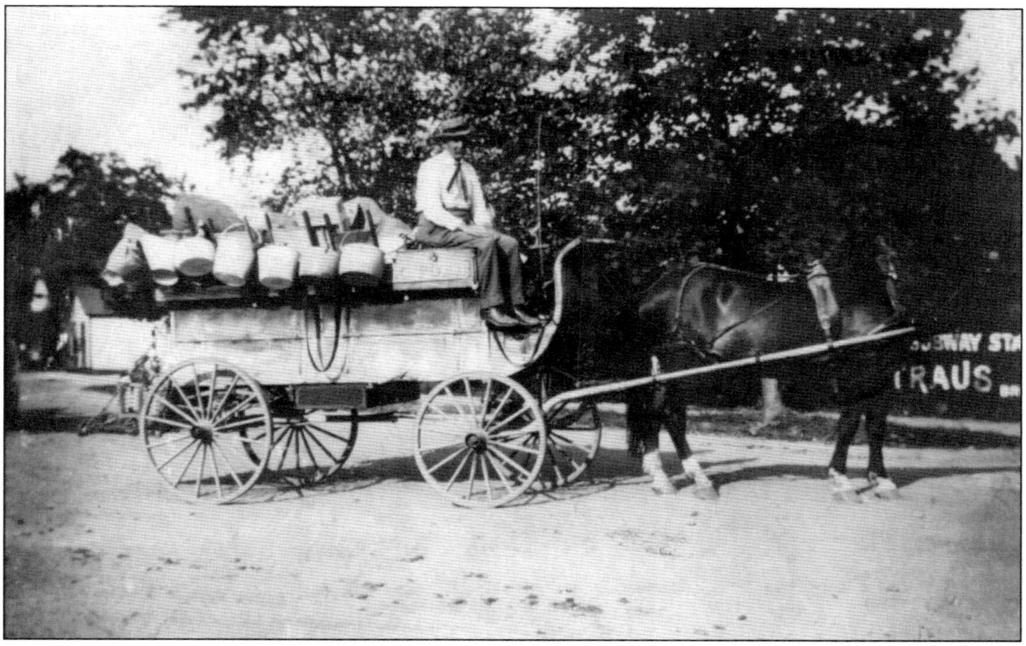

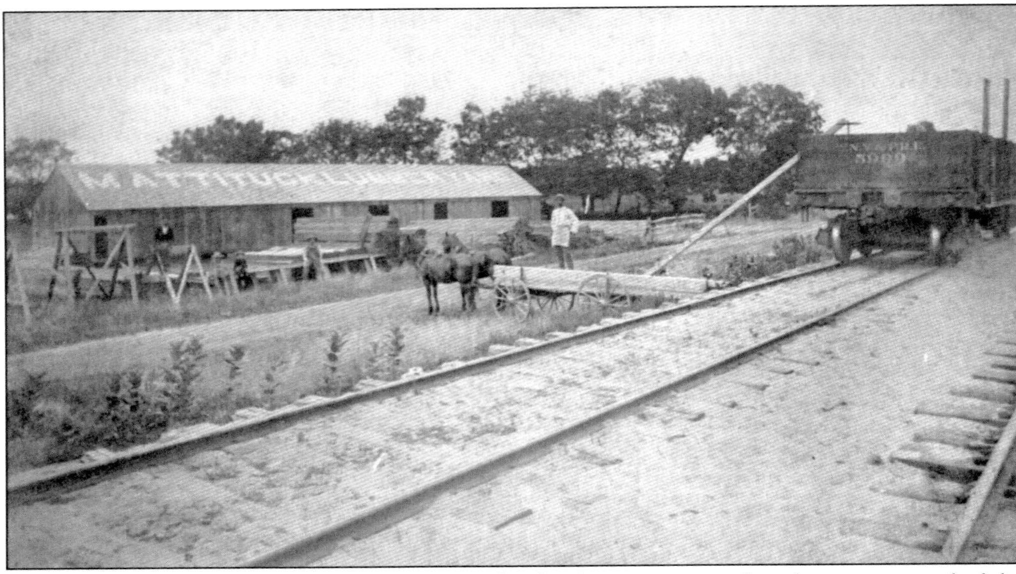

Penny Lumber, c. 1900. In 1890, the Penny lumber business opened at the western end of the village. A *Long Island Traveler* article states: "George L. Penny succeeds beyond expectations with his lumber yard here. He had three big car loads of lumber arrive here last week and can hardly keep supplied with a full stock as he is constantly carting it away from Southold to Aquebogue." (Courtesy of Carolyn LaTulip.)

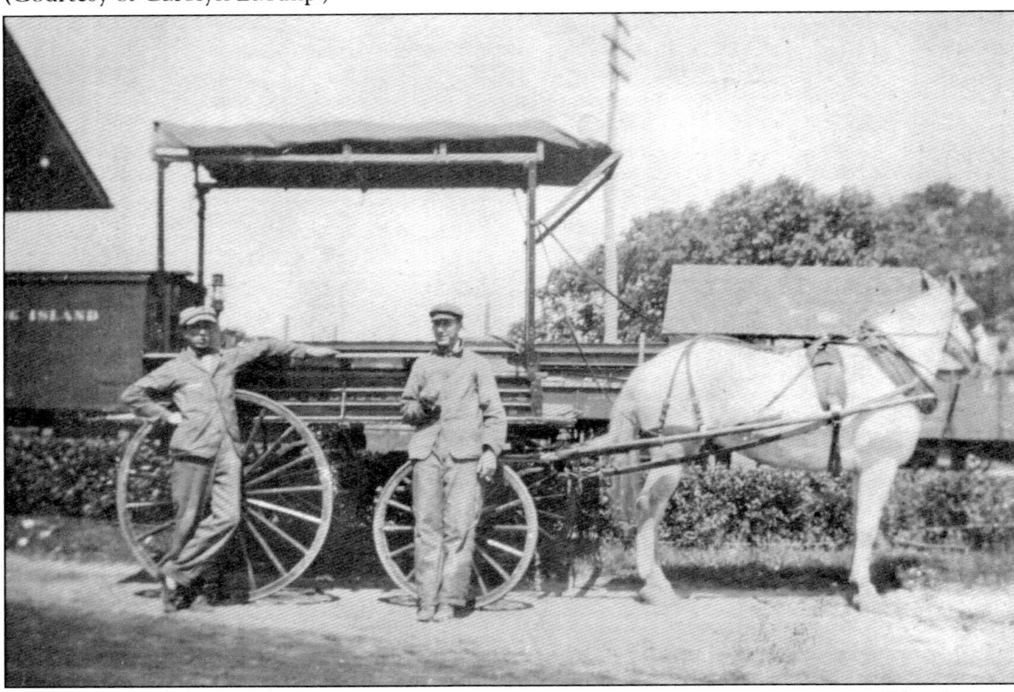

Frank "Duke" MacMillan and George L. Penny, c. 1910. Horsepower moved lumber and supplies from the train to the Penny lumberyard. Penny was reported to have had a faithful old horse named Kit, who spent 27 years in the service of the lumber business and died at age 37. (Courtesy of the Louis "Chub" Gildersleeve family.)

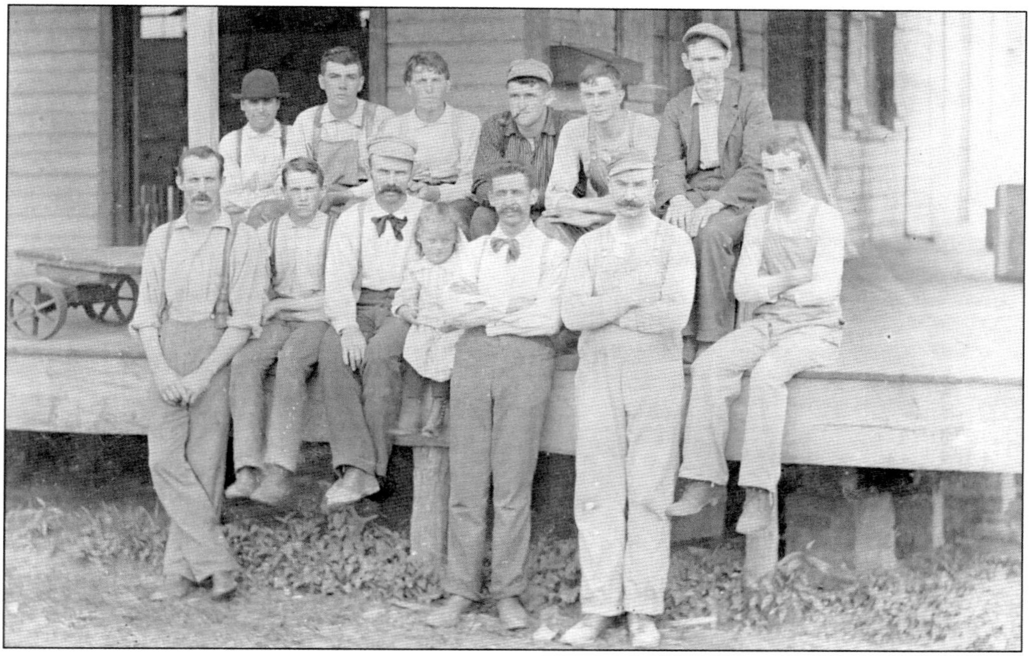

HUDSON BROTHERS CANNING FACTORY WORKERS, C. 1910. Built in 1888, the Hudson Canning Factory, located on Sound Avenue west of Pacific Street and adjacent to the railroad tracks, specialized in the canning of tomatoes, asparagus, cauliflower, and squash. The cans were shipped to markets in New York and Boston. This was an important industry for Mattituck, employing a large number of workers and providing a market for local farmers. (MLL.)

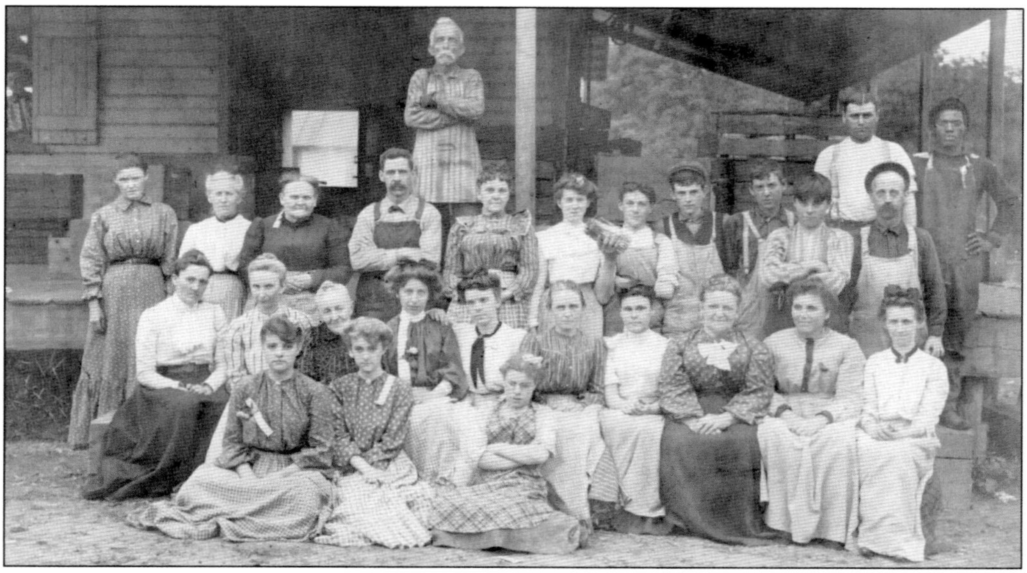

CANNING WORKERS, C. 1910. The Mattituck factory preserved about 5,000 quart-cans daily. In the fall, women were paid a penny and a half per pail for cleaning squash. In 1910, the output of the company was 125,000 cans of asparagus, 480,000 cans of tomatoes, 360,000 cans of peas, 192,000 cans of string beans, 100,000 cans of apples, 50,000 cans of strawberries, and 25,000 cans of raspberries. (MLL.)

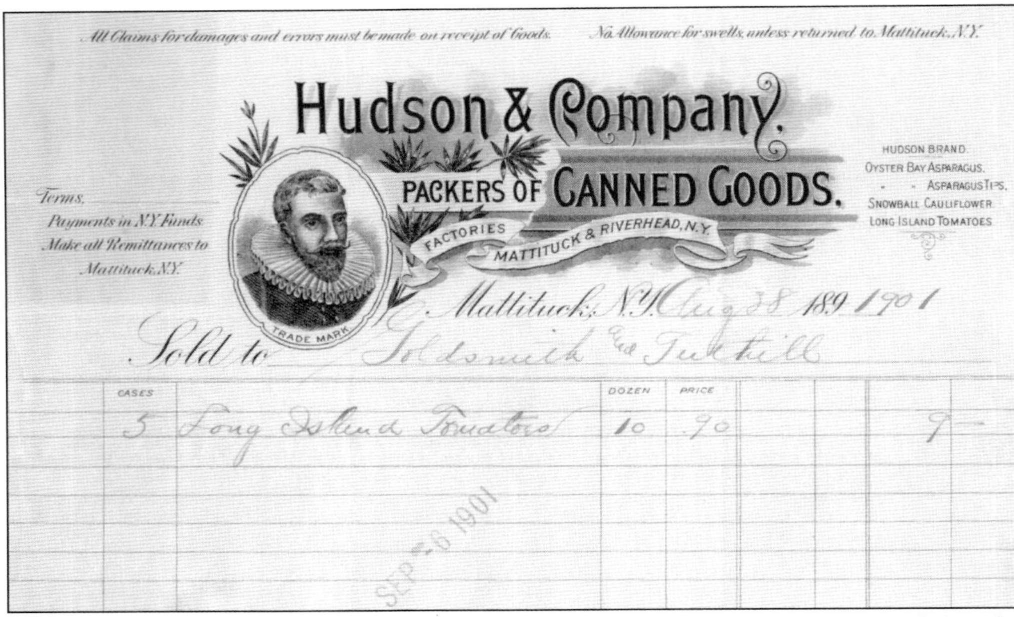

All Claims for damages and errors must be made on receipt of Goods. No Allowance for swells, unless returned to Mattituck, N.Y.

Hudson & Company.

PACKERS OF CANNED GOODS.

FACTORIES MATTITUCK & RIVERHEAD, N.Y.

TRADE MARK

HUDSON BRAND.
Oyster Bay Asparagus.
" " Asparagus Tips.
Snowball Cauliflower
Long Island Tomatoes

Terms.
Payments in N.Y. Funds.
Make all Remittances to
Mattituck, N.Y.

Mattituck, N.Y. Aug 28 1901

Sold to Goldsmith & Tuthill

CASES		DOZEN	PRICE	
5	Long Island Tomatoes	10	.90	9 —

SEP 6 1901

HUDSON & COMPANY LABEL, 1901. The label on the Hudson cans included an image of a bearded man wearing a ruff, a mark of high quality. The company's Long Island canned tomatoes were said to beat the world for flavor and coloring. By 1917, however, farmers were making more money for potatoes and cauliflower, so they stopped taking out contracts on tomatoes, and the Hudson canning factory subsequently closed. (MLL.)

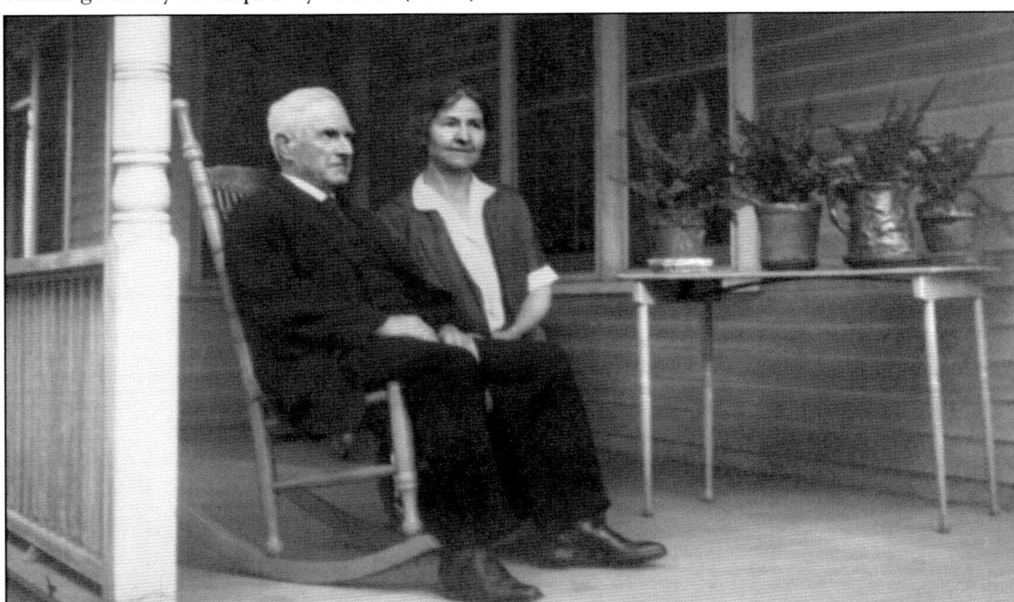

HENRY HALSEY REEVE AND SARAH E. REEVE, C. 1910. By 1884, T.E. and Henry Reeve operated greenhouses on the west side of New Suffolk Avenue. In 1888, they grew 50,000 cabbage plants, 20,000 tomato plants, beets, cucumbers, lettuce, cauliflower, radishes, cacti, rare geraniums, and roses. Shipping these products to New York City and other points west proved very successful. (Courtesy of Norman Wamback.)

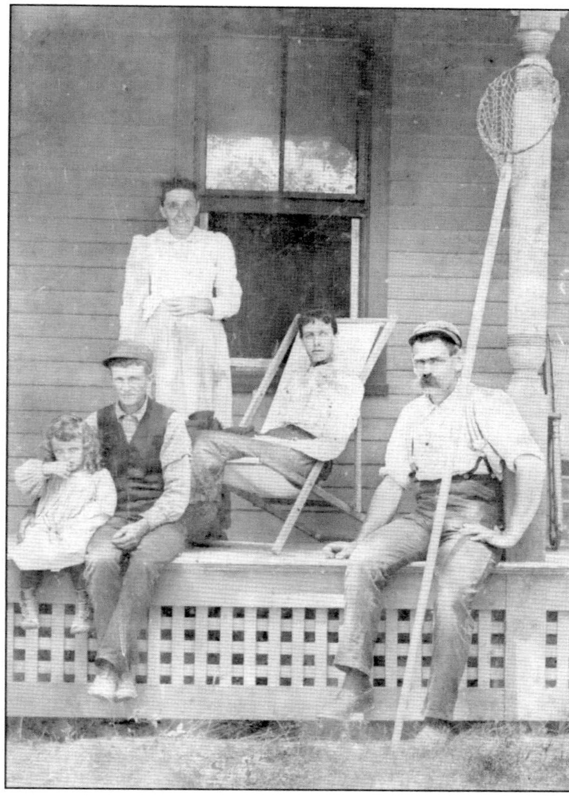

Peter Harvey Duryee, 1897. Here, from left to right, are young Vivien Duryee, Ben Wells, Mrs. Albin, Beulah Duryee, and Peter Harvey Duryee. With his partner, Otto P. Hallock, Peter owned a three-story fertilizer factory near the Long Island Rail Road tracks on a road that still retains the name Factory Avenue, though the building was destroyed by fire many years ago. Some of the fertilizer was produced by grinding up horseshoe crabs. (MLHS.)

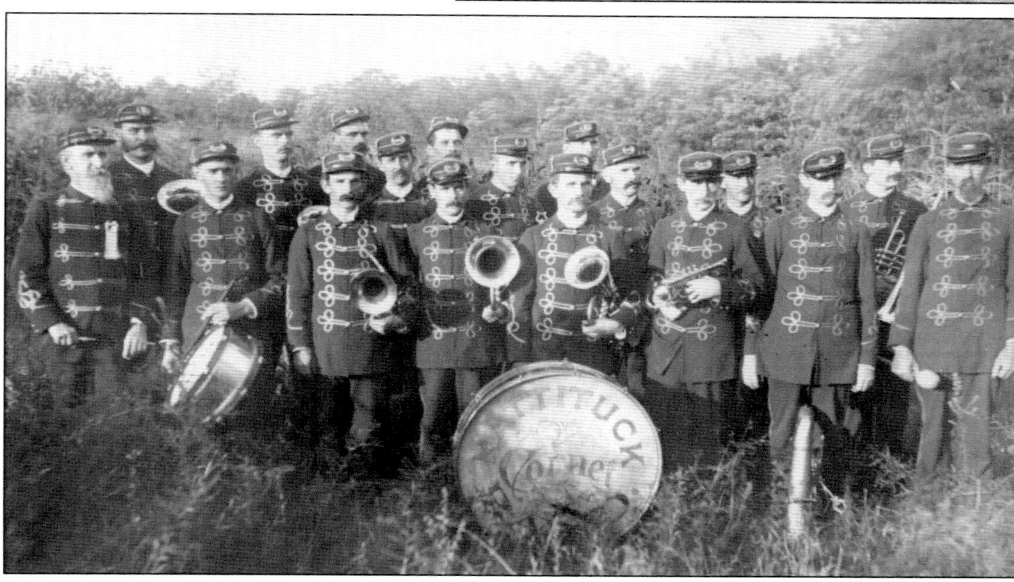

Mattituck Cornet Band, c. 1890. Organized in 1884, the cornet band played at the opening of the fertilizer factory four years later. The band includes, from left to right, (first row) Prof. George B. Reeve, Howard Terry, Wallace Tuthill, George Terry, Willis Tuthill, Jim Reeve, Otto Hallock, and Lucius Young; (second row) E.V. Knipe, Oscar Robinson, Peter Harvey Duryee, Gene Robinson, Herbert M. Reeve, Will Duryee, Wickham Reeve, Harry Lupton, and M.P. Goff. (MLL.)

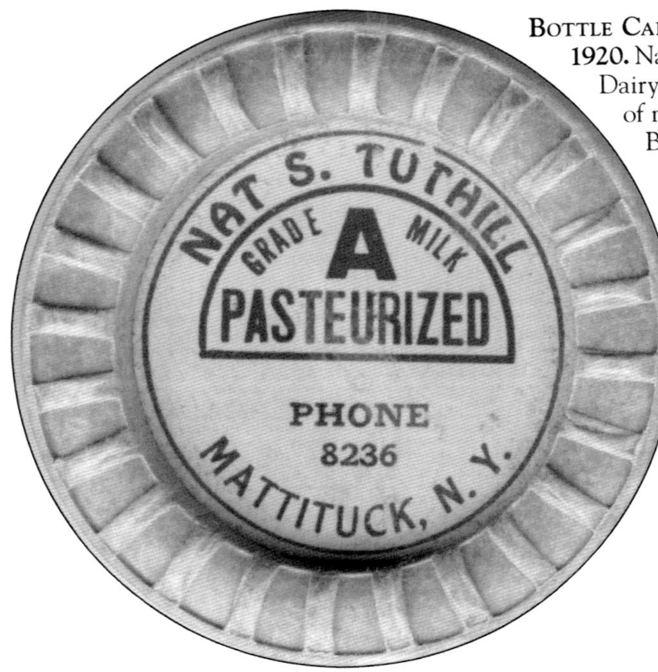

BOTTLE CAP FROM WOLF PIT LAKE DAIRY, C. 1920. Nat S. Tuthill opened the Wolf Pit Lake Dairy around 1920, selling a few bottles of milk each week at the Gildersleeve Brothers store. As demand for the milk grew, he decided to start a delivery route, eventually covering Riverhead east to Cutchogue. His son Nathaniel S. Tuthill Jr. continued the business successfully into the 1960s, with his Guernsey cows producing rich, creamy milk. (Courtesy of MLL.)

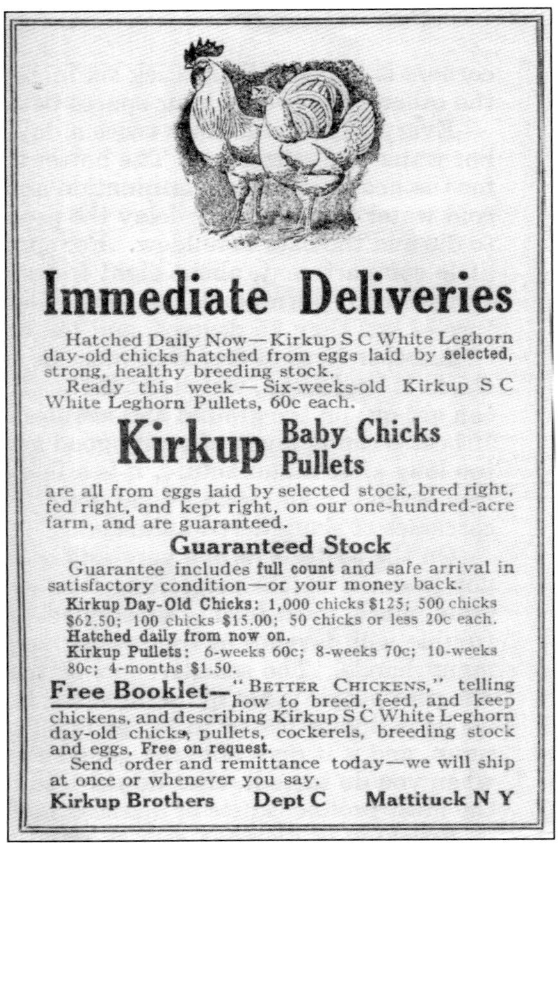

KIRKUP BROTHERS ADVERTISEMENT, 1914. Brothers Victor and J. Trowbridge Kirkup ran a very large and successful poultry business for many years. In the spring of 1914, they were planning to ship more than 20,000 day-old chicks, 5,000 cockerels, and 5,000 pullets. (MLL.)

Five

Farm, Family, and Home

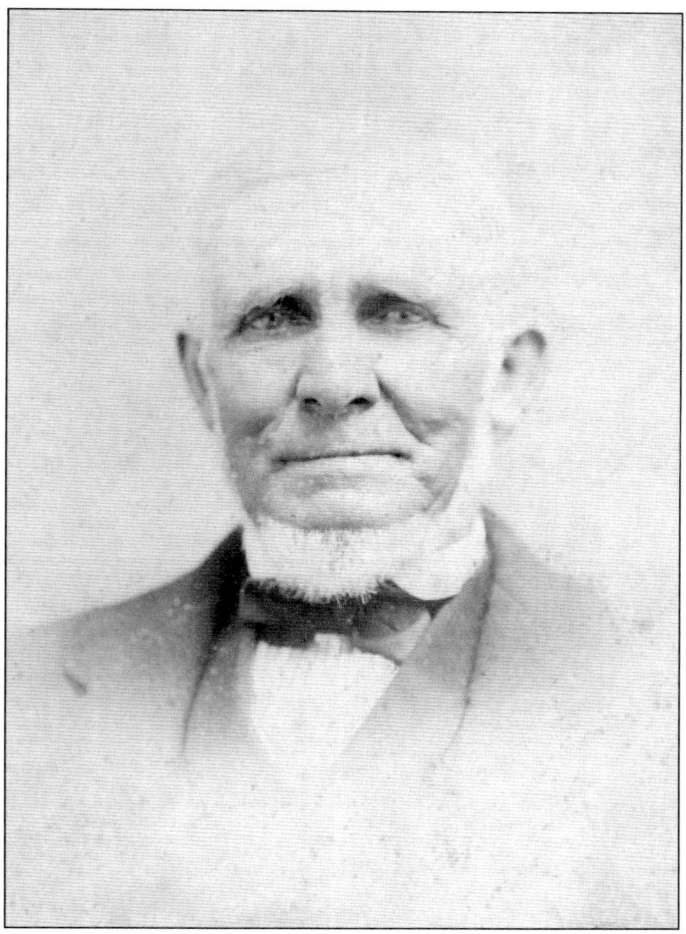

Elijah Tuthill, c. 1890. Elijah Tuthill, the son of Jesse Tuthill, and his relatives established farms in the eastern part of Mattituck. *Lain's Business Directory* for 1897 lists 150 farming families in Mattituck. The land seemed predestined for farming after the glaciers that passed through thousands of years ago left a thick layer of loess, a rich, dustlike soil that was ideal for planting. So robust were the crop yields that the factories came to the farmers. The average yield of asparagus was between 1,500 and 2,500 bunches per acre, so the Hudson canning factory was established to package the crop. In 1885, Mattituck farmers shipped about 1,000 barrels of cauliflower a day in nine railcar loads, so the Alart and Maguire pickling factory opened on Wickham Avenue to pickle both cauliflower and cucumbers. (MLHS.)

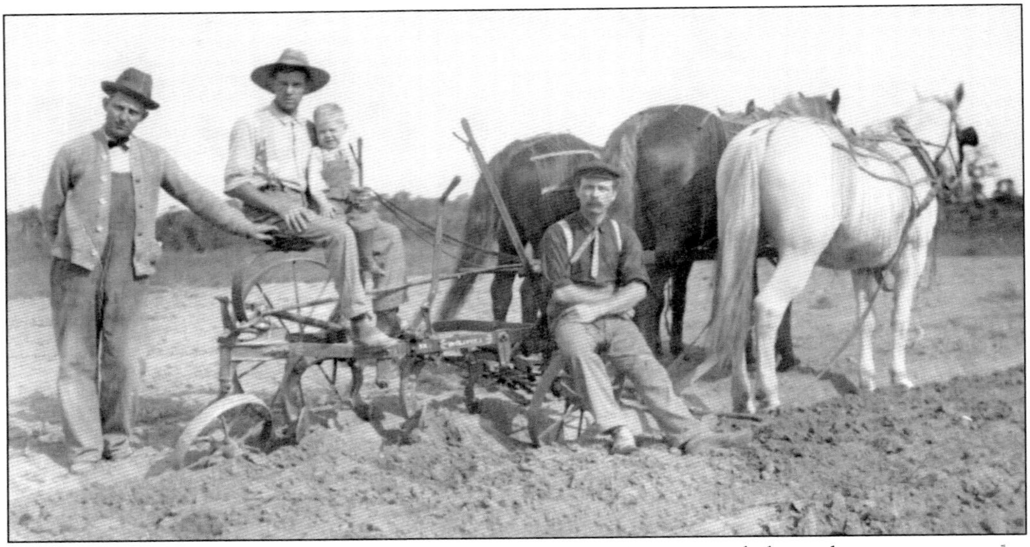

FARMERS AND THEIR PLOW, 1907. This iconic image of farmers and their plow represents the challenging work of all farmers who struggled with the soil to produce their harvest. From left to right, they are Henry P. Tuthill, Elmer D. Ruland Sr., baby Floyd Ruland, and Edward Gallagher. The Oliver Chilled Plow seen here was an improvement in the farm implement industry, equipped with a riding seat instead of the traditional, labor-intensive walk-behind plow. (MLL.)

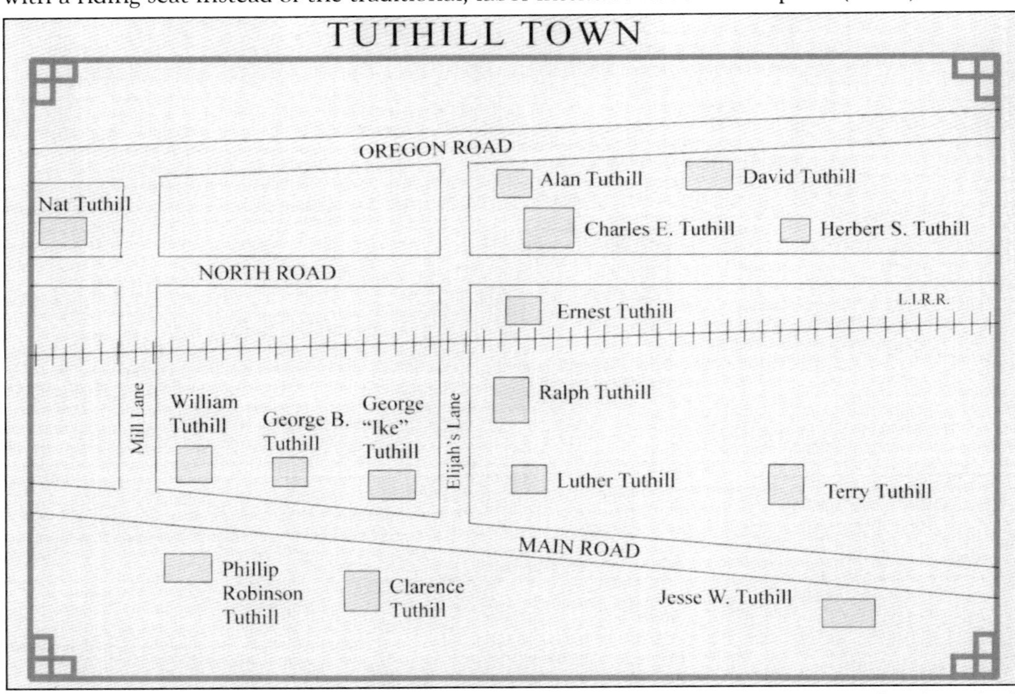

TUTHILL TOWN, C. 1900. Mattituck village actually began on its present eastern border, which was the original center of town, before the railroad pulled business west to Railroad Avenue (now Love Lane). The descendents of Jesse Tuthill settled on farms on the east side, giving the original town, with its two general stores, gristmill, and schoolhouse, the family name of Tuthill Town. (MLL.)

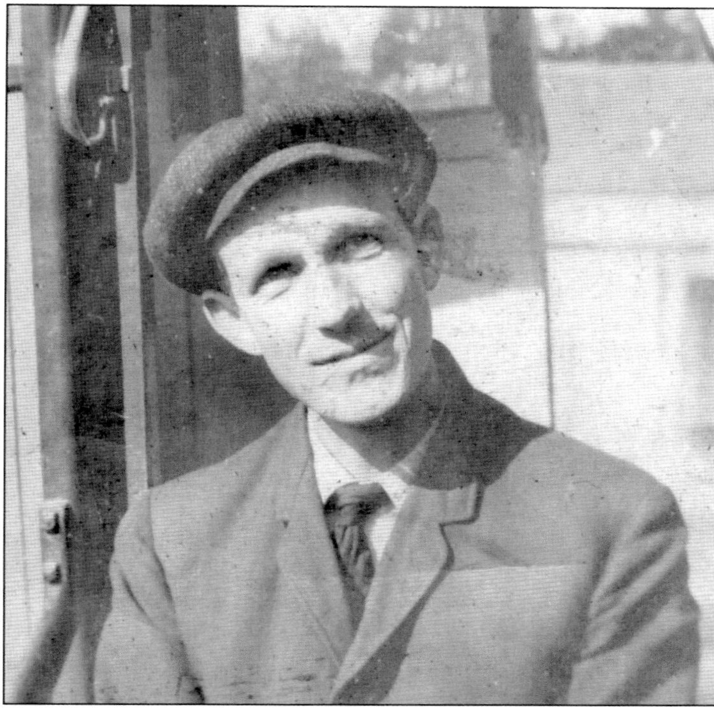

Ernest Tuthill, c. 1920. Like many farmers around 1900, Ernest Tuthill grew what he needed for his family. He raised potatoes, peas, lima beans, green beans, and brussels sprouts. He eventually grew cauliflower, which was shipped in barrels to the city. His wife, Leila, would often make cream potatoes for breakfast and dinner. Ernest had a small milk route down Bay Avenue, where he delivered milk by horse and wagon. (Courtesy of John C. Tuthill.)

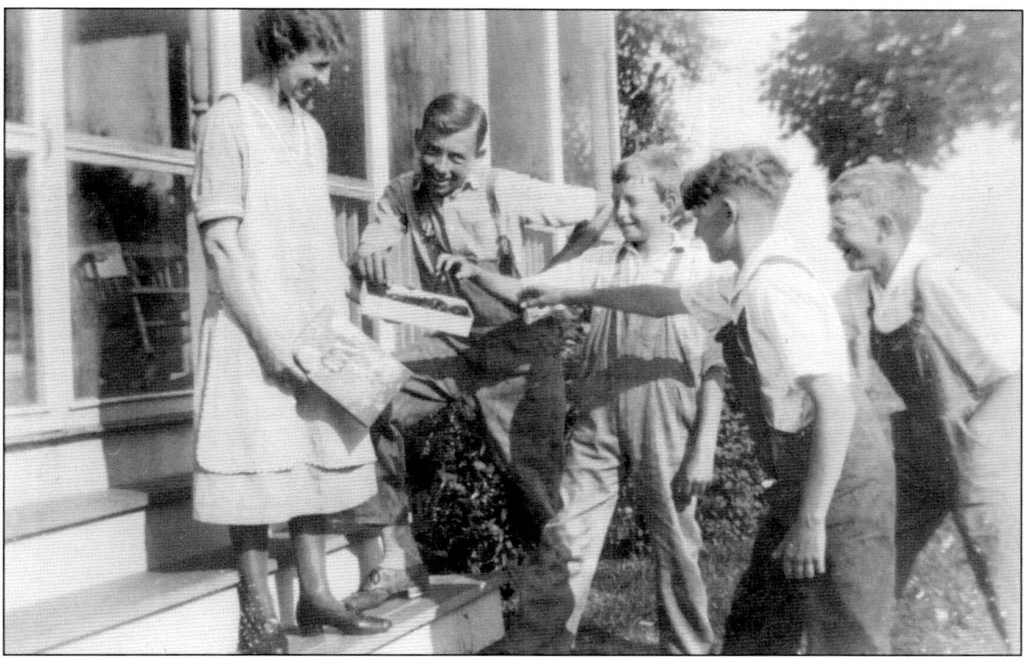

Ernest Tuthill Family, 1923. In what John C. Tuthill recalled as a "real event" on a farm in 1923, his mother, Leila Hallock Tuthill, the wife of Ernest Tuthill, distributes candy to, from left to right, her sons Ernest Quentin and John C., her nephew Raymond E., and her son Hallock. Ernest Tuthill decided to grow cucumbers for a few years, and his son John C., at age 98, recalled how he hated the chore of picking cucumbers as a boy. (Courtesy of John C. Tuthill.)

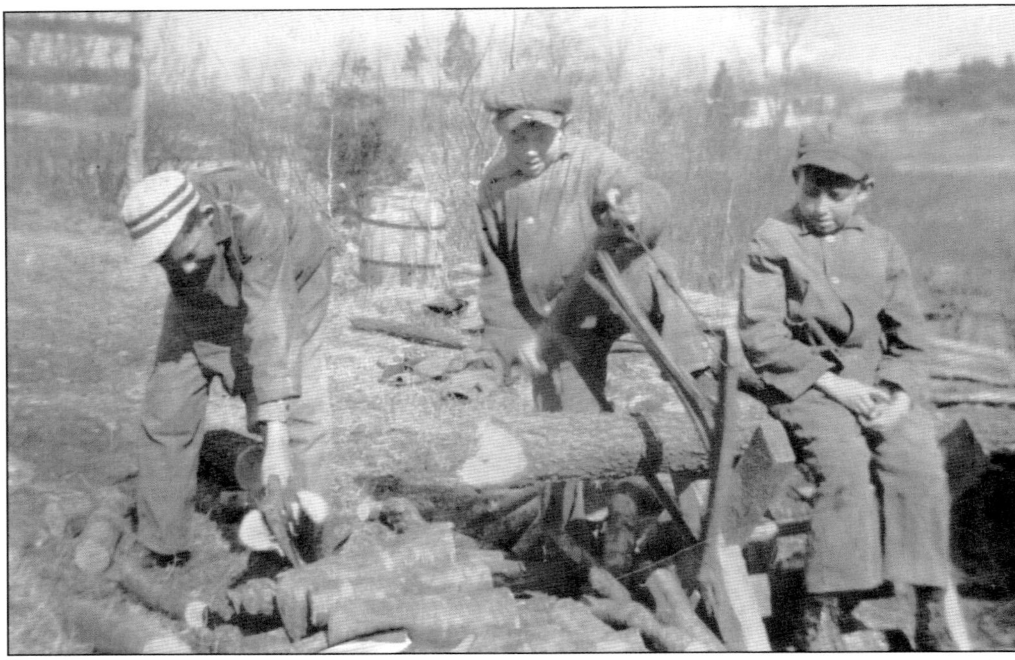

Ernest Tuthill's Boys, c. 1920. From left to right, Ernest Quentin, John C., and Hallock Tuthill cut wood for the fireplace and cookstove. John C. was the last of the Tuthills to farm in Mattituck. On Elijah's Lane, John C. planted potatoes, cauliflower, and brussels sprouts, but potatoes were his bread-and-butter crop. He also had 30 milking cows, selling the milk to the Wolf Pit bottling plant. (Courtesy of John C. Tuthill.)

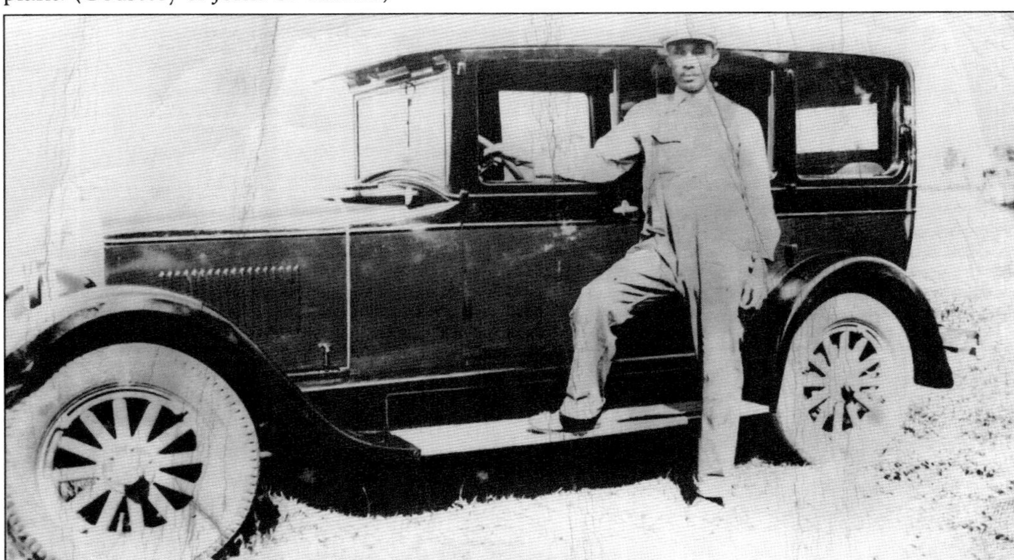

Jefferson Stovall, c. 1935. Jefferson Stovall, seen here with his car, moved his wife, Diantha, and his four children—Jefferson Jr., William, Andrew, and Alice—from Powhatan, Virginia, to Mattituck in 1930. The family lived with his brother Harrison in the old schoolhouse on the Ruland farm. Jefferson worked as a caretaker on the Charles Wells estate in Maratooka Park. (Courtesy of Alice Funn.)

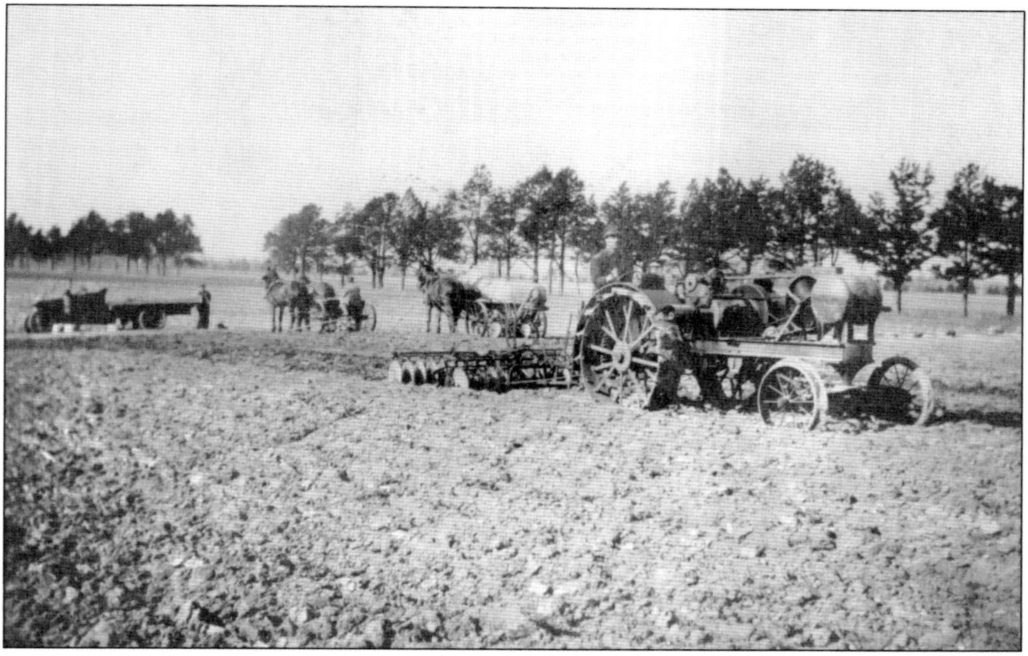

Wickham Farm, 1914. Charles W. Wickham employed both old and new methods of farming on his land, using horses to draw some implements and a tractor to pull a disc harrow to cultivate a field. The tractor, an early model Waterloo Boy with a two-cycle engine that ran on kerosene, cost approximately $750 at the time. (Courtesy of Jay Wickham.)

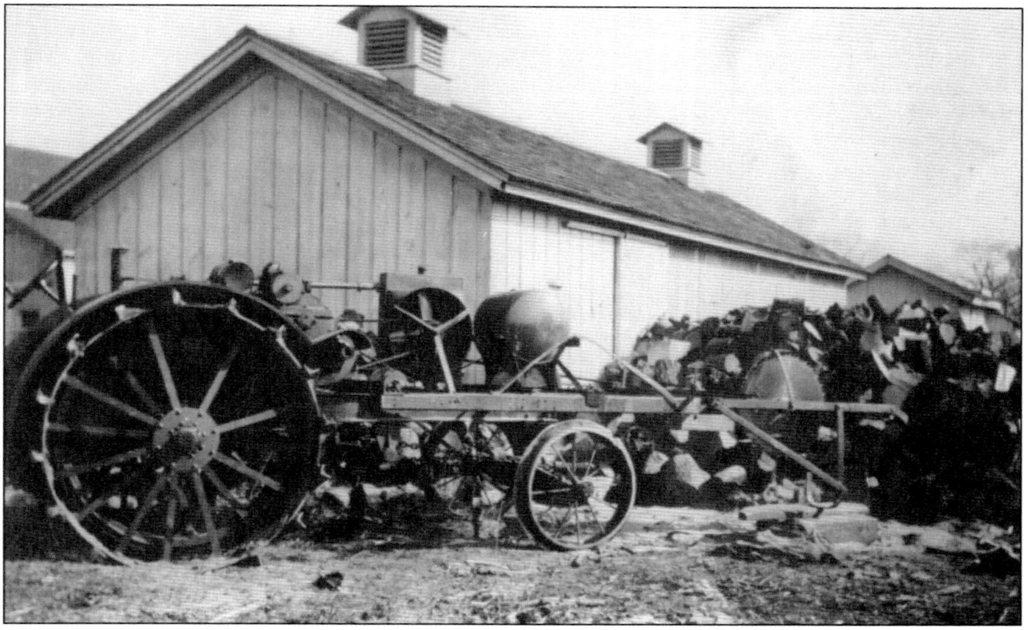

Cutting Cordwood, 1914. Charles W. Wickham had the foresight to utilize machinery to become more efficient on his farm and creamery. Here, he adapts his tractor to spin a large circular saw blade to cut trees into cordwood to be used on the farm and perhaps to be sold at his son Cedric's ice, coal, and wood warehouse. (Courtesy of Jay Wickham.)

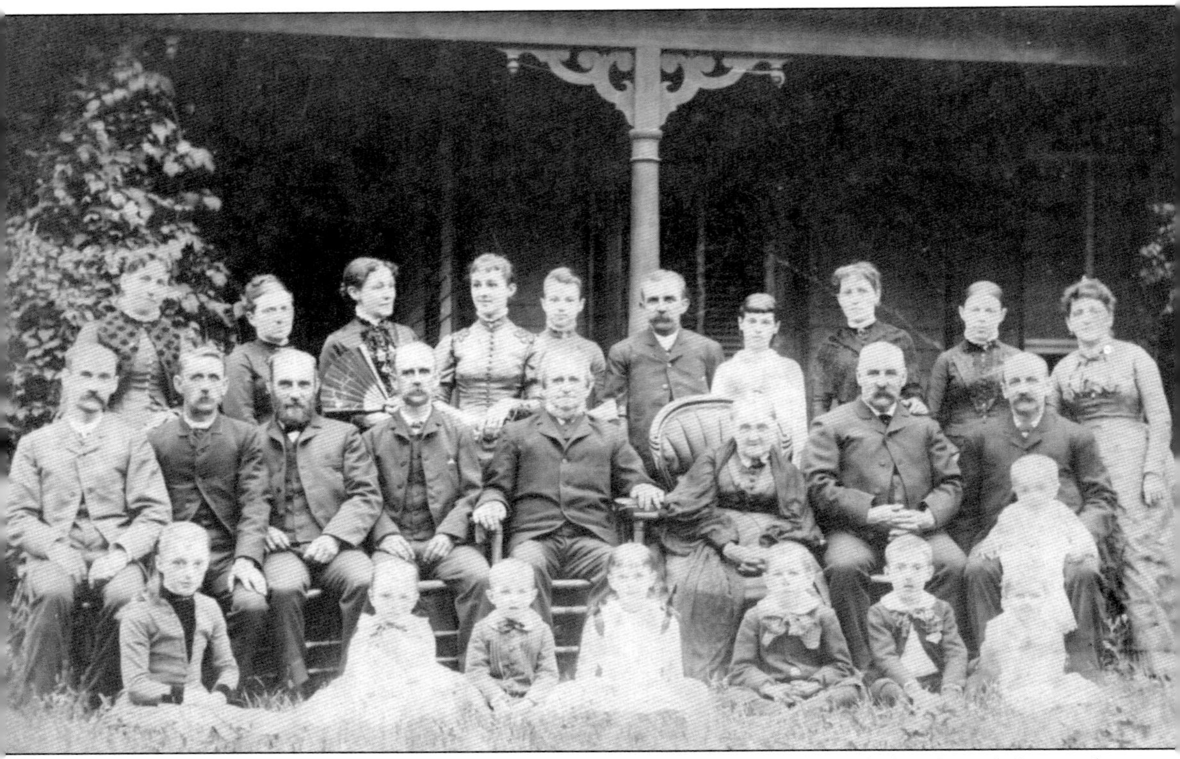

ANDREW GILDERSLEEVE FAMILY, C. 1890. The Gildersleeve family includes, from left to right, (first row) Fan, John, Sid, Puss, Jim, Wickham, Louis "Chub," and Cornelia "Doll"; (second row) Charles, Jim Kirkup, John, Irad, patriarch Andrew, matriarch Ann, Lester, and James; (third row) Miriam "Mitt" Kirkup, Jane, Alice, Allie, Annie, Henry, Esther, Sophia, Fan, and Mary. Andrew Gildersleeve and his family had a lasting impact on the village of Mattituck. Andrew was a native of Middle Island, where he had lived on a farm. He learned the house carpenter's trade and became a master builder. He built two of Mattituck's landmarks: the Presbyterian church, in 1853, and the Octagon Building, in 1854. He was a man of many interests and abilities, and spent time working as a postmaster, an assessor, a highway overseer, a Presbyterian church elder and trustee, farmer, a coffin maker, a flour mill operator, and a storekeeper. (Courtesy of Jim and Pauline Gildersleeve.)

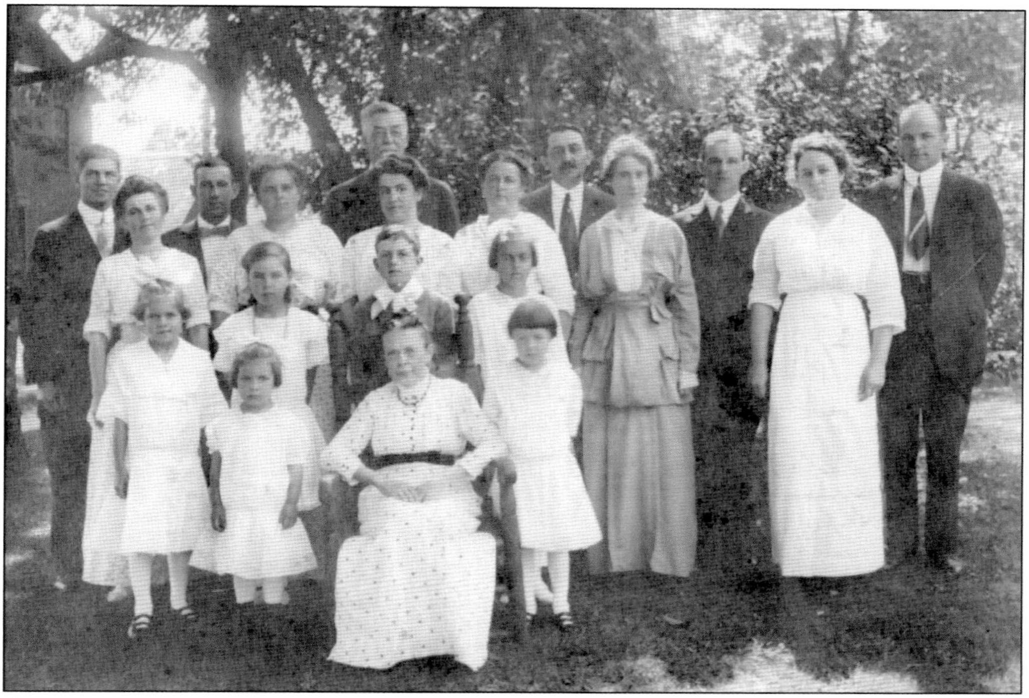

Gildersleeve Family, 1918. This family photograph includes, from left to right (first row) Lois, matriarch Ann, and Marian; (second row) Ruth, Ester, Nathaniel Tuthill, and Helen Terry; (third row) Cornelia "Doll," Ethel, Annie G. Tuthill, Helen "Puss" Terry, Ruth, and Hattie T.; (fourth row) Donald, James A., Nat, Fred Terry, Sid, and Louis "Chub." (Courtesy of Jim and Pauline Gildersleeve.)

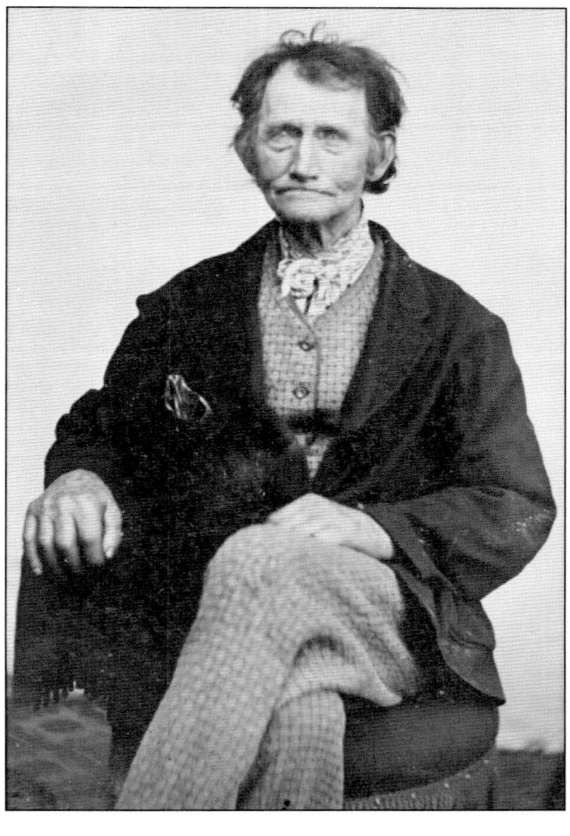

William Weed, c. 1880. This tintype preserves the image of William Weed, who devoted himself to years of loyal service in the household of John Wyckoff Duryee and his wife, Elizabeth Verity Duryee. As a tribute to his steadfast duty, Weed was buried in Bethany Cemetery in the Duryee family plot. His tombstone reads: "William Weed, August 22, 1885, 75 years, faithful servant." (MLHS.)

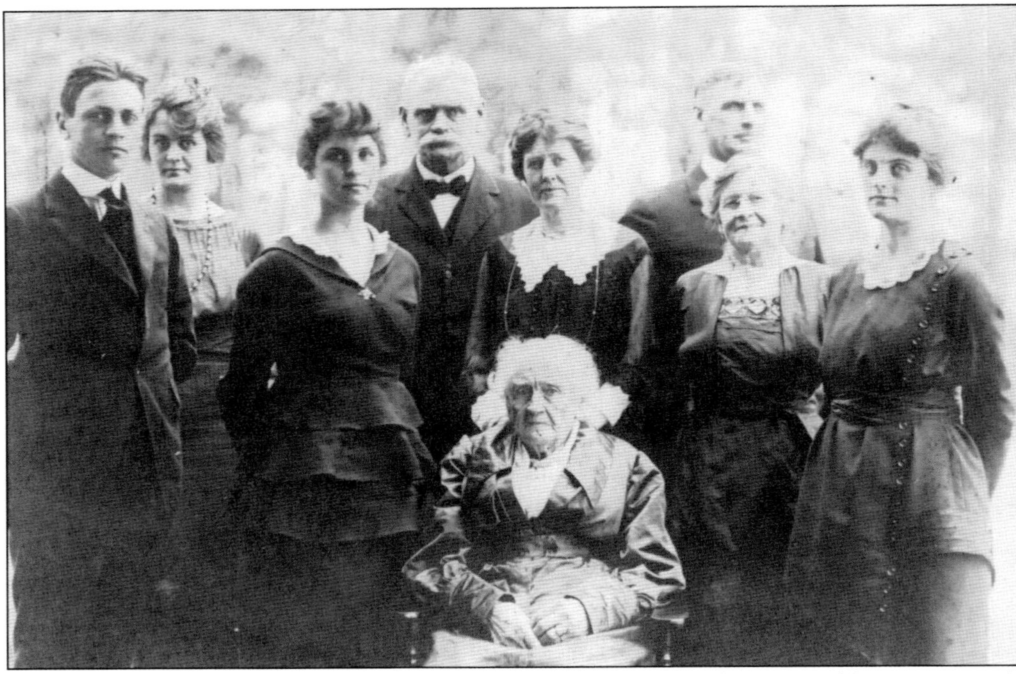

Duryee Family, c. 1920. One of several Dutch families that migrated from Brooklyn to Mattituck, the Duryee family established successful enterprises. The family includes, from left to right, John; Clara; Hope; Peter Harvey; his second wife, Mabel Hart; William Verity; his wife, Cornelia Gildersleeve; and Vivien. The family matriarch, Elizabeth Verity Duryee, is seated. (MLHS.)

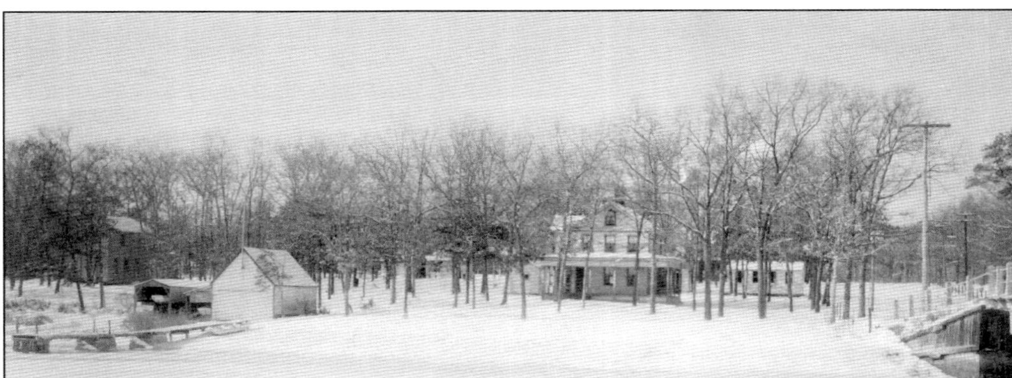

Peter Harvey Duryee Residence, c. 1920. The home of Peter Harvey Duryee is nestled in newly fallen snow on Mattituck Creek, just north of the Westphalia Avenue Bridge. Duryee purchased this property in 1889 for its proximity to the fertilizer factory he owned with Otto P. Hallock on Factory Avenue. To the left of the main house are the boathouse and dock of the family of avid boaters and sailors. (MLL.)

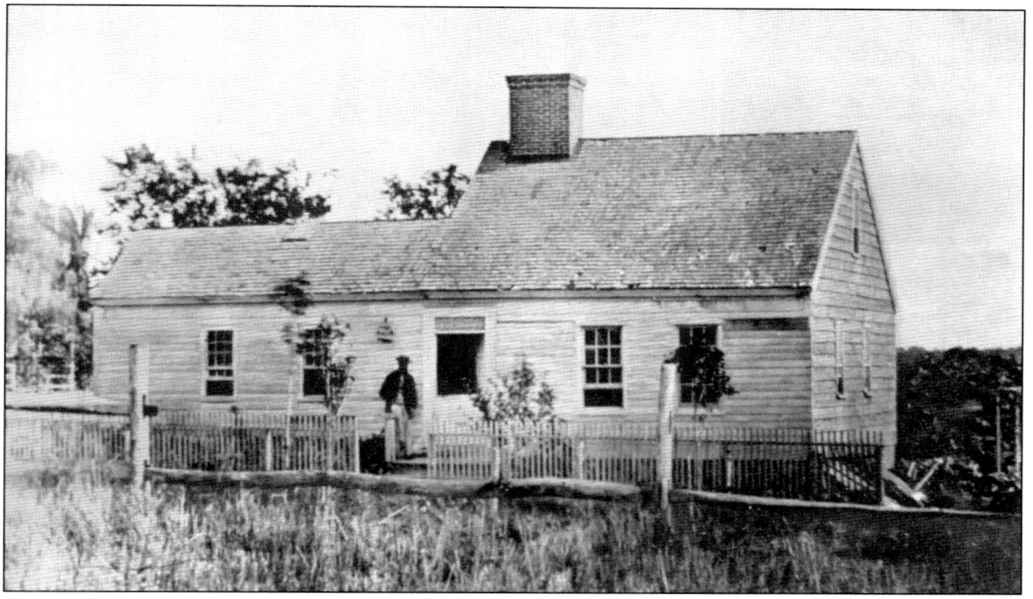

Deacon Nathaniel Hubbard House, c. 1880. Deacon Nathaniel Hubbard, whose house stood on North Road, was the brother of John Hubbard, who ran the Mattituck House. They were descended from Richard Terry, one of the original settlers of Southold. (Courtesy of the Suffolk County Historical Society.)

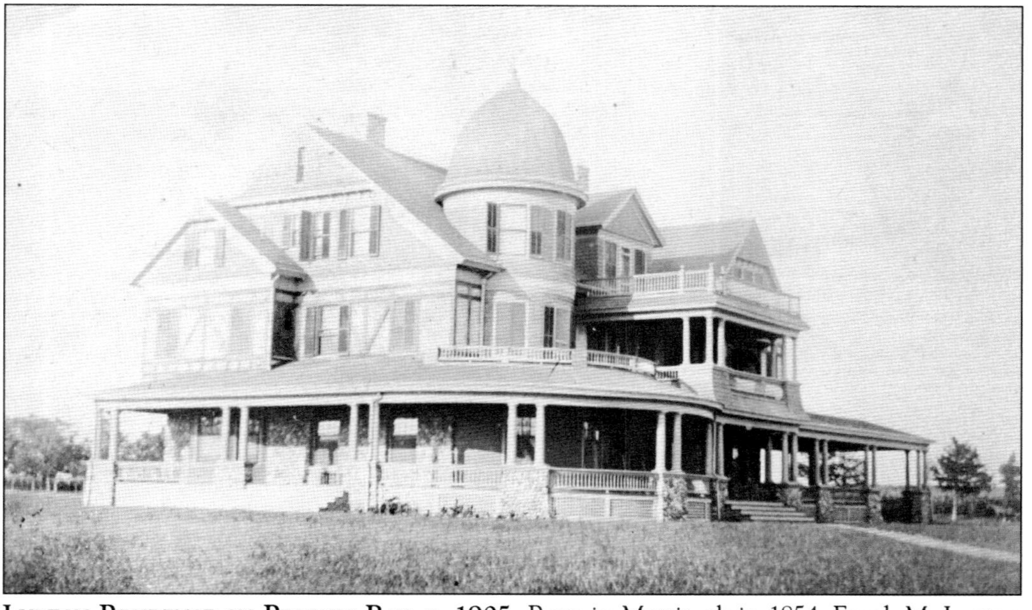

Lupton Residence on Peconic Bay, c. 1905. Born in Mattituck in 1854, Frank M. Lupton became a major publisher. After serving as an apprentice printer, he opened his own company and published *Fireside and Home*, a monthly literary periodical, and *Leisure Hour Library*, a series of complete novels at very low prices. In the latter venture, Lupton was a pioneer, and the circulation of the series reached one million monthly readers. (MLHS.)

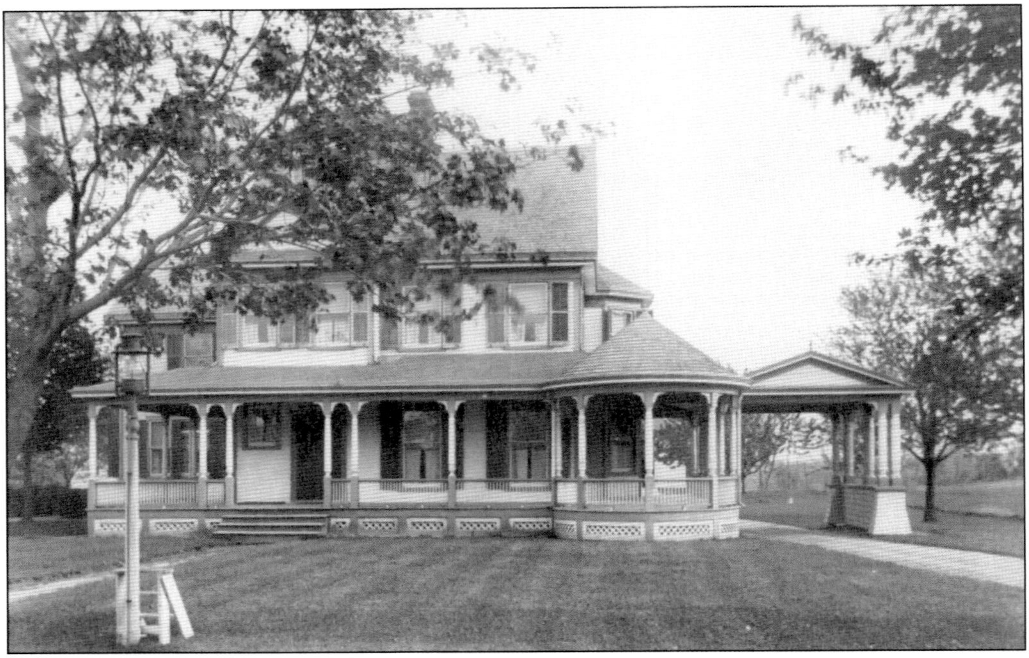

William M. Hudson Jr. Residence, c. 1900. This beautiful home on the west side of New Suffolk Avenue was built in the late 1800s by William M. Hudson. He and his brother Joseph managed the Hudson canning factory, which was founded by their father, William H. Hudson. They had other factories in Glen Cove and Riverhead. Later, Joseph supervised the canning factory in Holley, New York. (MLL.)

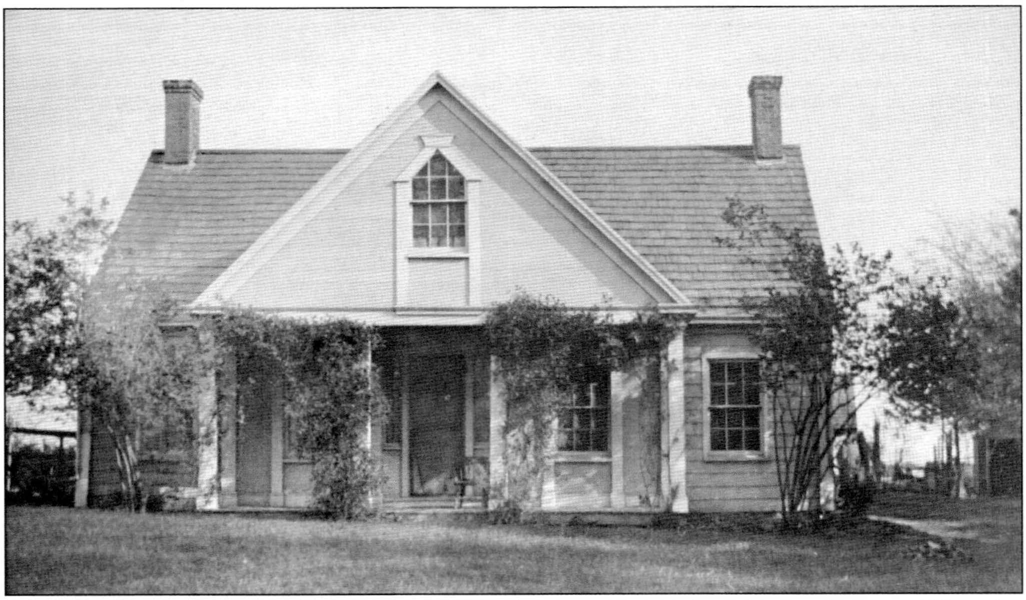

Wells-Howell Residence, c. 1900. Built by William Wells V before the Revolutionary War, this home still stands on the south side of Main Road. At the outbreak of the war, Wells moved his family to Connecticut to evade the British occupation. In the latter half of the 1800s, the cottage was owned by Joel and Phoebe Howell. (Courtesy of the Suffolk County Historical Society.)

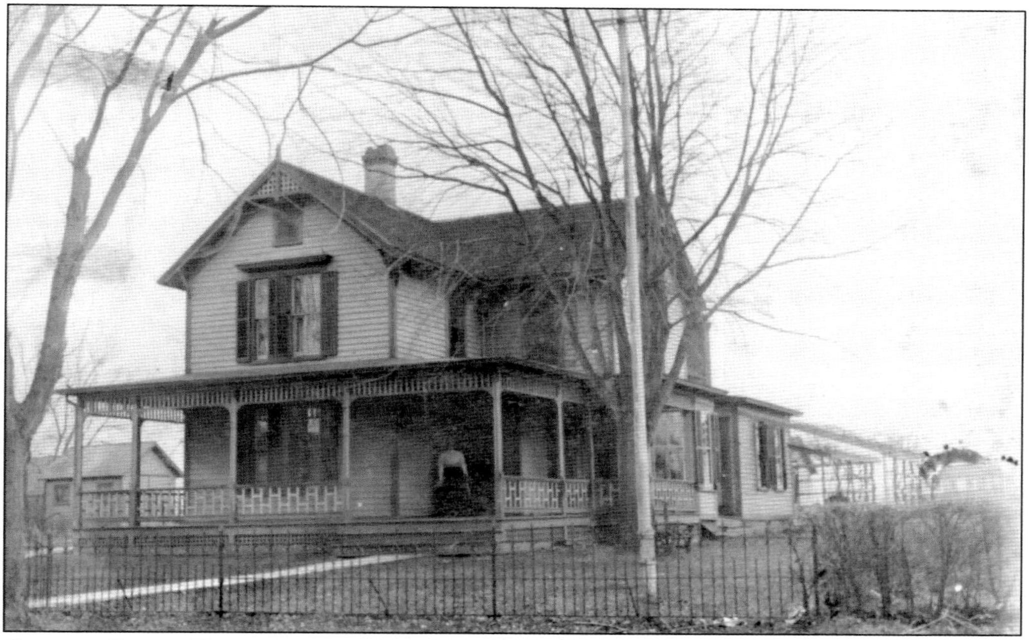

Conrad Grabie Residence, c. 1920. Conrad Grabie came to this country from Germany in 1878 and became the village blacksmith. His birthday was on Christmas Day, and he and his wife, Amelia, invited "everybody" to celebrate around the Christmas tree. Their house, on the south side of the Main Road, was also a famous place to hold church suppers. Conrad labored daily at his forge up until a few weeks before he died, at age 84. (MLHS.)

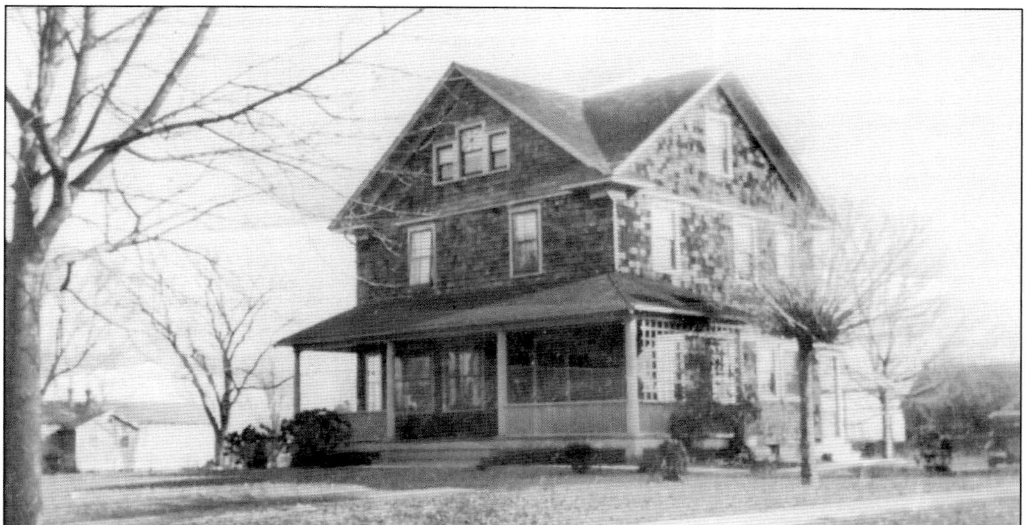

Sidney and Ruth Gildersleeve Residence, c. 1925. Sidney and Ruth Aird Gildersleeve lived in this house on the south side of Main Road. Ruth came to Mattituck from Newburgh to teach school, and she married Sidney in 1914. Sidney and his brother James had been running the Gildersleeve Brothers store since the death of their father, Andrew, in 1896. Sidney and Ruth were actively engaged in Mattituck Presbyterian Church as well as with the literary and dramatic societies. (MLHS.)

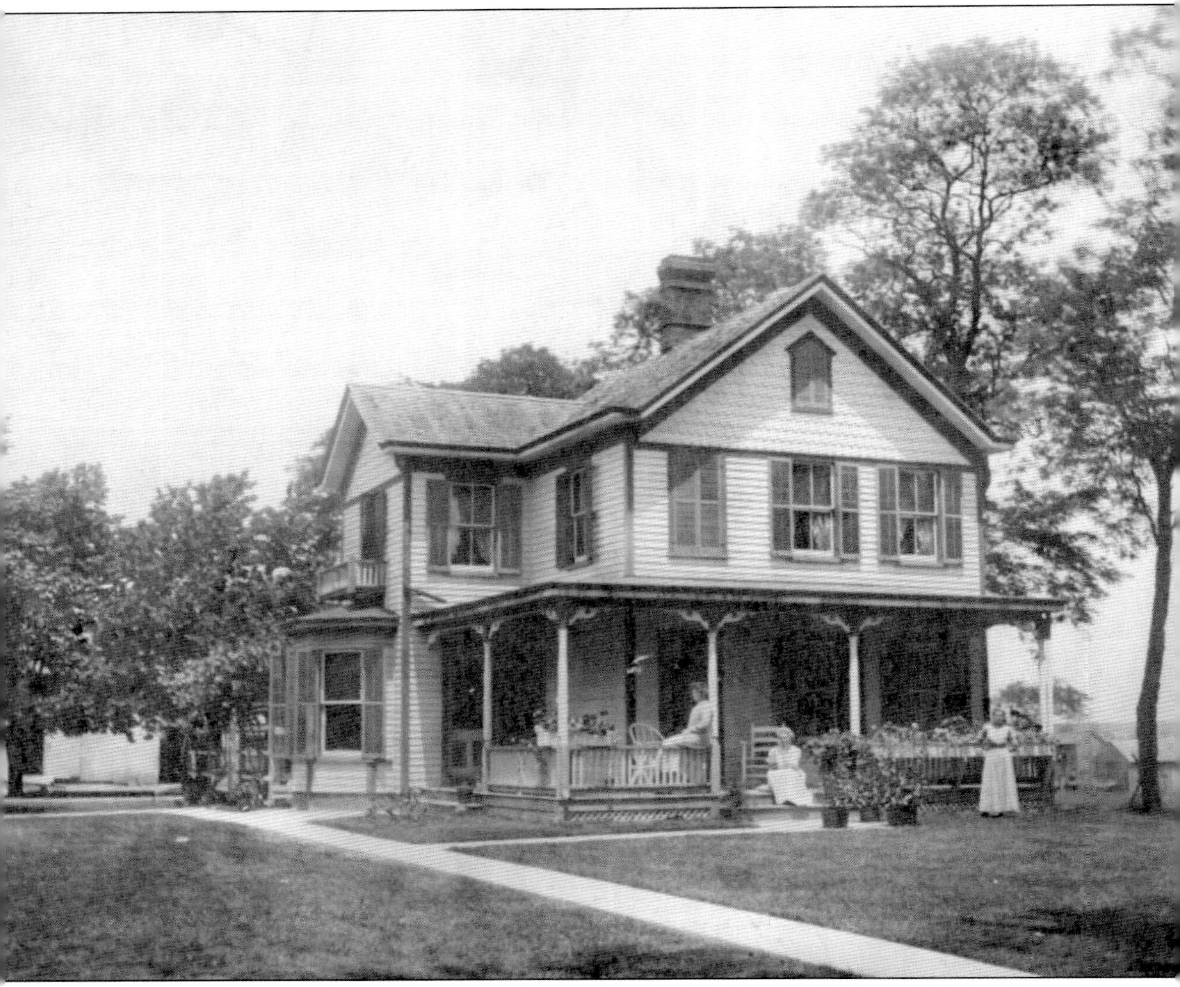

The Helfrich/Boutcher Home, c. 1900. About 1888, John Helfrich and his brother-in-law, Fred Greaves, purchased two lots from Bryant Conkling just east of his residence on the north side of Main Road. There, they built two beautiful homes for their wives, the Stewart sisters. John Helfrich moved his family to Southampton in the summer of 1898 because there was much carpentry work available. The house was eventually sold to William L. Boutcher, whose wife, Sarah Elizabeth, was the third Stewart sister. (Courtesy of the Massey family.)

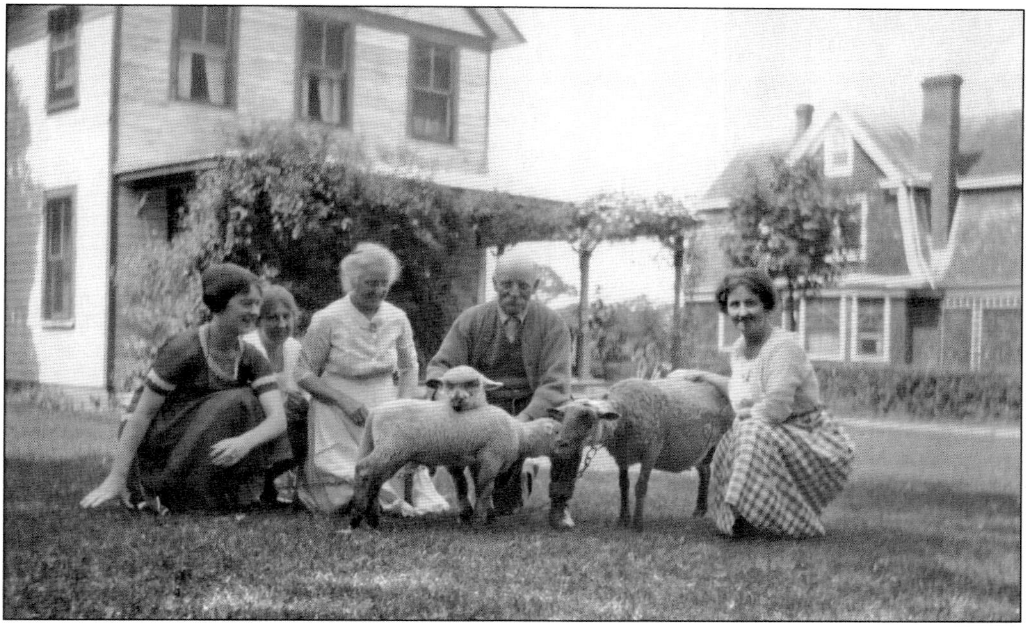

EDWARD SPENCER HORTON RESIDENCE, C. 1925. Edward Spencer Horton is seen here with his family and a few pet sheep in front of their home on the north side of Old Sound Avenue. Horton was a butcher at Reeve and Hall at one time and also a painter. The house in the background was built by George L. Penny, next to Penny's lumberyard. (Courtesy of Carolyn Gillespie Markowitz.)

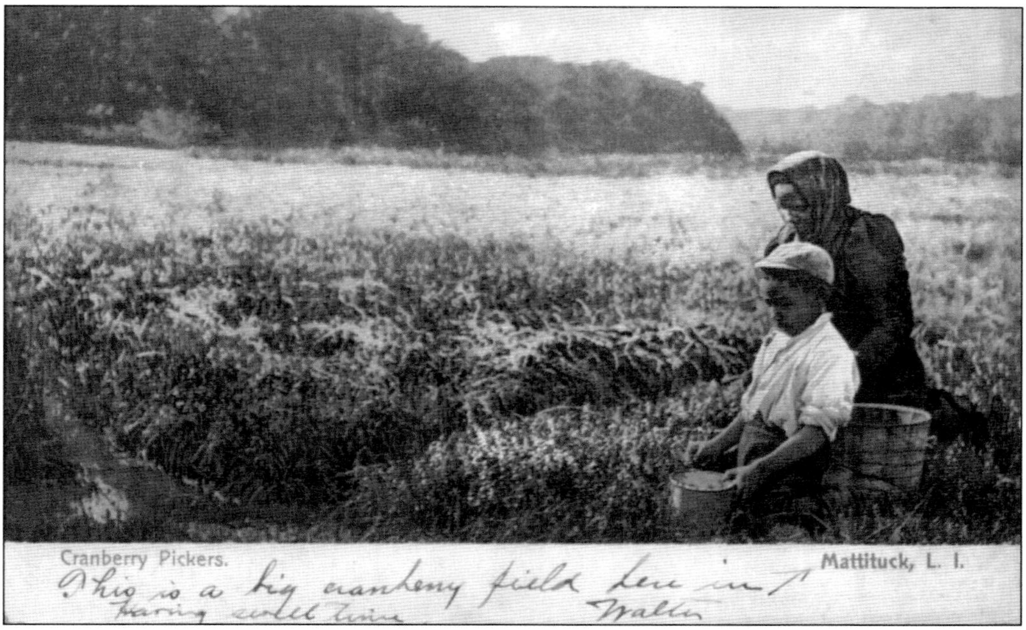

CRANBERRY PICKERS, 1907. In 1885, John C. Wells owned a cranberry marsh at the bay in Mattituck that yielded 1,000 bushels. By 1928, Suffolk County was the third-largest producer of cranberries in the country. Pickers were paid 12¢ for a peck-size pail of cranberries. Ladies who spent the summers plucking duck feathers picked cranberries in the fall. (Courtesy of the Queens Borough Public Library, Long Island Division, Postcard Collection.)

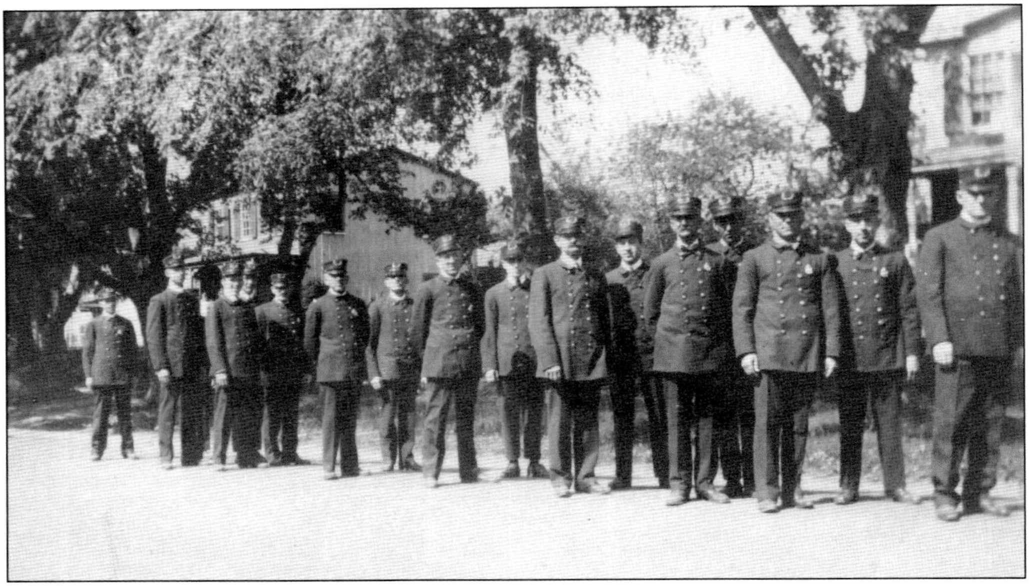

Mattituck Fire Department, 1908. Protecting the farms, homes, and families of Mattituck-Laurel through the years have been the members of the Mattituck Fire Department, who have volunteered their time and expertise to keep community members safe from harm. The fire department was organized in April 1907 by three chosen fire commissioners from Mattituck: Otto P. Hallock, James L. Reeve, and James J. Kirkup. James A. Gildersleeve and William H. Reeve were elected chief and assistant chief, respectively. (Courtesy of the Louis "Chub" Gildersleeve family.)

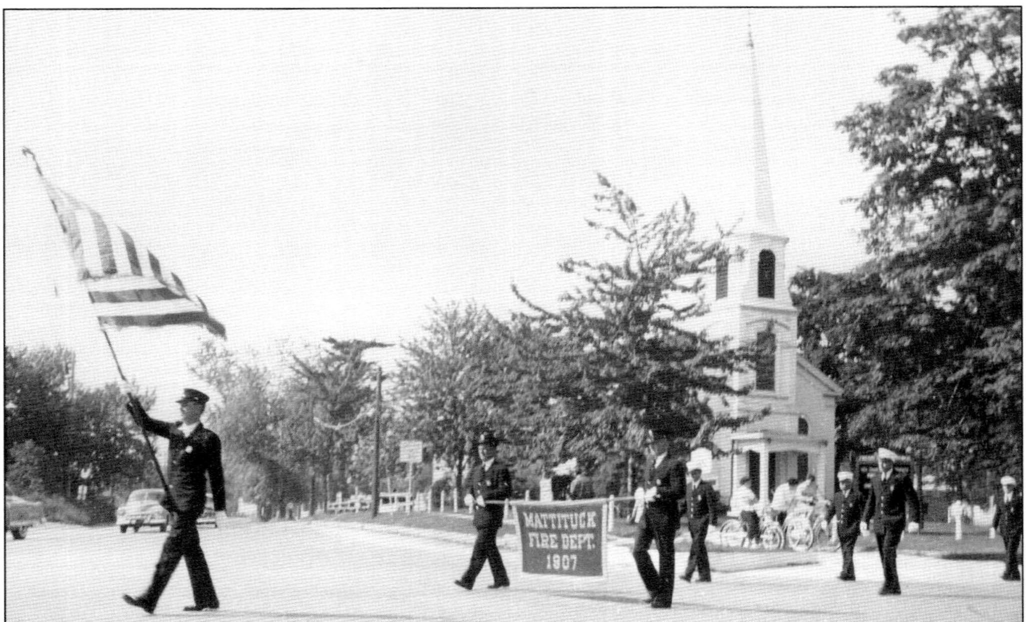

Fire Department in Parade, c. 1950. In 1907, when the Mattituck Fire Department was organized, Rev. Charles E. Craven, William M. Hudson, and Charles W. Wickham were appointed to a committee to draw up the company's rules and regulations. (Courtesy of Jim and Pauline Gildersleeve.)

Six

WORSHIP, EDUCATION, AND LESIURE

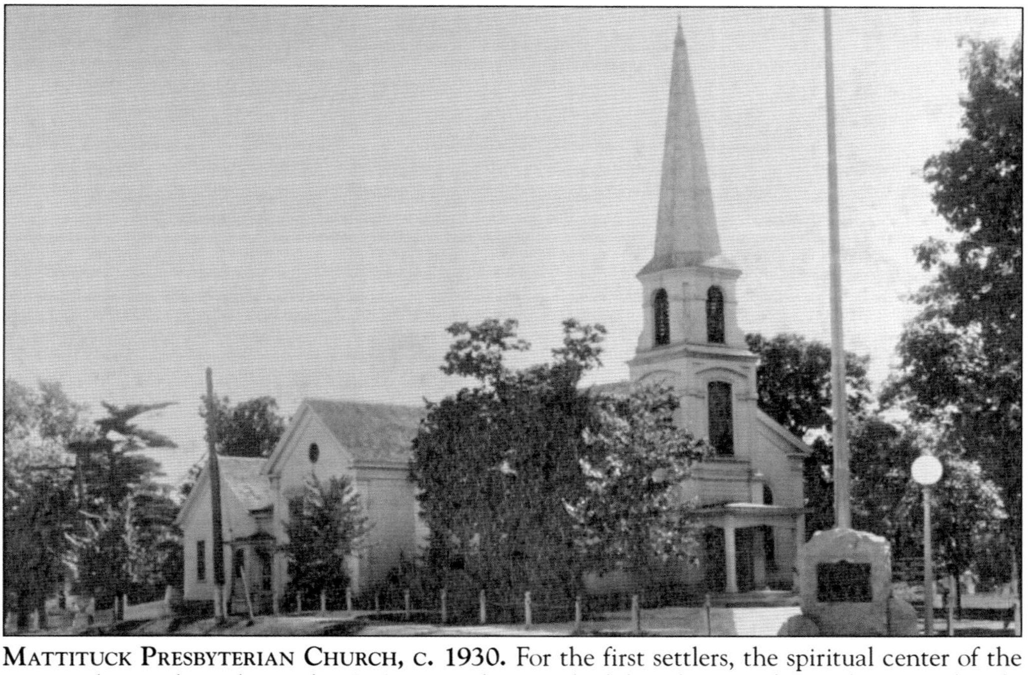

MATTITUCK PRESBYTERIAN CHURCH, C. 1930. For the first settlers, the spiritual center of the Mattituck-Laurel parish was the 1715 meetinghouse, which later became the Presbyterian church. Parishioners attended services and listened to the doctrinal sermons of their formally educated minister. The church was also a place for cultural events presented by the Mattituck Literary Society, such as lectures, recitations, and musical entertainments. The church alone could not satisfy the need for families and friends to gather socially, especially during the long, dark nights of winter in an agricultural community, so halls were built for that purpose. Through the years, Mattituck established several halls as venues for cultural events, dances, basketball games, and meetings, and eventually for the viewing of motion pictures, including St. Charles Hall, Apollo Hall, Library Hall, and Fischer's Hall. (Courtesy of the Mattituck Presbyterian Church.)

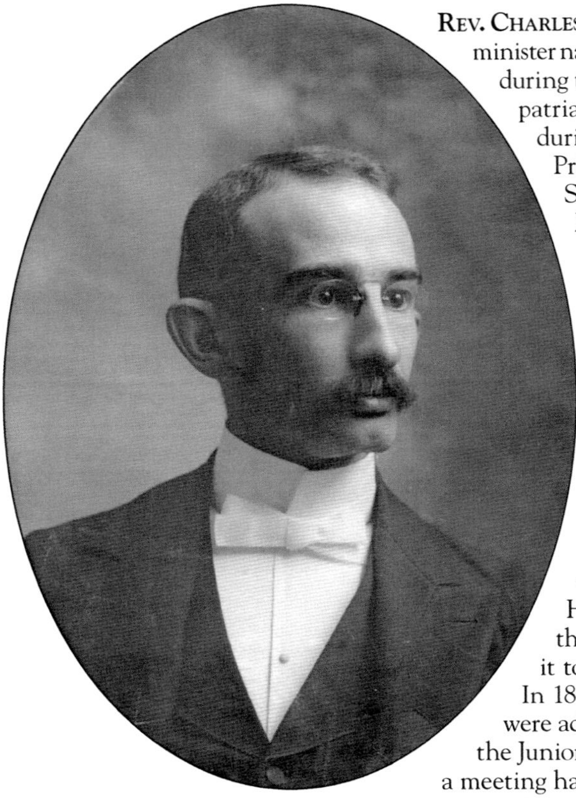

Rev. Charles E. Craven, c. 1900. A young Presbyterian minister named Charles E. Craven arrived in Mattituck during the latter part of 1895 and became the true patriarch and spiritual leader of the community during his 18 years of ministry. A graduate of Princeton College and Princeton Theological Seminary, Dr. Craven wrote *The History of Mattituck*, a scholarly work that traces the history of the hamlet from its settlement in 1662 until its economic transformation in 1906. (MLL.)

Methodist Episcopal Church, 1913. The Methodist Episcopal church (below) was organized in 1853 when Thomas Hallock purchased the second edifice of the former Presbyterian church and relocated it to the west side of the old burying ground. In 1896, an impressive new church and steeple were added to the front. The building was sold to the Junior Order of United American Mechanics as a meeting hall in 1918. (MLL.)

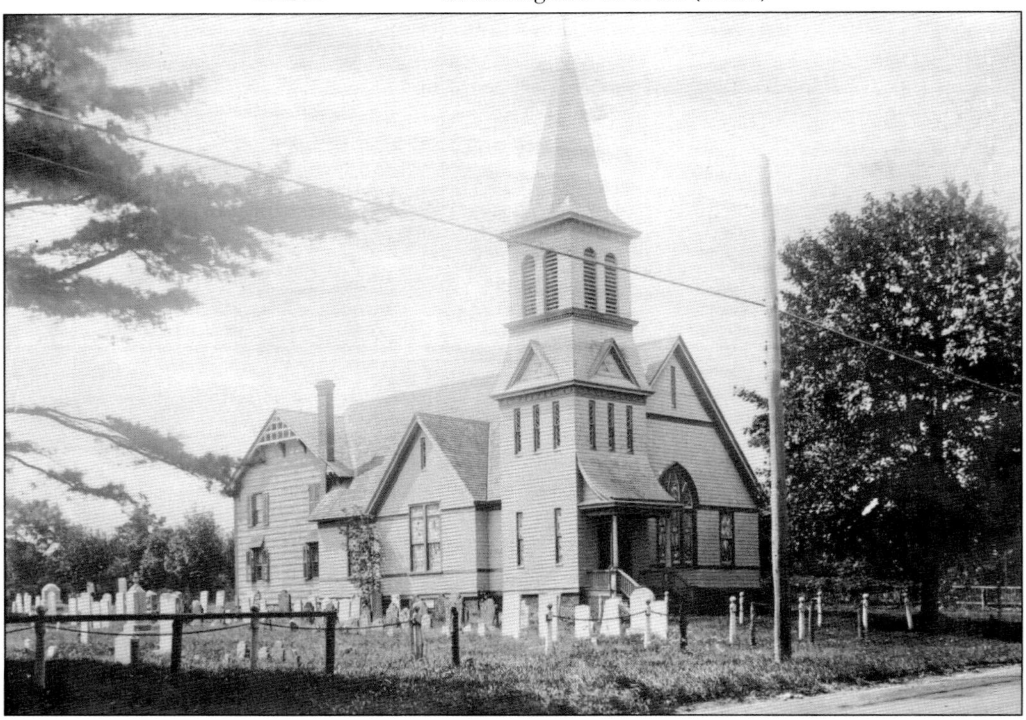

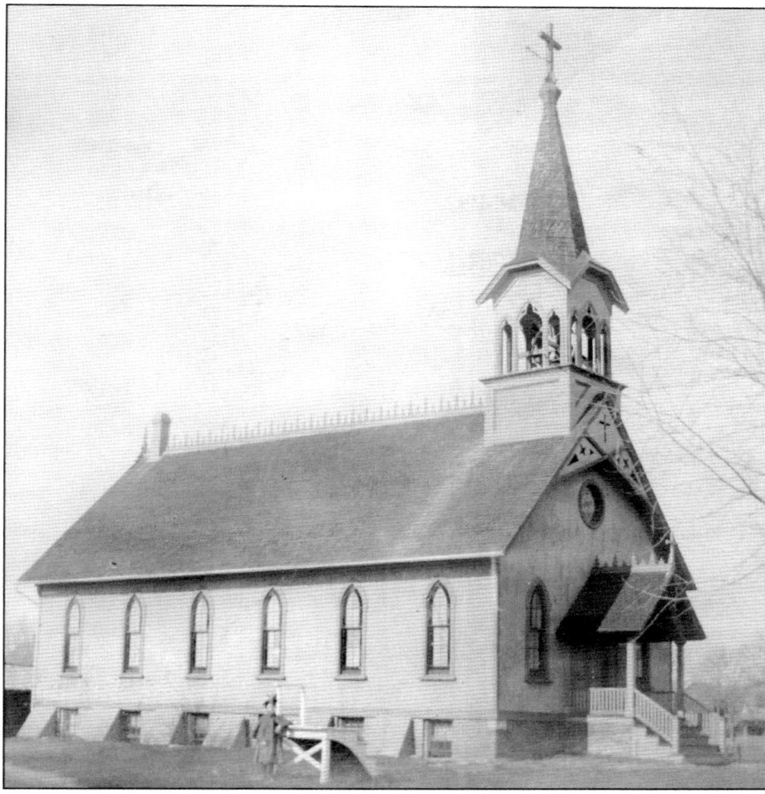

Episcopal Church of the Redeemer, c. 1900. In 1877, Henry Dingee, the proprietor of the Mattituck House, donated a 150-foot-by-70-foot piece of property on the southwest corner of the hotel property for the purpose of an English Episcopal church. The Episcopal Church of the Redeemer was opened for service in July 1879. The original bell tower in the front was removed after remodeling in 1932. (MLL.)

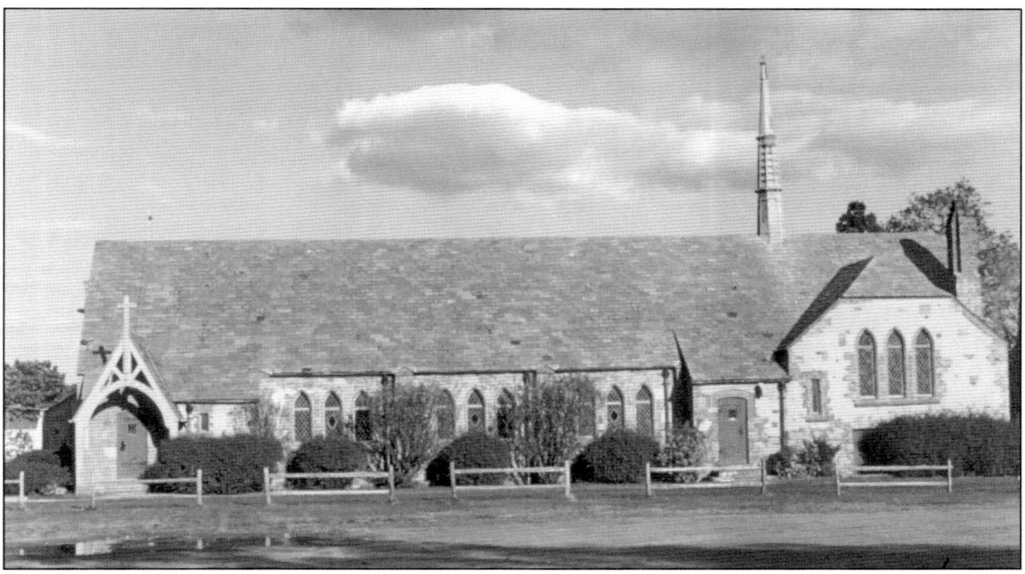

Our Lady of Good Counsel Church, c. 1940. In 1929, Father John C. Brennan of Sacred Heart Parish in Cutchogue started a mission church in Mattituck. A year later, the diocese bought a piece of property on the corner of Main Road and Reeve Avenue. The building contract was awarded in July 1931, and the first mass of Our Lady of Good Counsel was held on Christmas 1931. (MLL.)

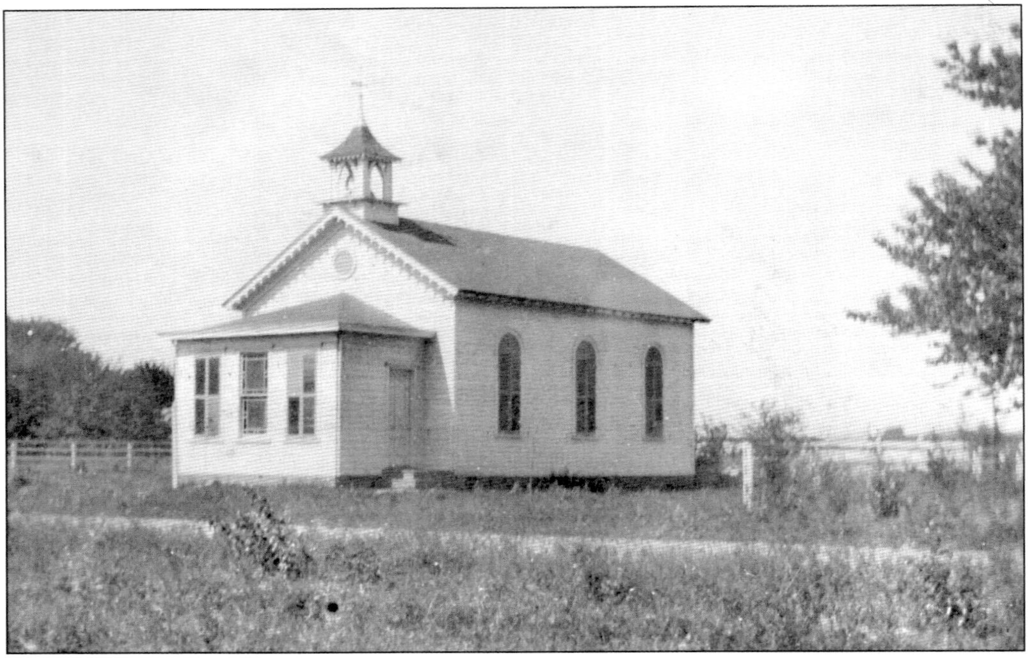

Oregon Chapel, c. 1920. The Oregon Chapel, located just east of Elijah's Lane on the north side of Oregon Road, was in existence by 1878. The Oregon public schoolhouse was erected just west of the chapel. In 1885, the congregation was accompanied in its singing by a newly acquired Estey organ. (Courtesy of Marilyn Gatz.)

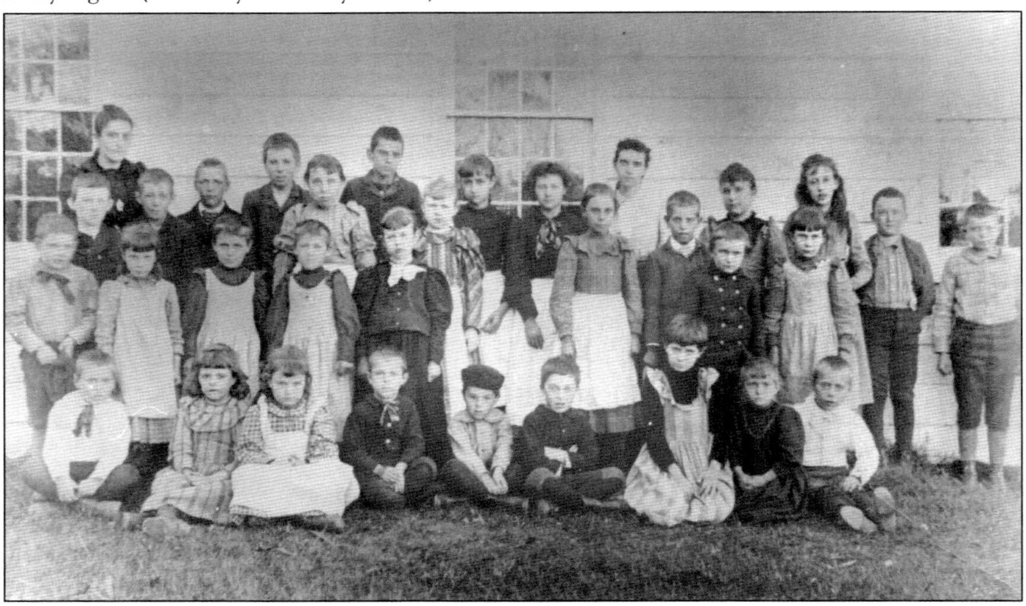

New Egypt Schoolhouse c. 1905. Schoolhouse No. 10, known as the New Egypt School because of its remote distance from Mattituck, was built on the north side of Sound Avenue near Kirkup's Hill. Irma Reeve, who attended in 1904, recalled, "The teacher's desk stood on a platform at the front of the room. In the vestibule was a basin for washing and a bucket of water and a dipper." (MLL.)

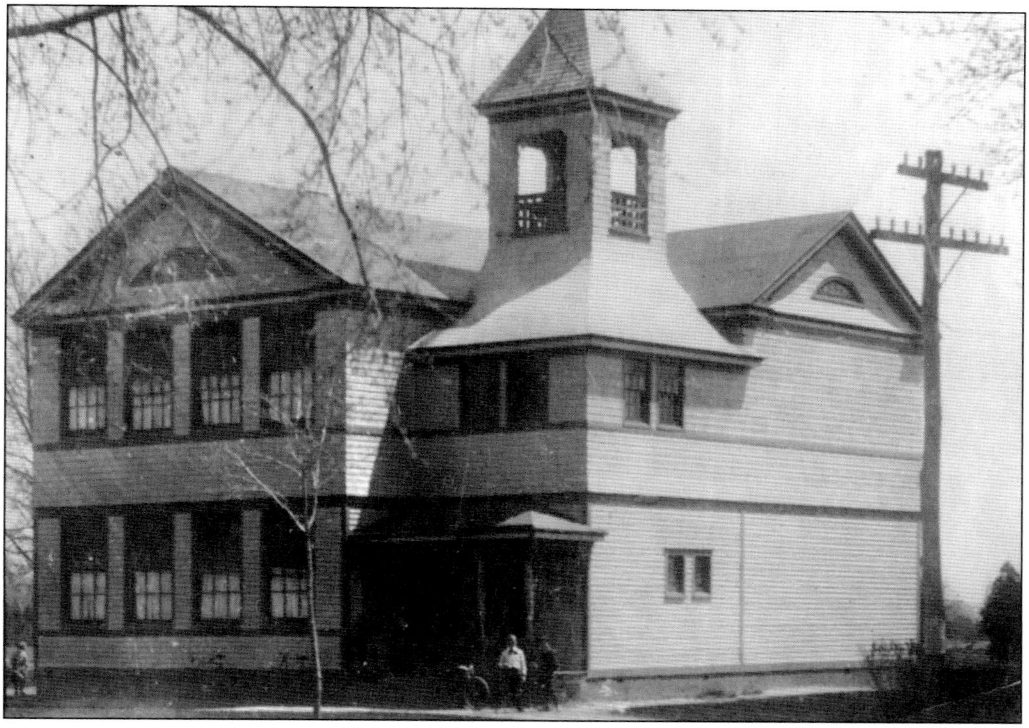

Mattituck Public School, c. 1900. A new two-room schoolhouse was built by Lester Gildersleeve in 1890 on the northeast corner of the T.E. Reeve farm for $1,000. By 1896, District School No. 9 was becoming overcrowded again, and in 1897, another story was added, making it a four-room building. In 1899, the district hired George B. Reeve as an instructor in vocal music, paying him $1 per lesson. (MLL.)

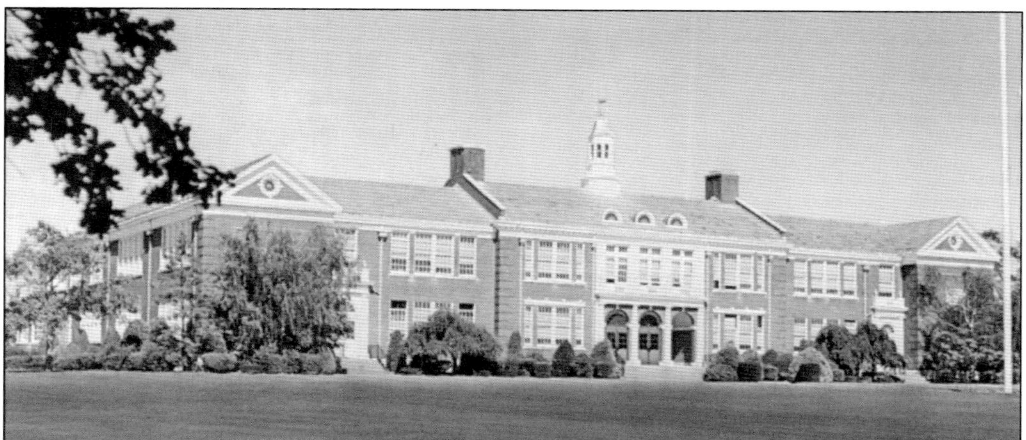

Mattituck High School, c. 1940. After many years of overcrowding at the old school building, the grand new Mattituck School was officially dedicated on July 3, 1935. The new school accommodated students from kindergarten through 12th grade, and had many new features, including an auditorium/gymnasium, a library, a cafeteria, a shop, a science laboratory, and ample classroom space. On the school site, there were also tennis courts, a track, a baseball field, and a playground for the smaller children. (MLL.)

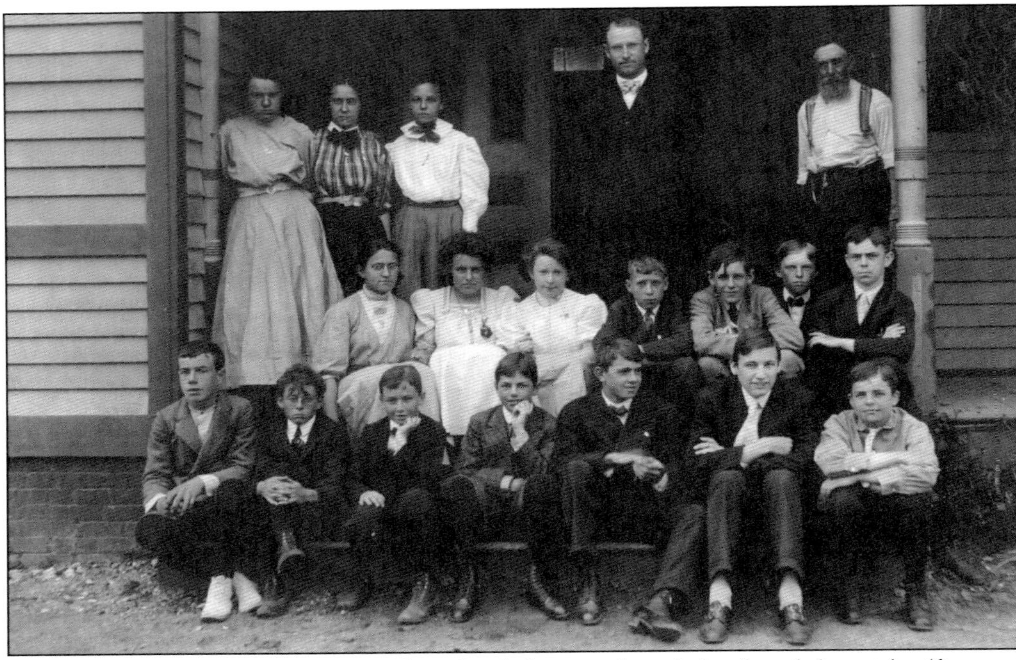

MATTITUCK GRADE SCHOOL, 1907. This school photograph includes, from left to right, (first row) George Gildersleeve, Walter Silkworth, John McNulty, Donald Gildersleeve, Harry Aldrich, Vera Hazzard, and Charles Reeve; (second row) Flora Aldrich, Ida Jackson, Bessie Zenzius, Raymond Hudson, Bryron Grathwohl, Winfield Robinson, and Carleton Wickham; (third row) Ruth Tuthill, Alice Penny, Irma Reeve, Principal Gibbs, and custodian Joel Howell. (MLL.)

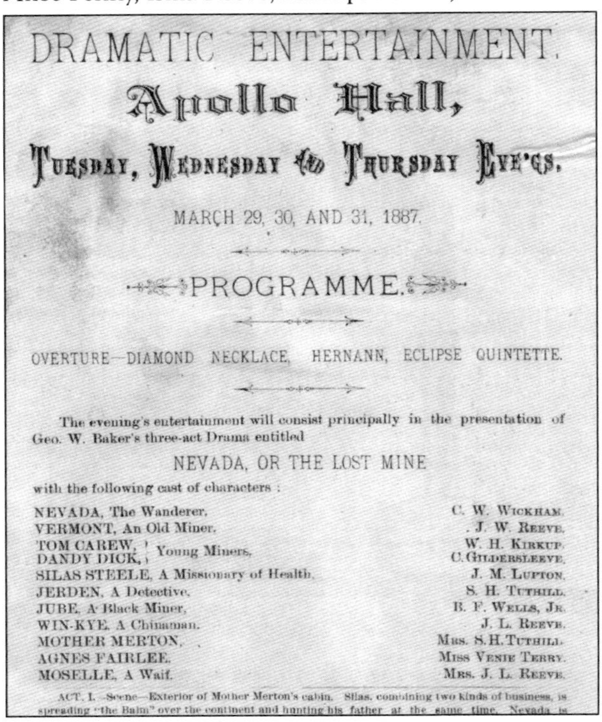

DRAMATIC ENTERTAINMENT.

Apollo Hall,

Tuesday, Wednesday and Thursday Eve'gs.

MARCH 29, 30, AND 31, 1887.

PROGRAMME.

OVERTURE—DIAMOND NECKLACE, HERNANN, ECLIPSE QUINTETTE.

The evening's entertainment will consist principally in the presentation of Geo. W. Baker's three-act Drama entitled

NEVADA, OR THE LOST MINE

with the following cast of characters :

NEVADA, The Wanderer,	C. W. WICKHAM.
VERMONT, An Old Miner.	J. W. REEVE.
TOM CAREW, } Young Miners,	W. H. KIRKUP.
DANDY DICK, } Young Miners,	C. GILDERSLEEVE.
SILAS STEELE, A Missionary of Health,	J. M. LUPTON.
JERDEN, A Detective,	S. H. TUTHILL.
JUBE, A Black Miner,	B. F. WELLS, JR.
WIN-KYE, A Chinaman.	J. L. REEVE.
MOTHER MERTON,	MRS. S. H. TUTHILL.
AGNES FAIRLEE.	MISS VENIE TERRY.
MOSELLE, A Waif.	MRS. J. L. REEVE.

ACT. I.—Scene—Exterior of Mother Merton's cabin. Silas, combining two kinds of business, is spreading "the Balm" over the continent and hunting his father at the same time. Nevada is

APOLLO HALL PLAYBILL, 1887. To the east of the railroad depot on Love Lane and Pike Street was the Reeve and Wilson grocery store. The owners opened Apollo Hall on their second floor in 1879, and the Mattituck Dramatic Society presented plays such as *Nevada, or the Lost Mine* (playbill seen here), with actors from familiar local families. The Mattituck Literary Society also presented programs of vocal and instrumental music, recitations, charades, skits, and short plays followed by a dance. After the dance, young people stopped at Dick Cox's ice cream parlor, and in later years, at Dr. Robert Lahy's drugstore in Library Hall or at Harry DePetris's for an ice cream soda or sundae. (MLHS.)

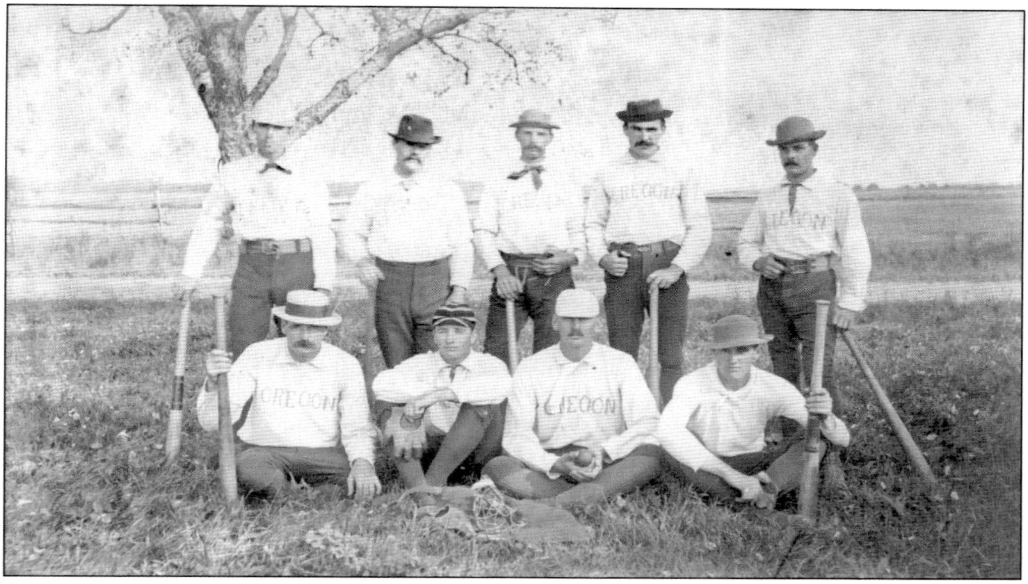

Oregon Baseball Club, 1886. Members of the baseball team from Oregon, the northeastern section of Mattituck, are dressed stylishly on a summer night in 1886, when they played the Manhansets from Shelter Island. The farm boys from Mattituck arrived fatigued from work in the fields, but they scored eight runs in the bottom of the seventh inning and six runs in the bottom of the ninth inning to beat the Manhansets 17-15. (MLHS.)

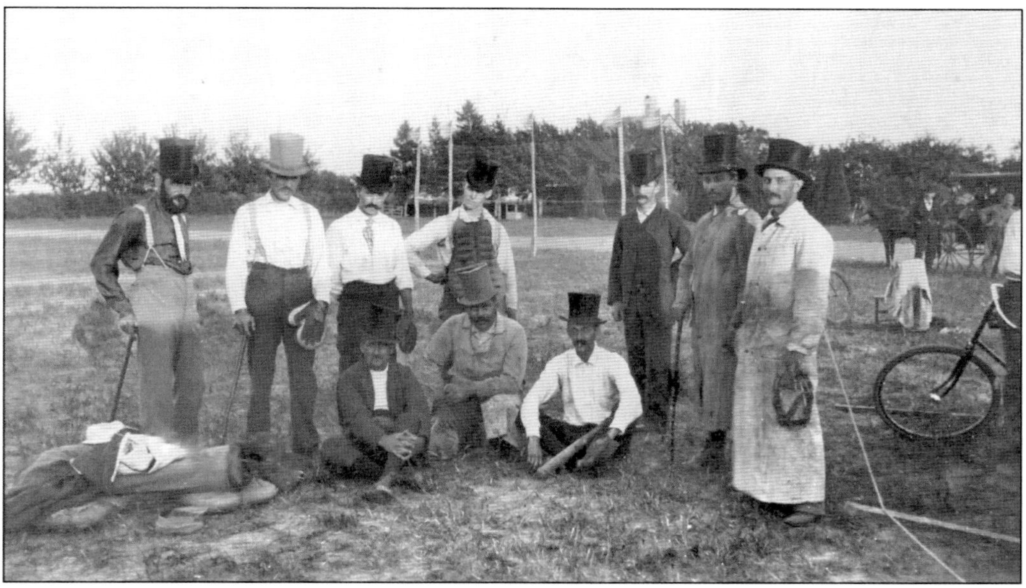

Mattituck Baseball Club, 1893. This baseball team, whose players arrived at the field in style, with their top hats and canes, includes, from left to right, (seated) Jesse W. Tuthill, Leon R. Hall, and Dr. E.K. Morton; (standing) Charles Wickham, Herbert Conkling, Peter Fanning, J. Wood Wickham, Alex K. Brown, William G. Hazard, and J.M. Lupton; (leaning on bicycle) J.B. Hudson. The old Reeve-Lavalle-Pymm House is in the background. (MLL.)

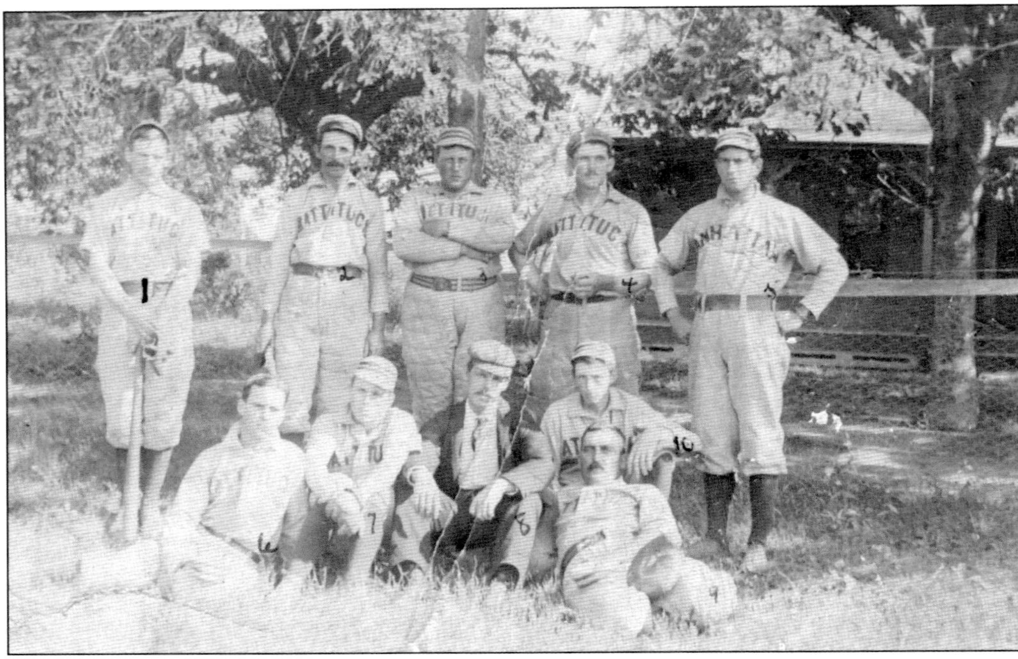

Championship Mattituck Baseball Club, 1900. This championship club includes, from left to right, (sitting) Howard Robinson, second base; Dudley Pike, left field; J.W. Wickham, manager; (leaning back) Luther "Lute" Tuthill, first base; and LeRoy "Slats" Reeve, shortstop; (standing) Oliver Ruland, third base; William B. "Lawyer" Reeve, center field; ? Sprague, a catcher who could "hit 'em a mile"; Phil Duryee, right field; and ? Castro, pitcher. (MLHS.)

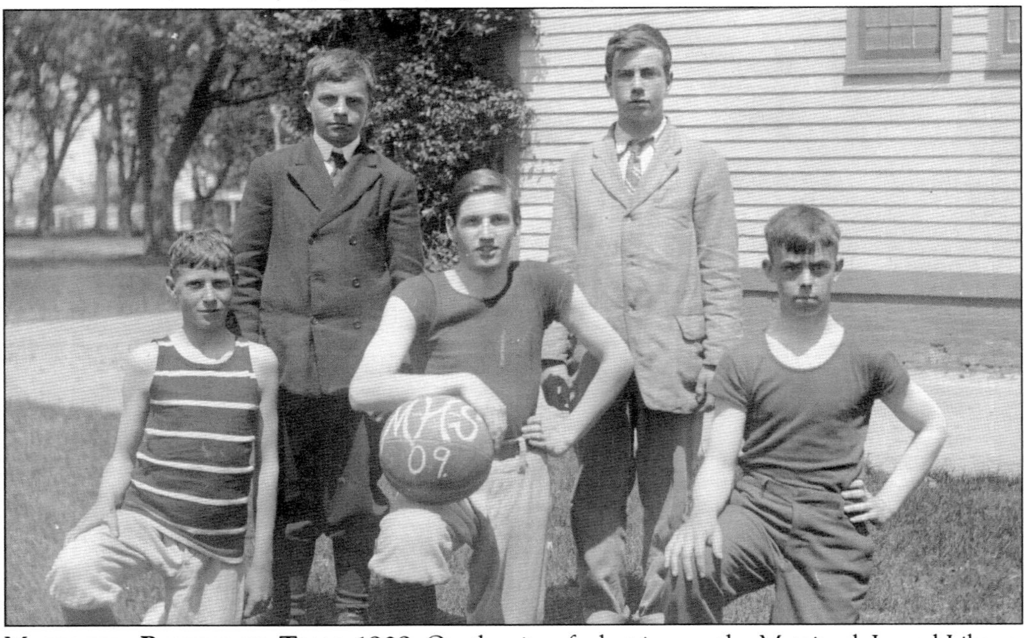

Mattituck Basketball Team, 1909. On the site of what is now the Mattituck-Laurel Library are, from left to right, (kneeling) Ray Hudson, Vere Hazzard, and Carleton Wickham; (standing) Charles Reeve and George Gildersleeve. (MLL.)

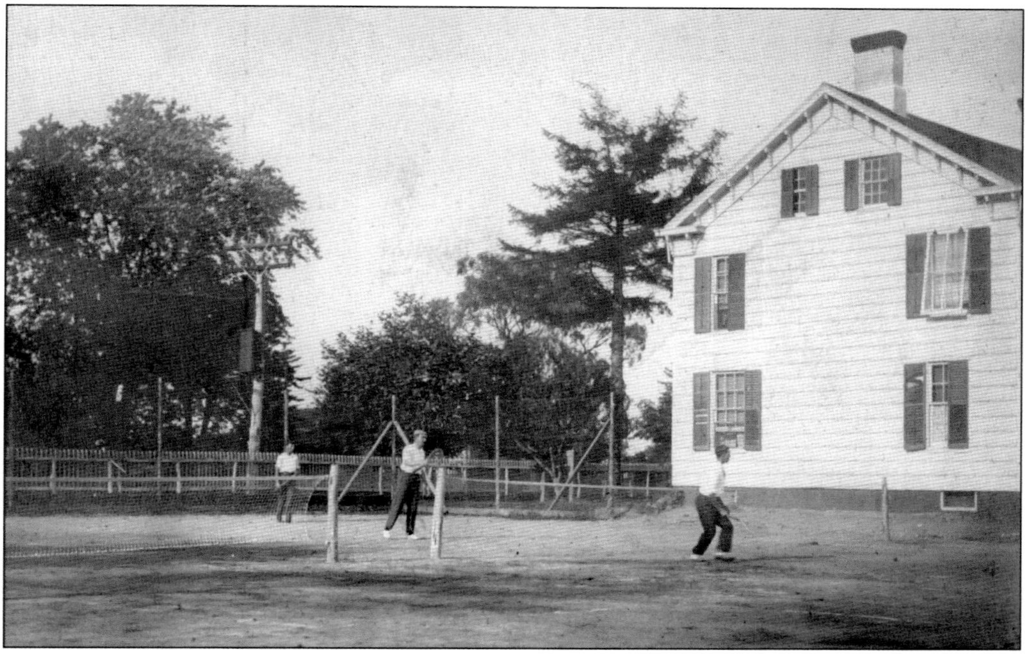

TENNIS COURT AT PHILIP TUTHILL RESIDENCE, C. 1920. Known as the Phips court, this court was built in 1910 on the grounds of the Philip Tuthill House. This house is now the home of the Mattituck-Laurel Historical Society. (MLHS.)

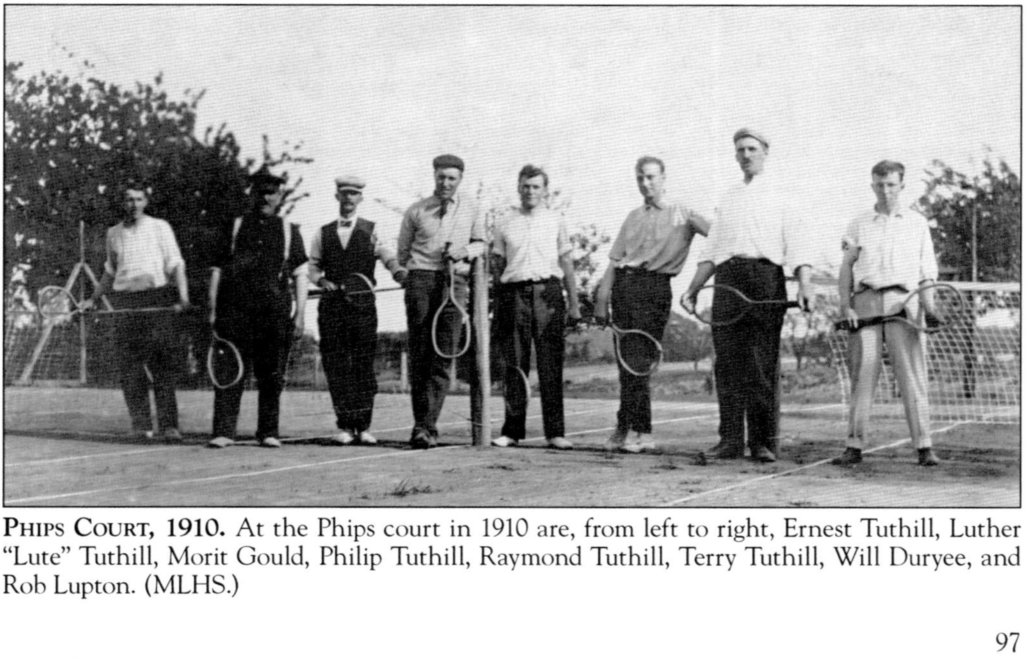

PHIPS COURT, 1910. At the Phips court in 1910 are, from left to right, Ernest Tuthill, Luther "Lute" Tuthill, Morit Gould, Philip Tuthill, Raymond Tuthill, Terry Tuthill, Will Duryee, and Rob Lupton. (MLHS.)

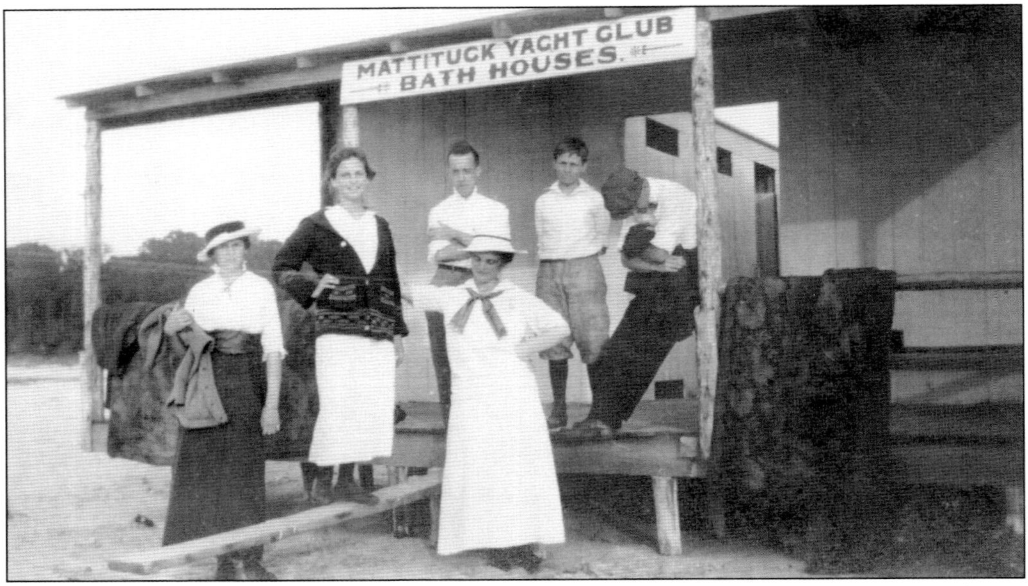

MATTITUCK YACHT CLUB BATHHOUSES, 1914. Located on Mattituck Creek near the sound were the bathhouses of the Mattituck Yacht Club. Here, strollers gather at the front of the bathhouse on July 4, 1914. Vivien Duryee is in the white hat and dress in the center, and her younger brother John is in knickers. (MLL.)

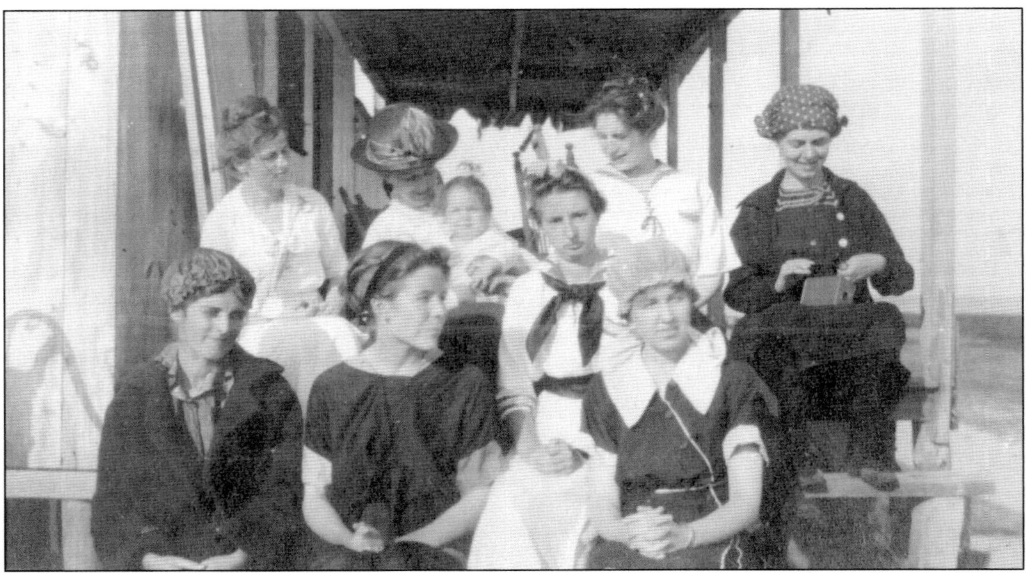

PICNIC ON THE BAY, 1915. Relaxed picnickers enjoy the bay on August 11, 1915. From left to right, they are (first row) Vivian Duryee, May Conklin, Julia Craven Penny, and Evelyn Reeve; (second row) Mildred Lupton Fischer, Mary Brady, Avis Fischer, and Isabel Jones. (MLL.)

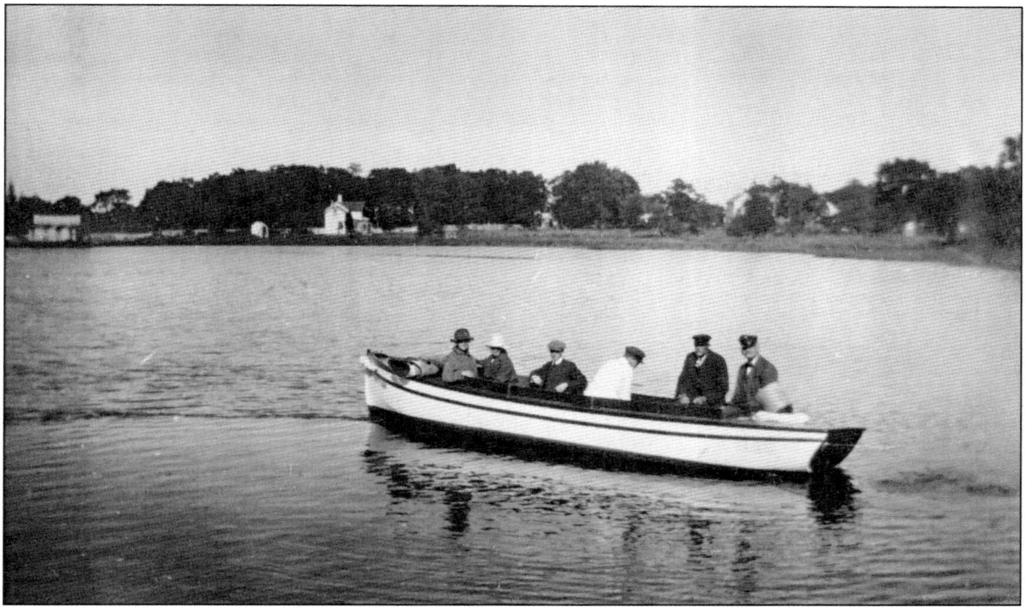

AFTERNOON CRUISE, C. 1920. One of Peter Harvey Duryee's favorite recreations was boating, and he delighted in taking his family and friends on excursions about the creek and the sound. Here, Duryee (steering) takes a tour of Mattituck Creek in his boat, *City of Mattituck*. His home and boathouse were conveniently located on the west end of the creek. He was a founding member of the Mattituck Yacht Club. (Courtesy of Michael J. Montgomery.)

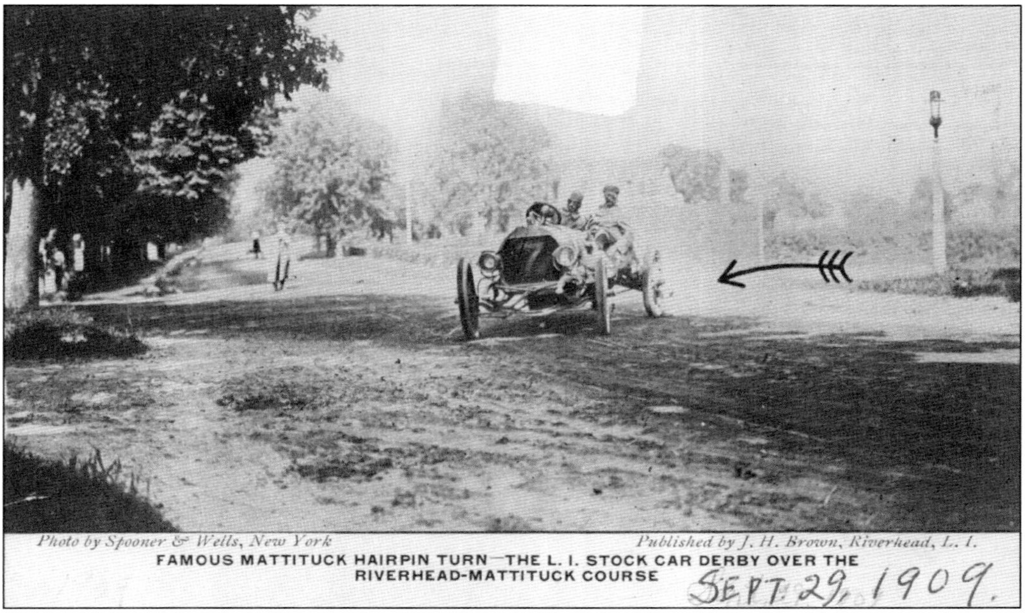

HAIRPIN TURN AT MATTITUCK, 1909. On September 29, 1909, the Long Island Stock Car Derby was held on a triangular course between Riverhead, Mattituck, and Centerville. Driving a 30-horsepower Buick, Louis Chevrolet traveled at 70 miles per hour, the fastest speed in an American road race to that time. Herbert H. Lyle was badly injured, and his mechanic, J.E. Bates, was killed when their car crashed a mile or two west of Mattituck. (MLHS.)

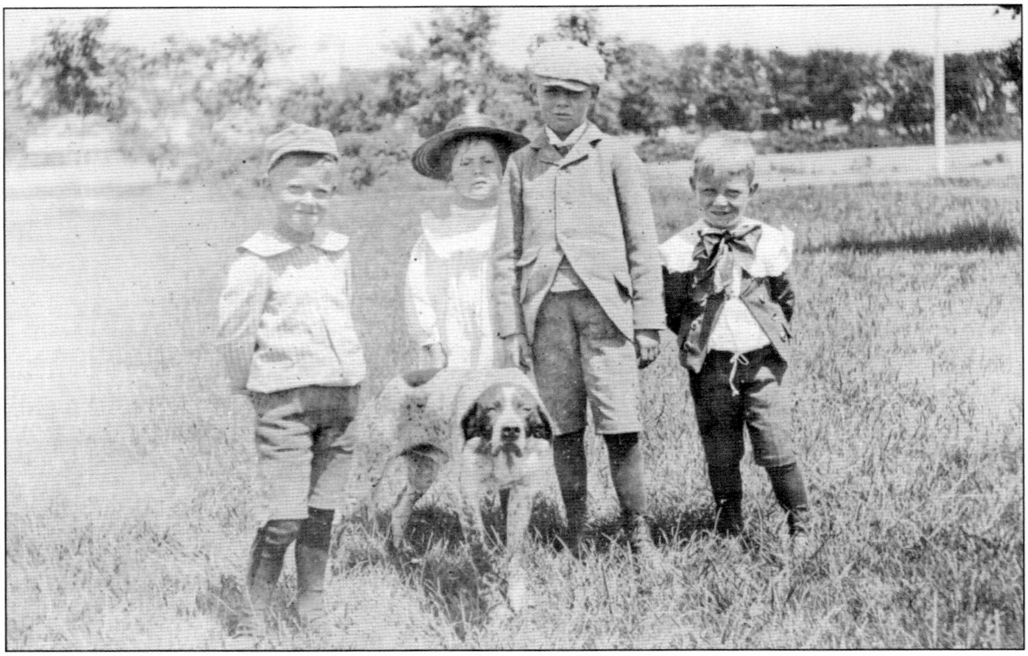

Hudson Children, c. 1900. Leisure time was easy to fill for children who had open fields to play in. Here, the Hudson children—from left to right, Raymond, Elberta, George, and Harold—pose with their dog Schneider. (MLL.)

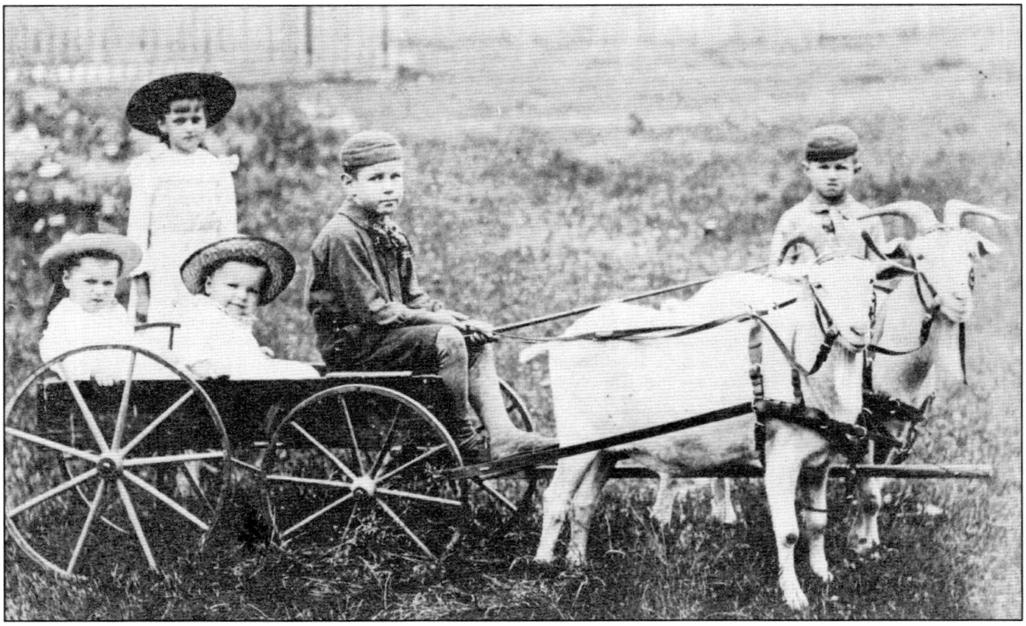

Gildersleeve Children with Goat Wagon, c. 1905. John Duryee presented Jim Gildersleeve Jr. with this trained team of goats with harnesses and trappings. The *Long Island Traveler* recounts about the goats: "We can vouch for their taste for good literature, for we saw one of them consume with gusto spare pages of the 'Christian at Work' which lay near the sidewalk." "Doll" and "Chub" Gildersleeve ride while Jim drives and "Puss" and Sid look on. (MLL.)

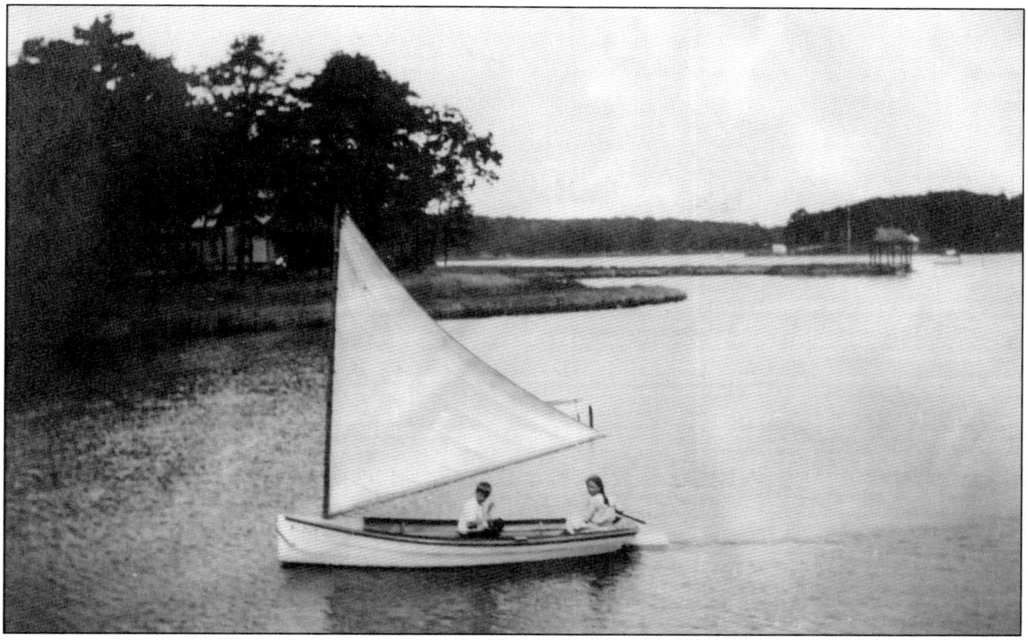

John and Hope Duryee, c. 1910. John and Hope Duryee lived on the west side of the Westphalia Bridge, so they had to row their boat under the wooden bridge into the cove before they could raise her sail. (Courtesy of Michael J. Montgomery.)

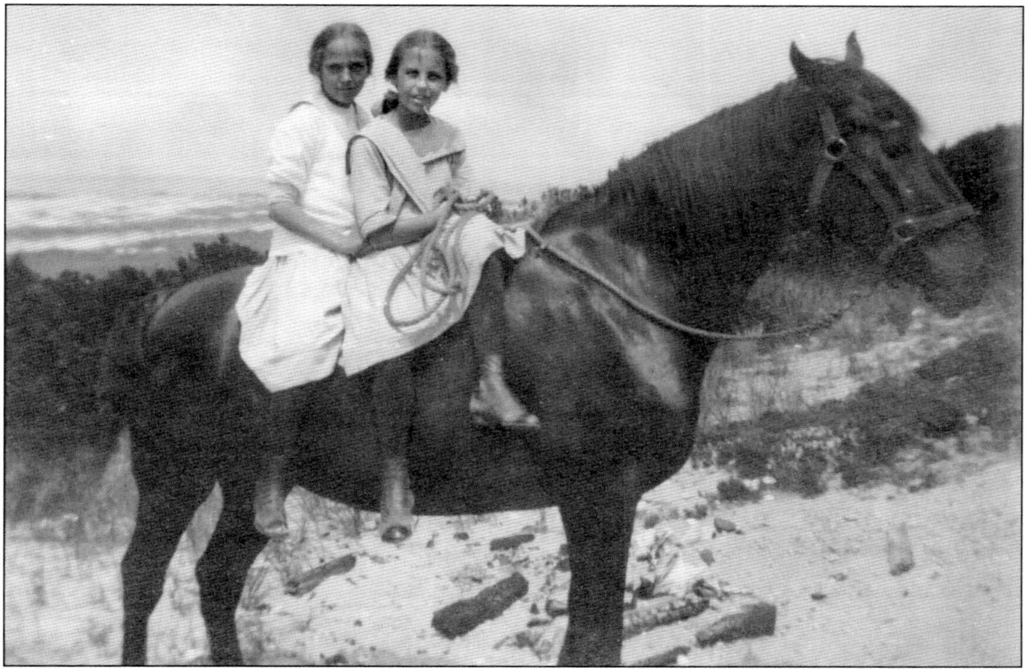

Clara and Hope Duryee on the Sound, 1914. These young ladies ride bareback on the cliffs near the sound shore, not far from the breakwater. Local families camped and picnicked along the shore, where the salt-spray breeze provided a brief respite from the heat. (Courtesy of Michael J. Montgomery.)

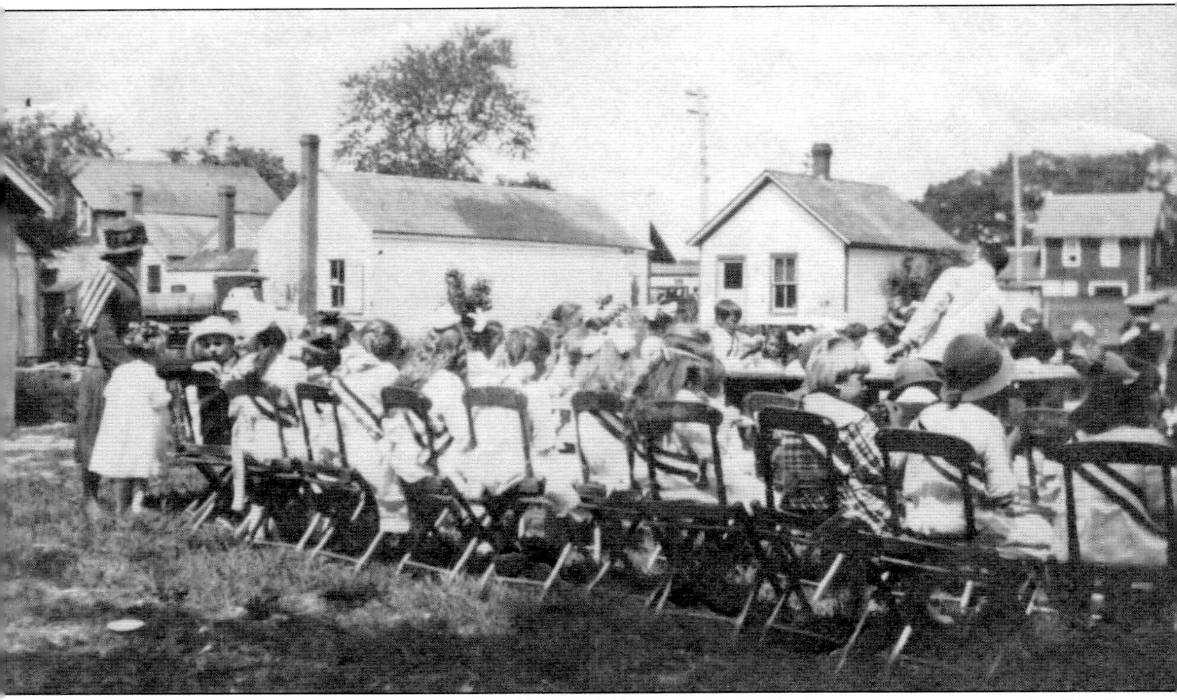

MEMORIAL DAY, 1920. A large group of local children enjoys refreshments being served by Frank Cantelmi, Harry DePetris's brother-in-law, on a beautiful Memorial Day in 1920. Frank was a well-known local athlete who excelled in baseball and football. These chairs are spread out on an empty lot on the west side of Love Lane, where William Barker would eventually build his new pharmacy in 1926. (Courtesy of the DePetris family.)

Seven

Franklinville Becomes Laurel

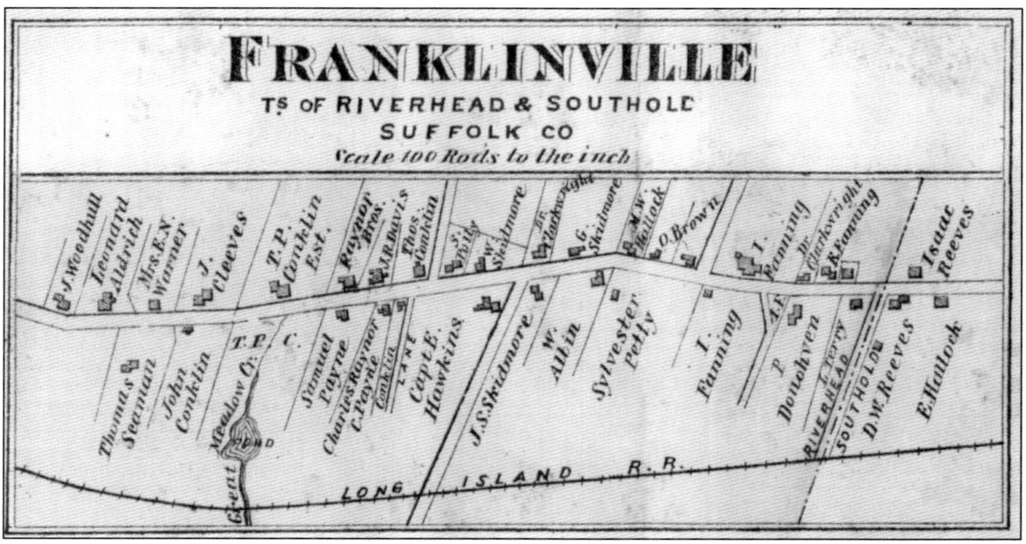

1873 Map. This map from the 1873 *Beers Atlas* shows the many old families who resided in the small farming hamlet of Franklinville, which was part of both the town of Riverhead and the town of Southold. Its residents had built their own church in 1831, followed by a school, the Franklinville Academy, in 1832. In 1898, the residents needed a post office, but there was already a town named Franklinville in upstate Cattaraugus County. Rev. W.H. Seely suggested the name Sequana, meaning "healing springs of water." Others preferred Laurel, after Laurel Lake and the abundance of flowering laurel nearby. The vote was taken, and there were 13 votes for Laurel and nine for Sequana. (MLL.)

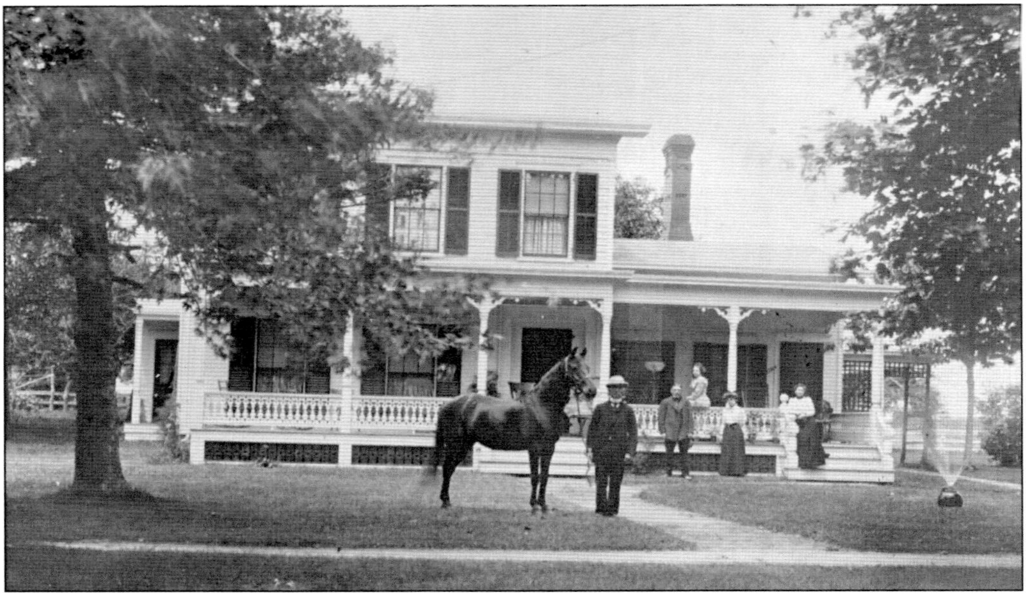

Capt. George E. Penny Residence, c. 1900. The Penny family is seen here in front of their beautiful home and farm on Main Road. Their relative Dave Clark stands in front with one of his favorite horses. George E. Penny went to sea as a young man, but gave it up soon after marrying Sarah E. Vail of Laurel in 1877. They settled in Laurel, and George gradually acquired several surrounding farms and was successful enough at farming to retire at age 56. (Courtesy of the Boutcher family.)

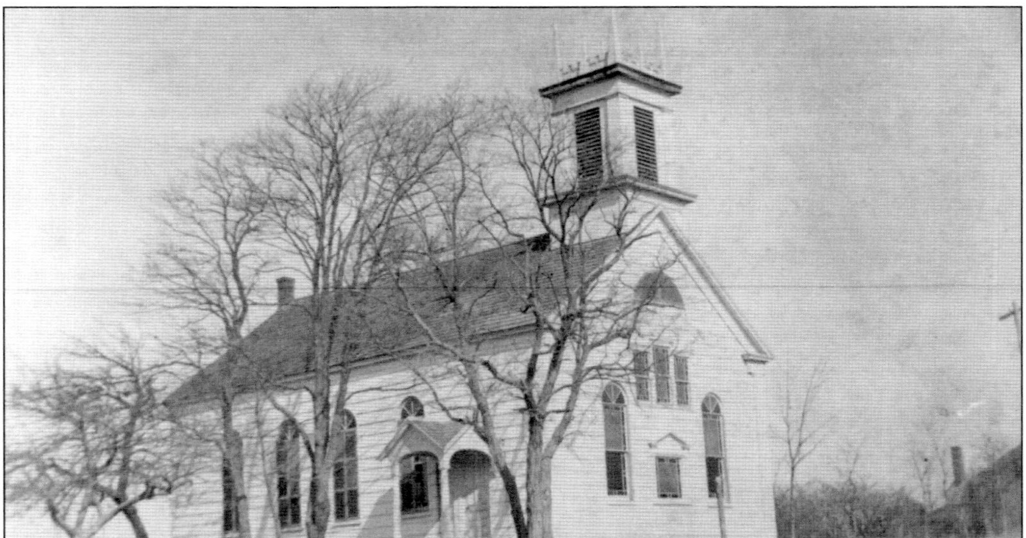

Franklinville Church, c. 1915. In 1830, the families of the Middle District (the area between Aquebogue and Mattituck) broke away from Union Parish and organized the Franklinville Church. By June 30, 1831, they had dedicated a new church building and sanctuary. The small parish flourished for 88 years before it closed in 1919. In 1921, the church was moved to the south side of Main Road in Jamesport, where it stands today, minus its steeple, as an apartment building. (Courtesy of Richard Wines.)

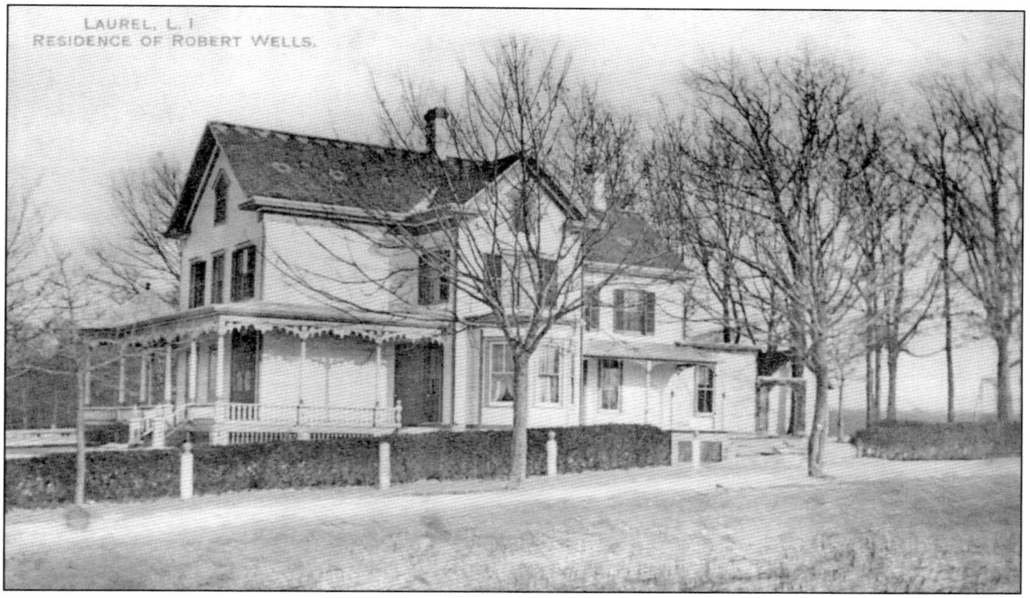

ROBERT WELLS RESIDENCE, c. 1920. Robert Wilbur Wells (1846–1941) was born in Laurel, the son of Joseph and Hannah Wilbur Wells. As a young man, he taught in one-room schoolhouses in Orient and Amagansett. In 1865, he married Elizabeth Amanda Parons of Orient. They settled at the old family farm on the south side of the main road in Laurel, where he farmed until his retirement around 1920. (MLL.)

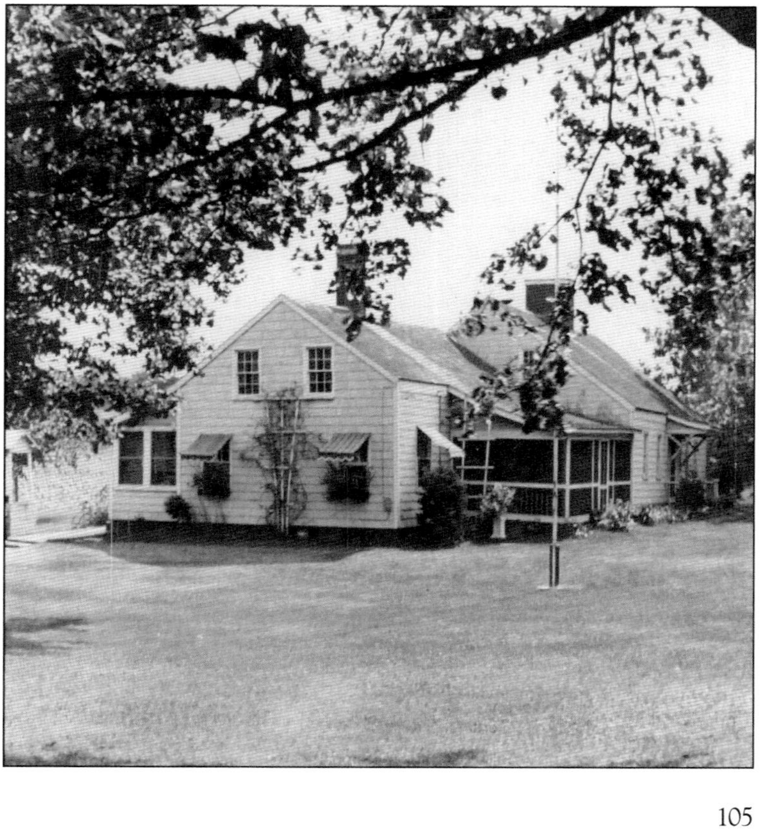

THE MCCARTHY-KUESTER HOUSE, c. 1940. Said to be the oldest house in Laurel, this English-model house was built at the headwaters of Brush's Creek for Capt. John Cleaves about 1703. In keeping with the English-style architecture, additional rooms were added around 1790 to the other side of the original chimney column. Another addition was made to the east of the original structure around 1820. (Courtesy of Althea Travis.)

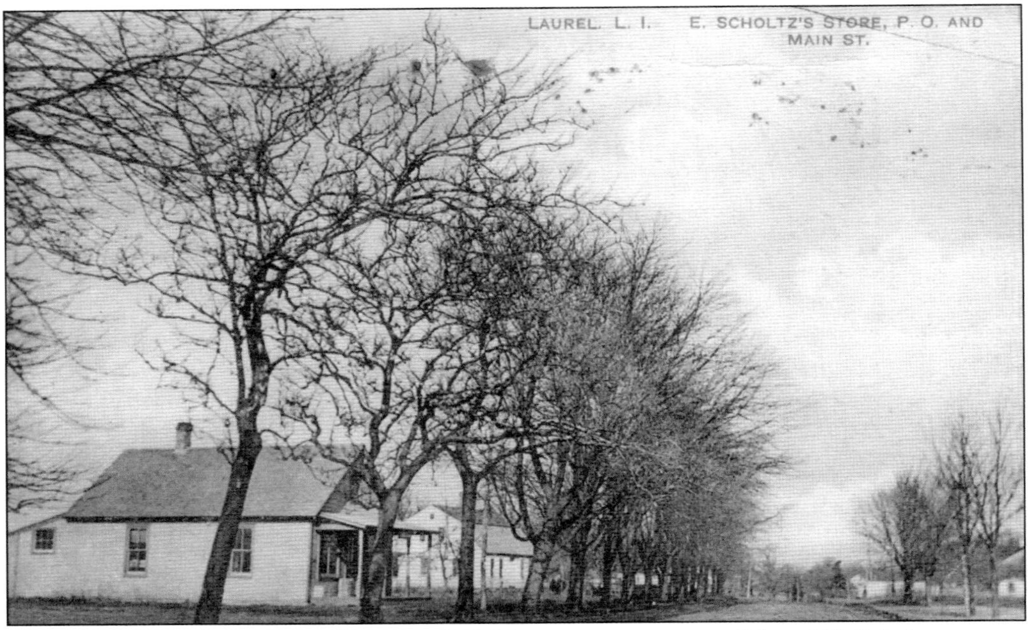

E. SCHOLTZ STORE AND POST OFFICE, 1907. Hungarian immigrant Edward Z. Scholtz came to Laurel from Sag Harbor in 1907 and purchased the Laurel post office and general store. Seen here is the original Laurel post office, which was built by Oliver Atwood around 1900. This building was eventually moved a half mile east to land owned by the Scholtz family. It is now Cliff's Elbow Room Too Restaurant. (Courtesy of Linda Bird.)

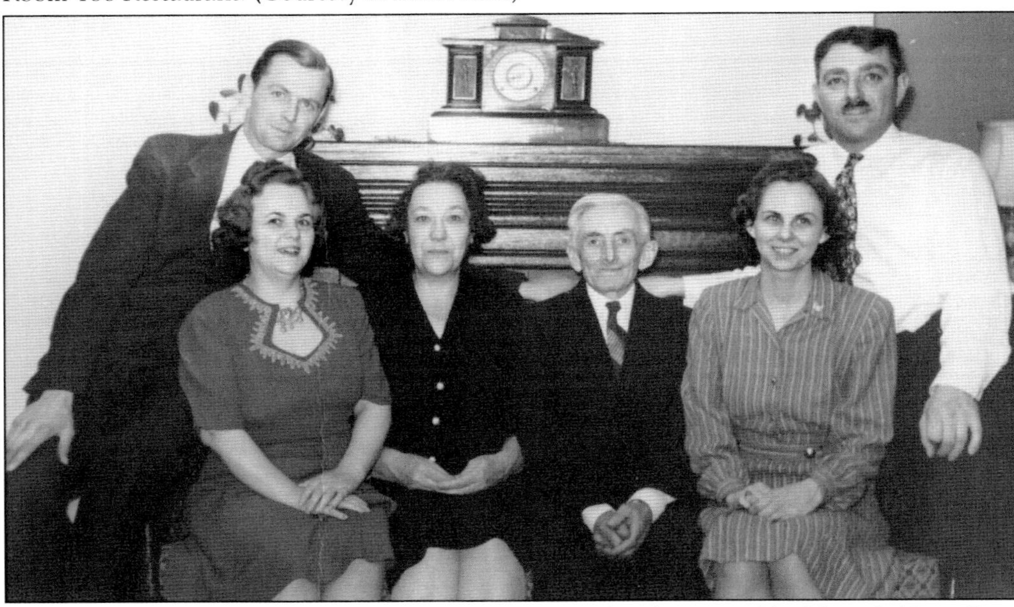

SCHOLTZ FAMILY. Edward Scholtz married Mary Emma Fleischman and had four children. From left to right, the family includes Irving Scholtz, Marguerite Scholtz , Mary Emma (Fleischman) Scholtz, Edward Scholtz, Marion Elberta, and Edward J. Scholtz. The two families ran the general store and post office in Laurel for 60 years, with Charlotte Fleischman serving as postmistress from 1939 to 1969. (Courtesy of Maryann Fleischman.)

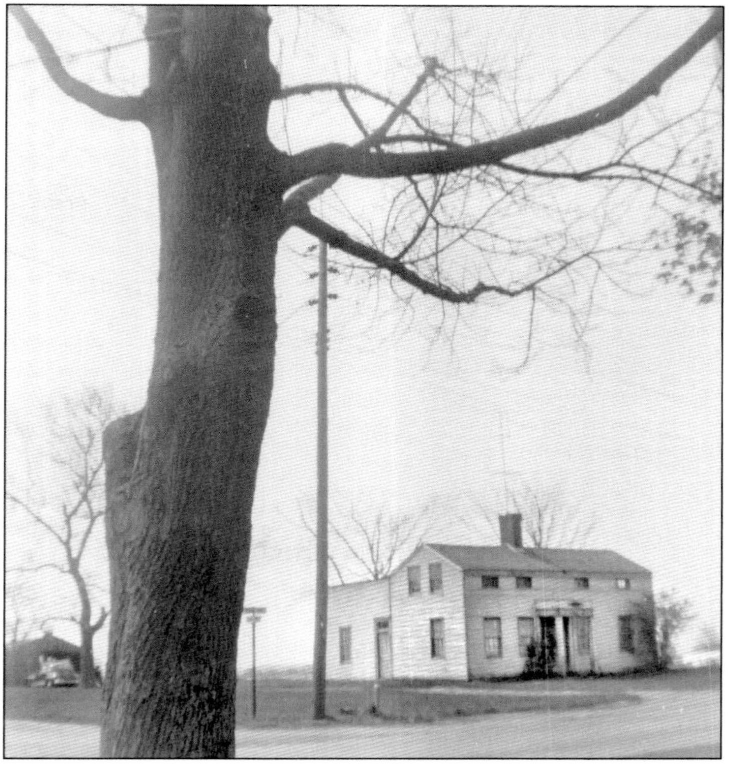

LEANDER TERRY RESIDENCE, C. 1940. On the west side of Laurel Lane was the home and farm of Leander Terry. Leander was a member of the 165th Regiment, New York Infantry during the Civil War. After the war, he married Lucilla Sayre of Southampton, and they lived and worked on their farm. The house was rented for many years after Lucilla's death in 1931 and was eventually razed sometime after 1950. (Courtesy of Maryann Fleischman.)

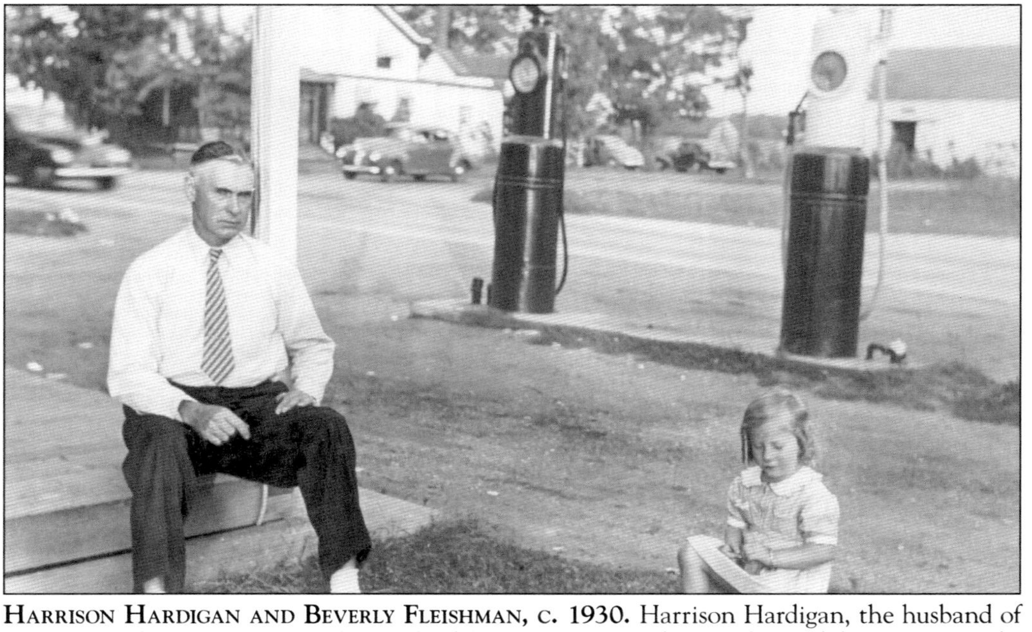

HARRISON HARDIGAN AND BEVERLY FLEISHMAN, C. 1930. Harrison Hardigan, the husband of Marguerite Fleischman, sits on the porch of the Laurel store and post office with his niece Beverly. The Mobil gas pumps in the background were part of the only gas station Laurel would ever have. Frank McNulty, whose father owned the farm on the corner of Laurel Lane in the background, recalled going to the store to purchase Wonder Bread. (Courtesy of Maryann Fleischman.)

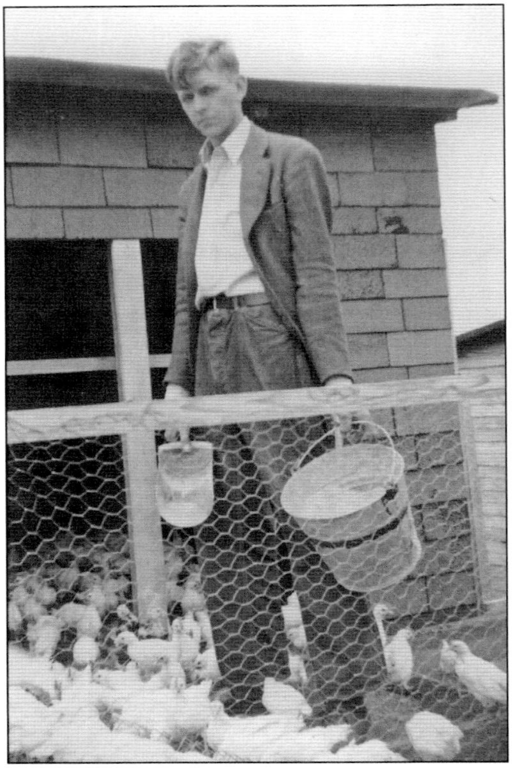

IRVING SCHOLTZ, C. 1935. A young Irving Scholtz feeds his chickens on the family property in Laurel. Scholtz started his egg business around 1935, when he was only 16 years old. (Courtesy of Linda Bird.)

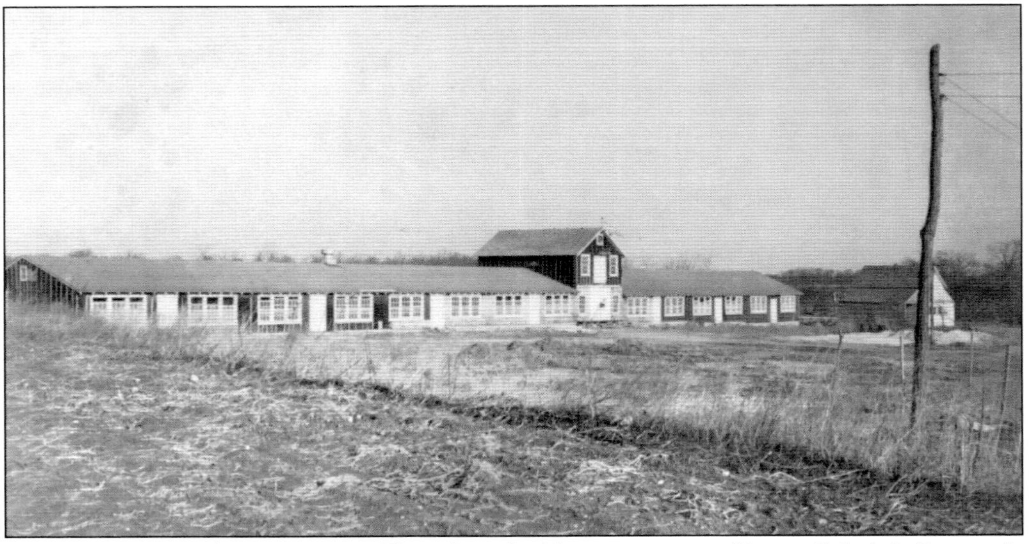

SCHOLTZ CHICKEN COOP, C. 1940. These large buildings were part of Irving Scholtz's Sunnyside Poultry Farm on the family property in Laurel. He needed these large coops to house the 20,000 laying chickens he tended. His wife, Eleanor, remembers the back room of the family home stacked floor to ceiling with eggs waiting to be sold to local restaurants. The two-story section of the chicken coop was moved to Main Road several years later and turned into a barbershop. The building still stands today on the west side of Cliff's Elbow Room Too Restaurant. (Courtesy of Eleanor Scholtz.)

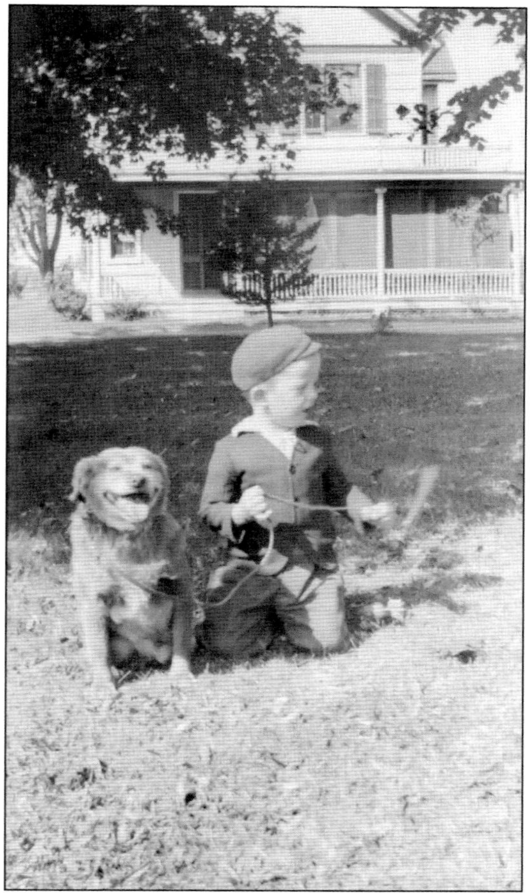

Harry Fleischman Jr., c. 1940. Harry Fleischman Jr. kneels with his dog in front of the family home, east of the post office on Main Road. The Fleischman house was originally the Franklinville Academy from 1833 to 1889, originally built by the people of Franklinville to support the minister of their new church. This was the first academy established on the North Fork. Oliver Atwood purchased the building after the academy closed. (Courtesy of Maryann Fleischman.)

Victor Kirkup House and Farm, c. 1920. On the south side of Sound Avenue in west Mattituck (below), brothers Victor and J. Trowbridge Kirkup ran a successful poultry business for many years. Victor also ran Lakeside Farm, a dairy farm on Laurel Lake. Their father, Benjamin C. Kirkup, came from Cambridge, England, as a small boy, and he and his brothers were the first people to grow cabbage seed in this area. (MLHS.)

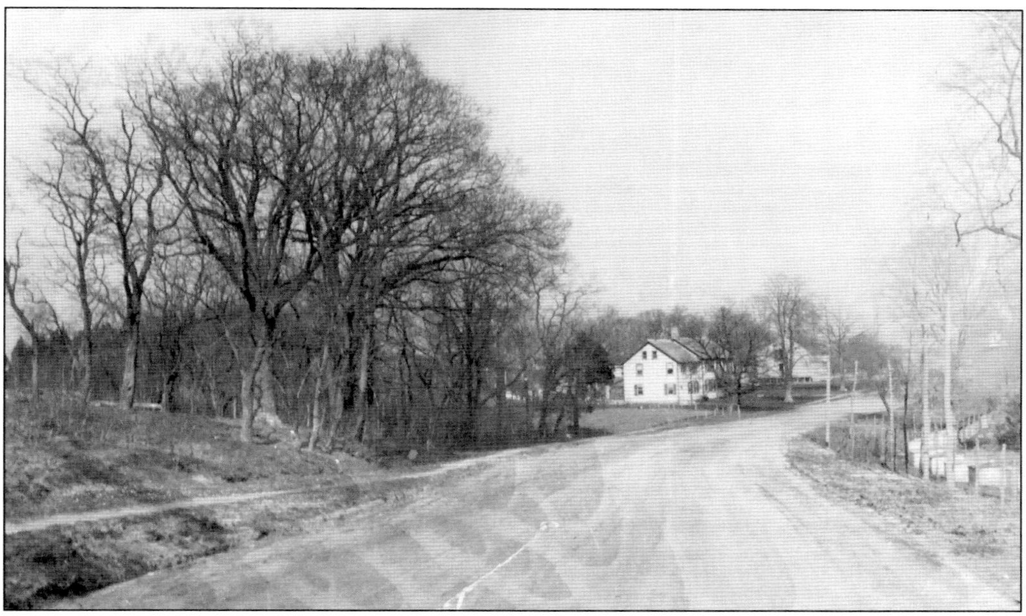

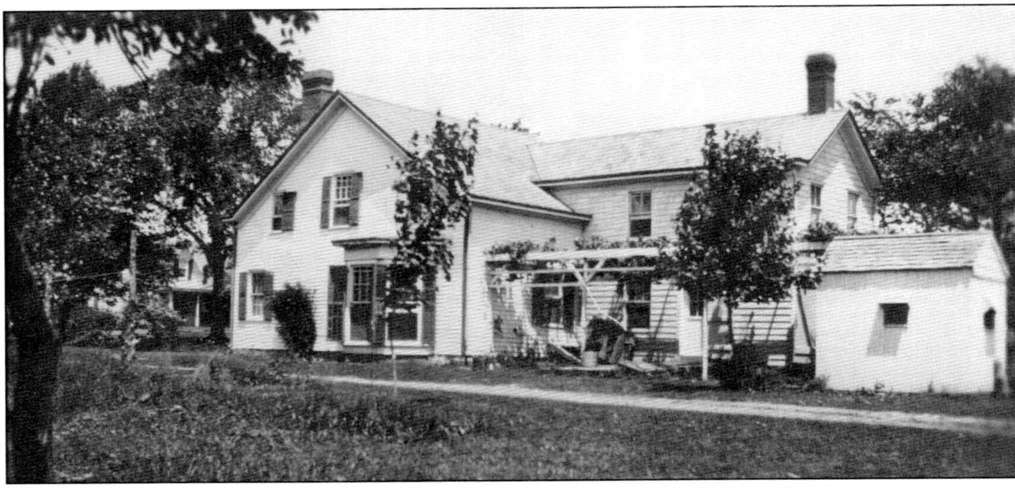

CHARLES MCNULTY RESIDENCE, C. 1930. Charles J. McNulty was born in the farming community of Oregon in 1868. His wife, Ann, and their six children lived in this farmhouse on the east side of Laurel Lane. McNulty was a very successful farmer and businessman. During his lifetime, he was the director of the Long Island Cauliflower Association, the director of the Mattituck Bank, and a Southold town trustee. (Courtesy of Maryann Fleischman.)

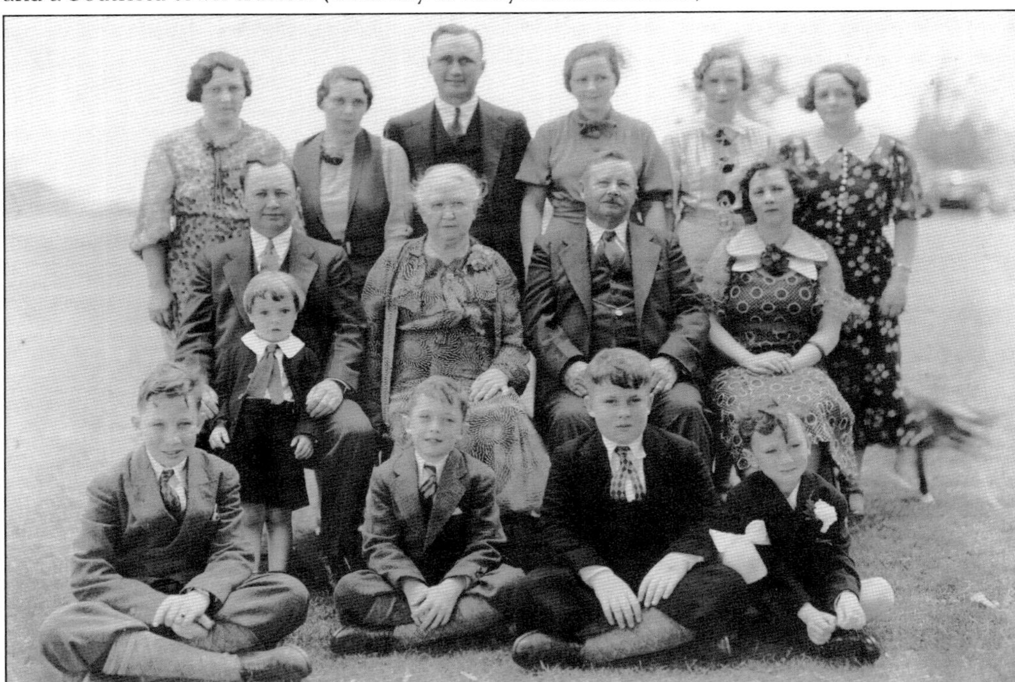

MCNULTY AND DILLER FAMILIES, 1936. Pictured, from left to right, are (top row) Mrs. John McNulty (Genevieve Schaumburg), Helen McNulty, Clarence "Doc" Diller, Edna McNulty, Mildred McNulty, and Anita McNulty; (middle row) John F. McNulty (father), John R. McNulty (boy), Mrs. Charles McNulty, Charles McNulty, and Marie McNulty Diller; (bottom row) Charles McNulty, William "Bill" McNulty, Frank McNulty, and Frank Diller. The occasion was Frank Diller's first communion. (Courtesy of Frank and Marilyn McNulty.)

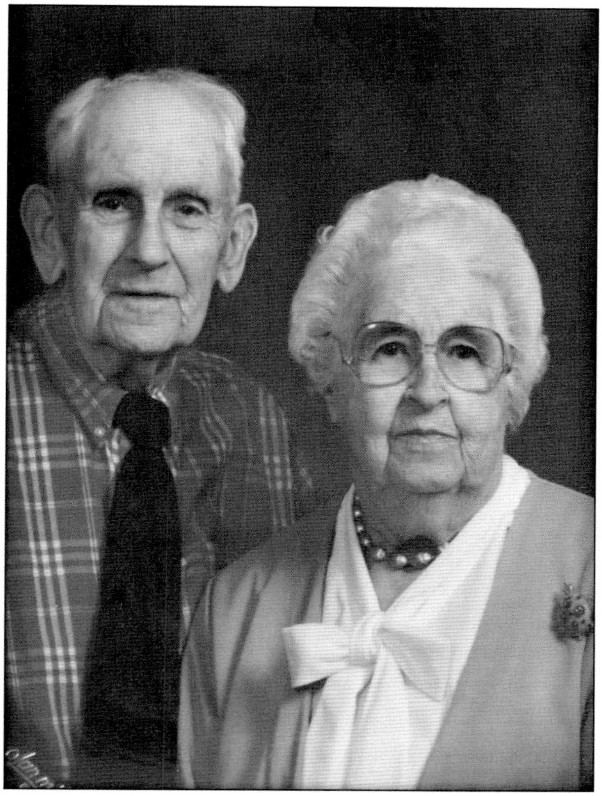

Cecil T. Young and Marion Gildersleeve Young, c. 1990. This couple owned a potato farm in Laurel from about 1920 until 1960. The farm ran from Laurel Lake down to Peconic Bay Boulevard and included all of the present Laurel Country Estates, east and west of Delmar Drive. Their son Myron remembers growing varieties of potatoes such as Katahdin, cobbler, Pontiac, Chippewa, russet, and Sebago. (Courtesy of Joan and Myron Young.)

Patrick L. Mahoney House, c. 1900. Hannah Mahoney and one of her daughters stand outside their home on Main Road in Laurel, just west of the Laurel schoolhouse. After retiring from farming, son George S. Mahoney lived in the house with his wife, Edith Penny, and they worked as the custodians for the school. (Courtesy of Robert Gerdts.)

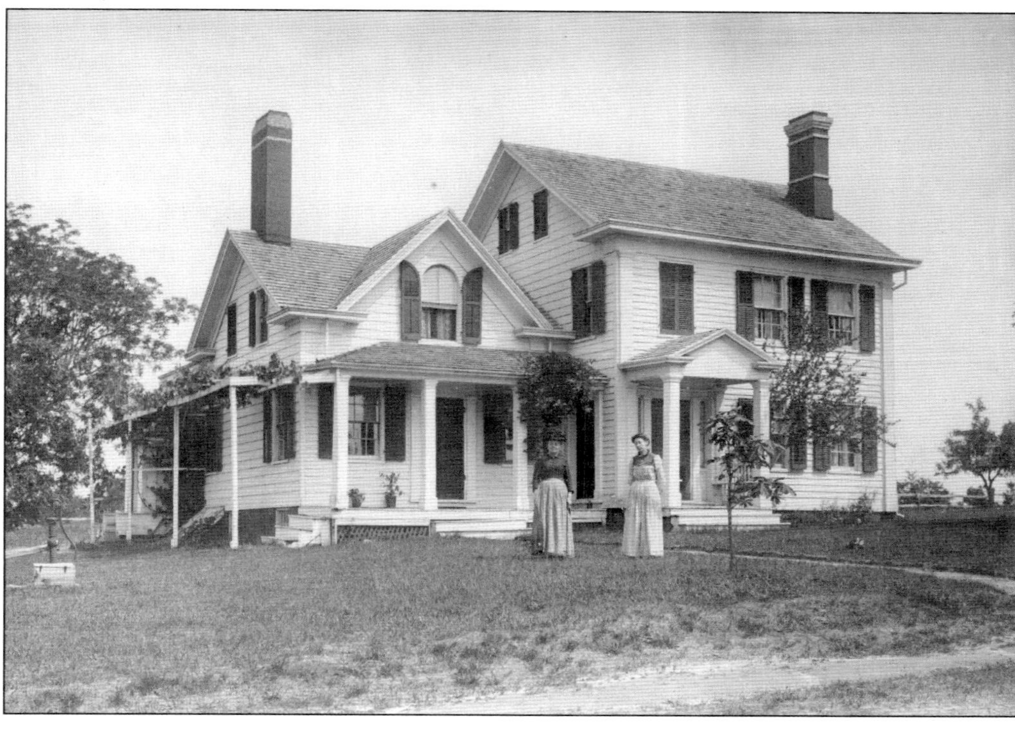

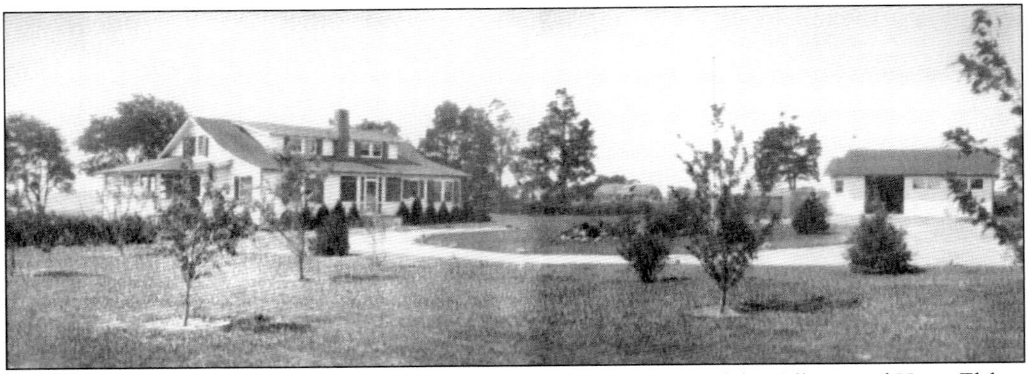

Ehlers Residence on Peconic Bay, 1934. This panoramic view of the Albert and Katie Ehlers summer home is part of a composite of four photographs taken from the roof of the Dr. John and Susan Horni garage by Russell Hawes in 1934. The house is located on Peconic Bay, just east of Laurel Lane on farmland purchased from Charles McNulty. The house was built by Wick Gildersleeve in 1931. The homes are still in the Thoet and Ehlers family today. (Courtesy of the Ehlers family.)

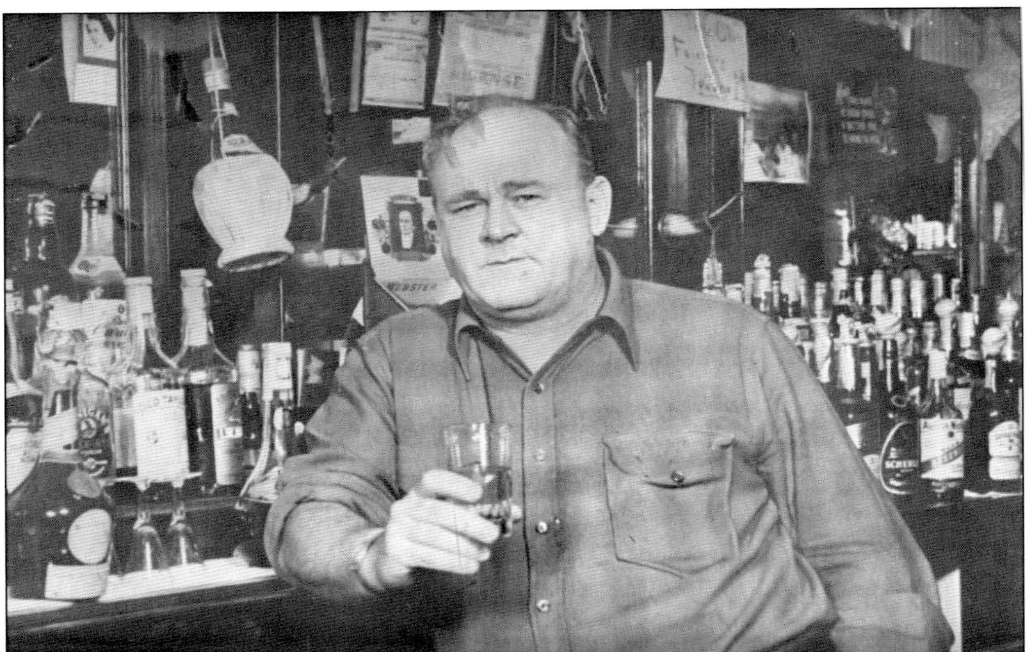

Cliff Saunders Sr. at the Laurel Inn, c. 1950. Cliff Saunders started the Laurel Inn around 1946, after managing the Anchor Inn for many years. Saunders loved to fish, and whatever he caught in the morning became the "catch of the day" at the restaurant. The Saunderses had a secret family recipe for their Manhattan clam chowder, which is still a customer favorite today. (Courtesy of Cliff Saunders III.)

Eight

MODERN MATTITUCK

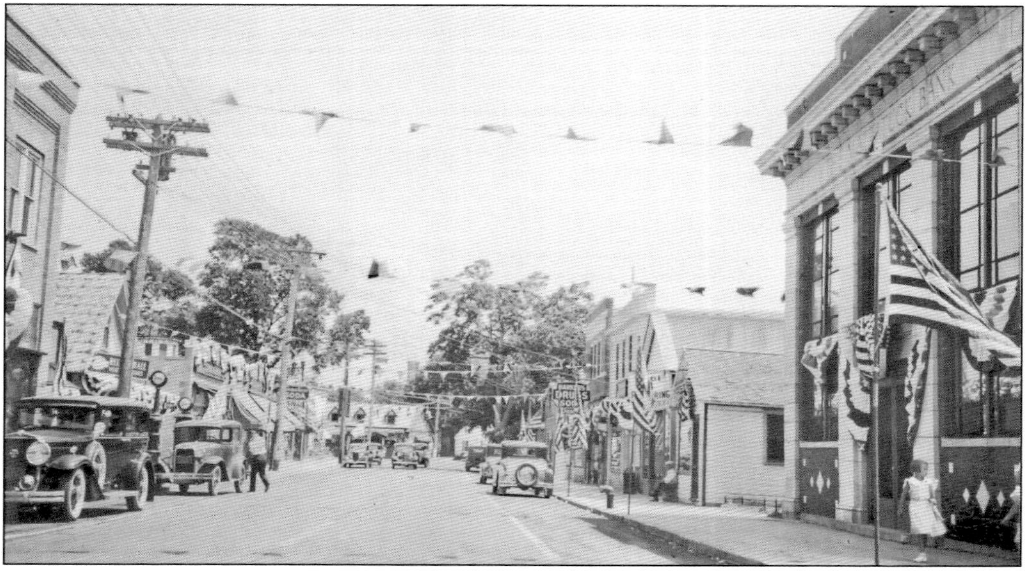

LOVE LANE, JULY 4, 1935. By the mid-1920s, the Mattituck business district, comprising Love Lane and Pike Street, began to undergo a dramatic transformation from small wooden shops to modern brick and stone structures. The unpaved roads once traveled by horses and carriages gave way to paved roads, concrete sidewalks, and automobiles. This photograph of Love Lane, looking south from Pike Street, shows the dramatic change from the old village center to the modern business district. (Courtesy of Jim and Pauline Gildersleeve.)

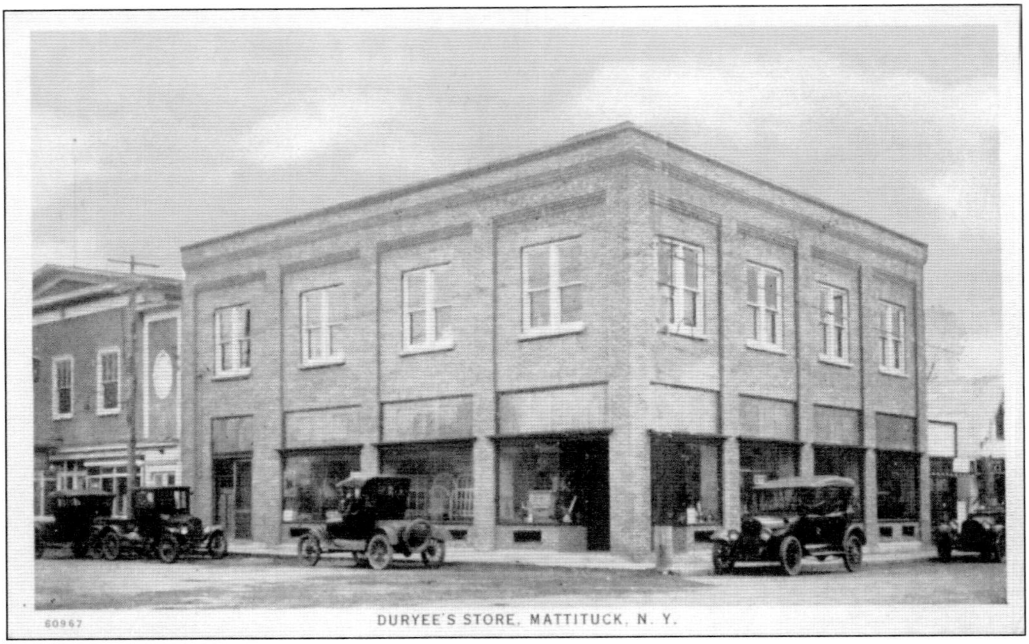

Duryee Hardware and Fischer's Hall, c. 1925. In 1925, William V. Duryee built this impressive hardware store on the southeastern corner of Love Lane and Pike Street, replacing Fischer's Market. Duryee already owned a seed business at his first building, on Westphalia Avenue. He was assisted at both stores by his brother Peter Harvey Duryee and his nephew John Duryee. In 1971, after 52 years of service, John sold the store to Marty Suter and Henry Raynor. (MLL.)

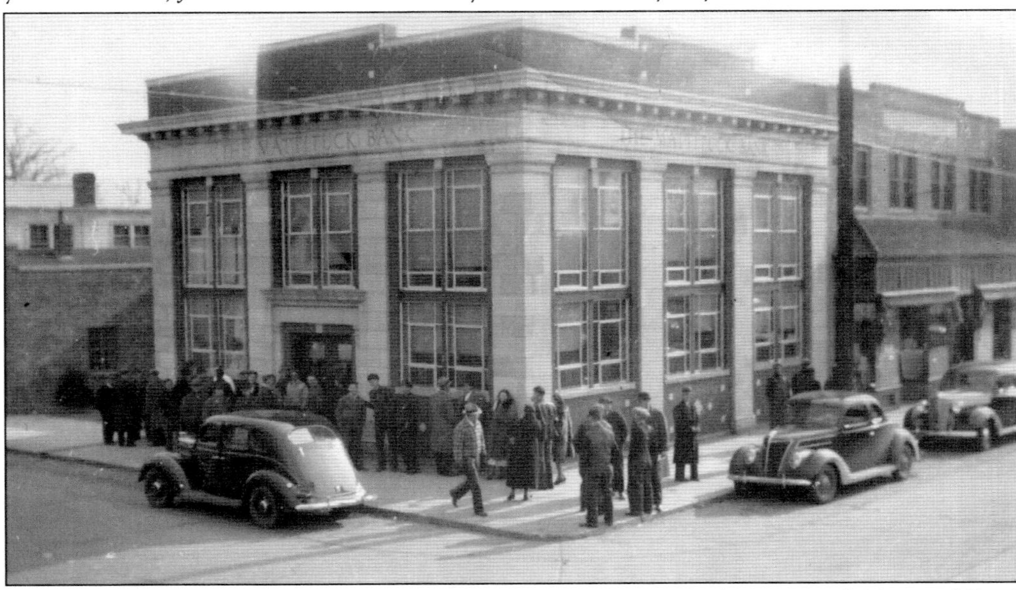

Mattituck National Bank After Robbery, c. 1930. In 1925, the Mattituck National Bank and Trust moved from Library Hall to this striking stone edifice on the southwestern corner of Love Lane and Pike Street, opposite Duryee Hardware. The bank grew, and in 1950, a 20-foot-by-34-foot expansion was added to its south side. On the right is the Liddell Building, the location of Samuel's Department Store. (MLHS.)

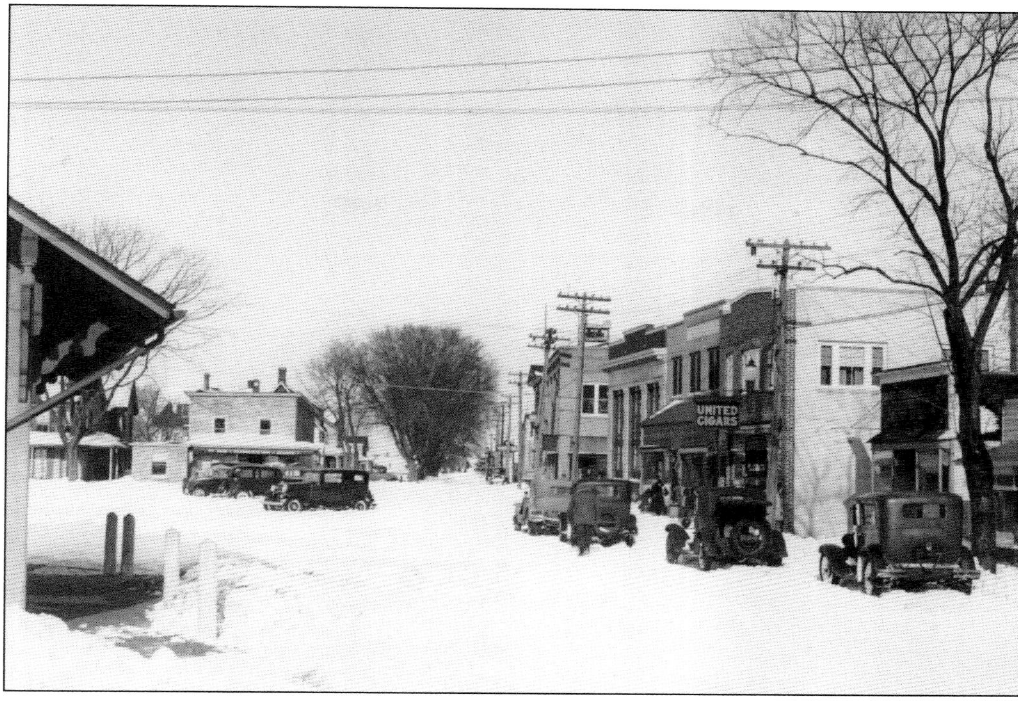

Pike Street, c. 1930. George Brown came to Mattituck from Jamesport in 1928 to engage in the stationery business. He constructed a two-story brick building on Pike Street. In this photograph, looking east on Pike Street, the United Cigars sign hangs outside his stationery store. The store was on the ground floor, and the family residence was on the second floor. The building was sold in 1953, when Brown decided to enter into business with his son K.G. (MLL.)

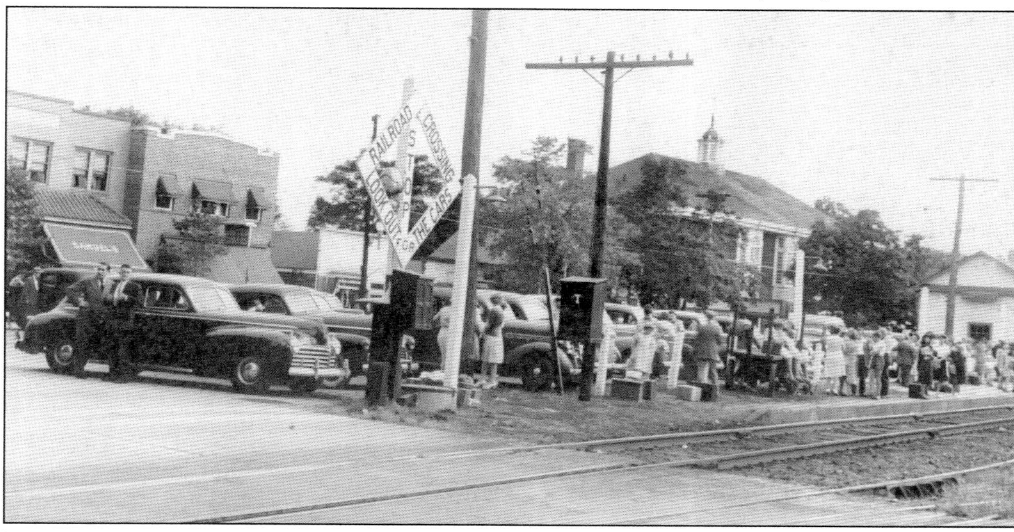

Pike Street, c. 1940. The Liddell Building, with the large awning in the background, contained Samuel's Department Store. Milton and Florence Samuel opened their store in 1924. Milton's sister Ruth married David Rothman, who owned and operated the Rothman Department Store in Southold. After 25 years in business, Samuel turned the store over to his daughter Rosalind Phillips, of Mattituck, who changed the name to Phillips' Department Store. (MLL.)

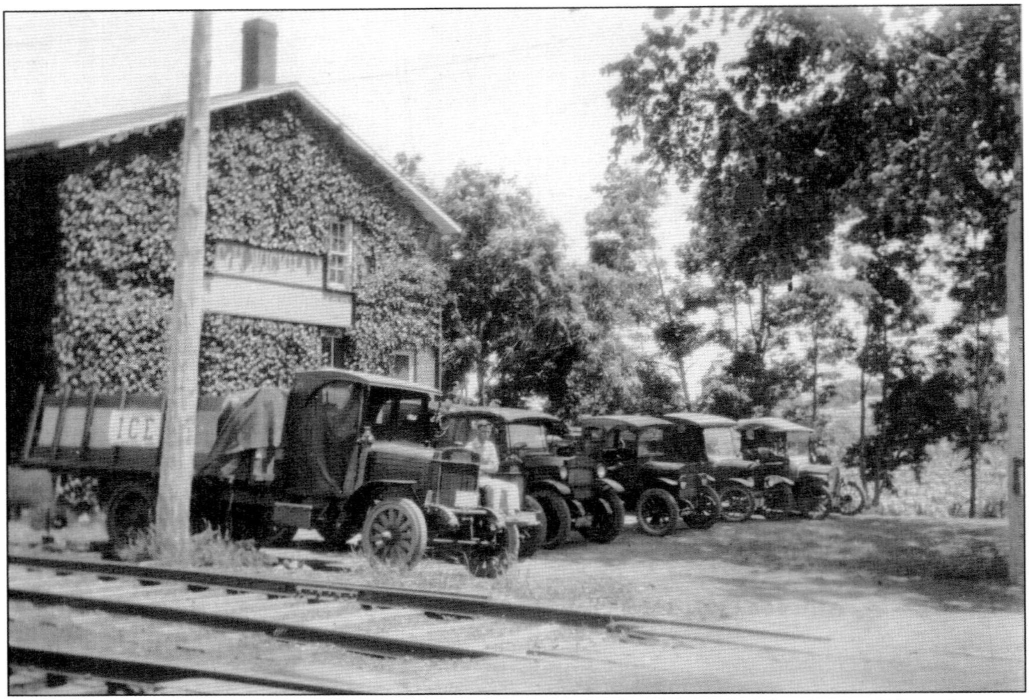

C.H. WICKHAM COAL AND PRODUCE, 1924. Formerly the Alart & Maguire pickling factory, then occupied by S.W. Tuthill & Co. Produce and Coal, this building on Wickham Avenue and the railroad tracks eventually became C.H. Wickham Coal and Produce. (Courtesy of Jay Wickham.)

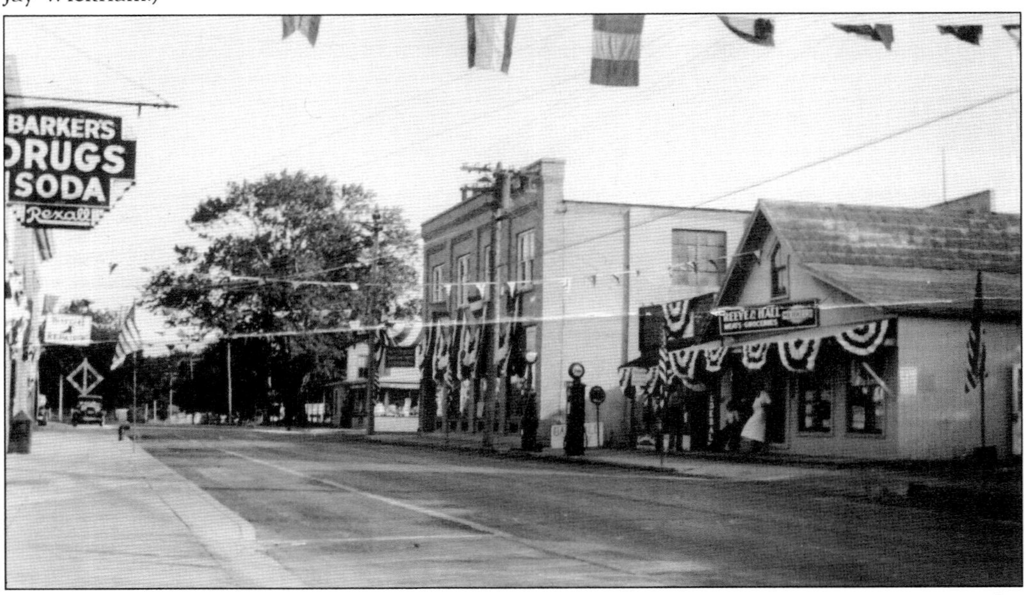

LOVE LANE, C. 1935. The Reeve and Hall meat market (right) was one of the more popular businesses in Mattituck for more than 60 years. Many local men gathered in the store's back room to smoke pipes and cigars, enjoying a game of dominoes or cards as they discussed issues of the day. It is now the location of the Love Lane Kitchen. (MLL.)

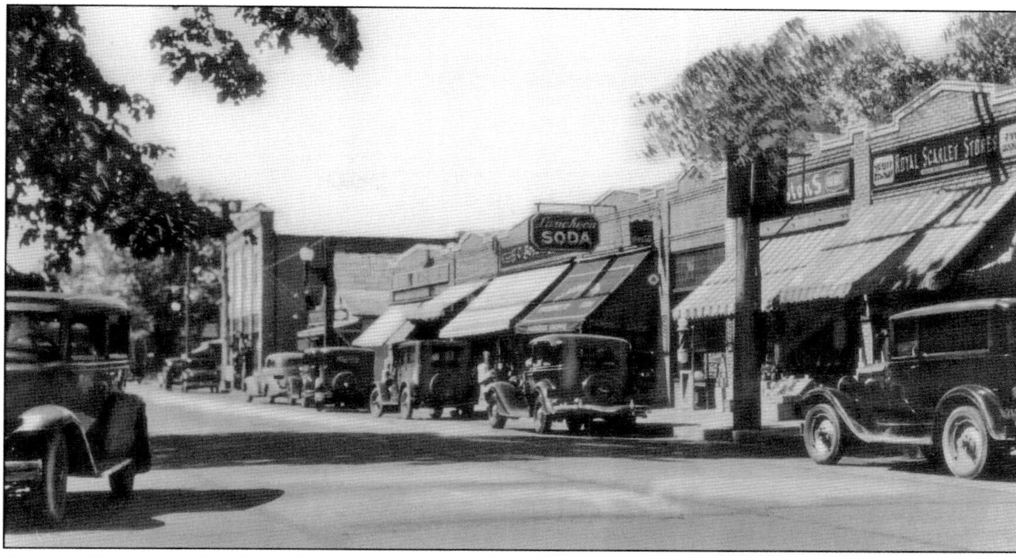

Kelsey Block c. 1935. Melville Kelsey, a realtor from Freeport, bought Carrie Wells Conklin's property on Love Lane in 1927. Kelsey razed the old buildings on the property and built several modern brick stores, which became known as the Kelsey Block. Many popular businesses occupied the stores over the years, including the A&P, Roulston's Market, Royal Scarlet Stores, Bohack, the L&L Food Market, and Paradise Luncheonette. (MLL.)

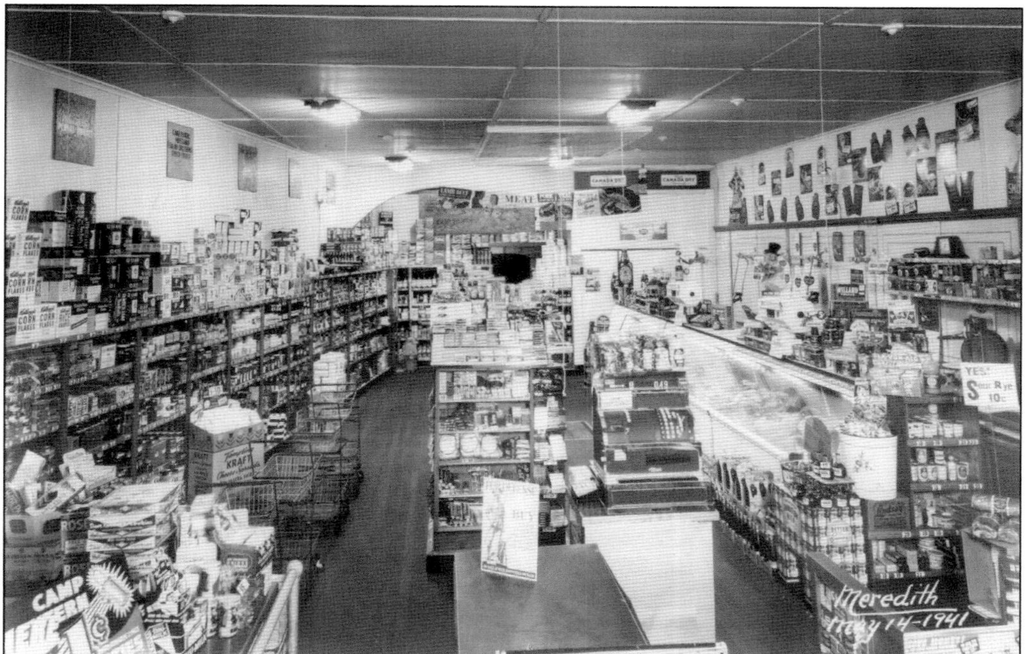

L&L Food Market on Love Lane, c. 1940. In 1939, the A&P moved from Love Lane to another location in Mattituck, and former A&P managers Alois Lutz and William "Bill" Long opened the L&L Food Market in its place. After Long passed away in 1959, Lutz expanded the store and ran it successfully before selling it to Leo Milowski Jr. in 1970. (Courtesy of the Southold Historical Society.)

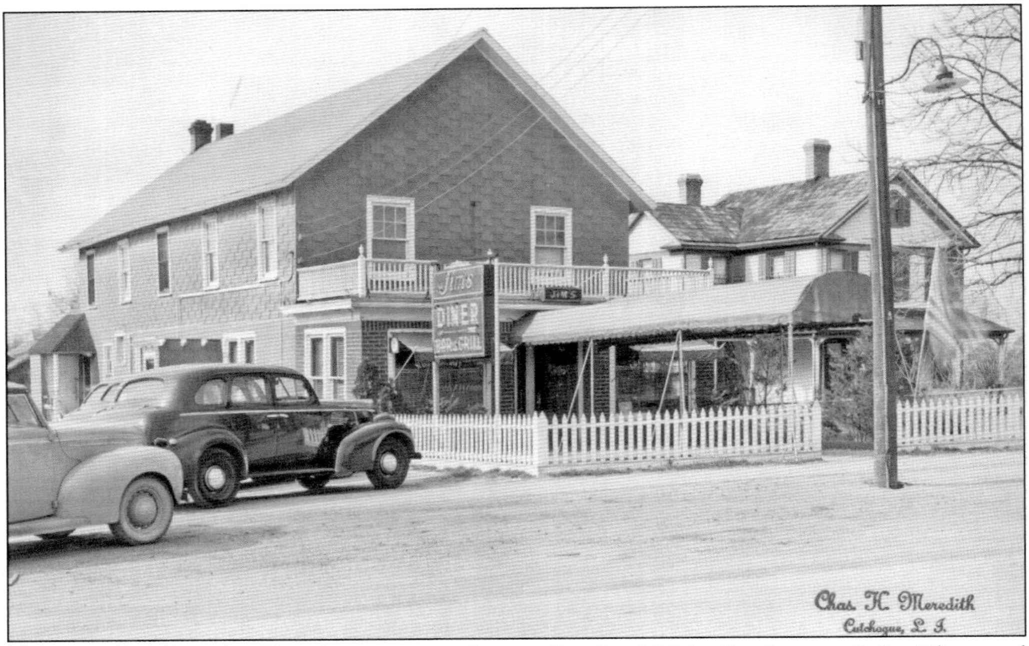

Jim's Diner, c. 1935. This diner was on the north side of Main Road, east of the Glenwood Lodge. The building was originally Reeve and Tuthill's grocery, located on Love Lane opposite the Gildersleeve store. Conrad Grabie moved the building to its present location around 1918. Jim Albin ran the popular eatery until his death in 1948. (Courtesy of the Southold Historical Society.)

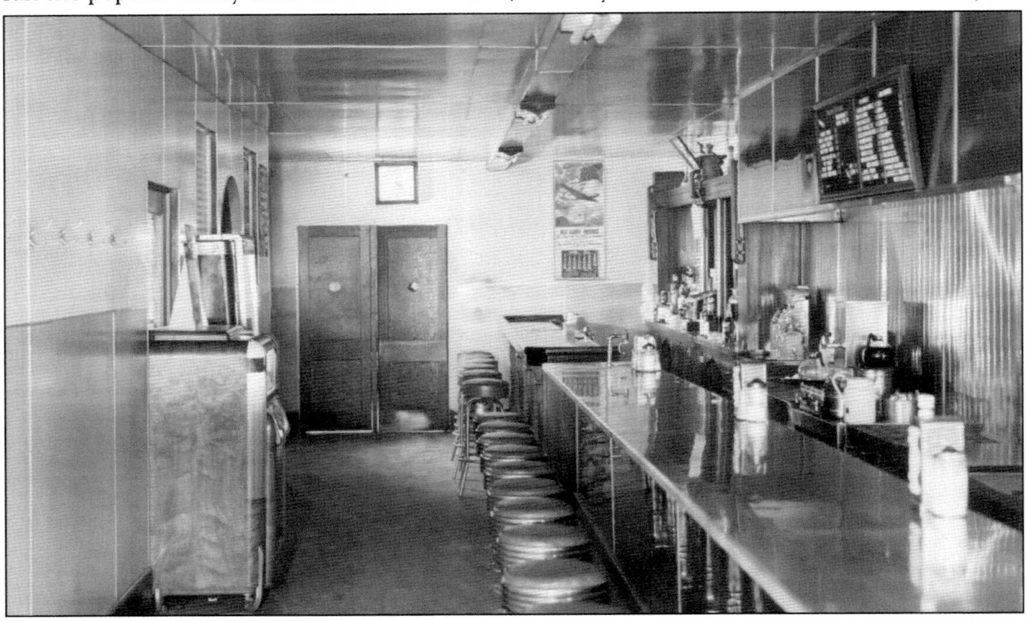

Interior View of Jim's Diner, c. 1935. The dining room was on the left, through the archway opposite the lunch counter. There were also pool tables upstairs, where local groups convened for dinner and meetings. Grampy Kootz, who worked behind the counter, was slow and loved to talk. Babe Ruth and Lou Gehrig stopped for breakfast at Jim's on their way to go fishing in New Suffolk. (Courtesy of the Southold Historical Society.)

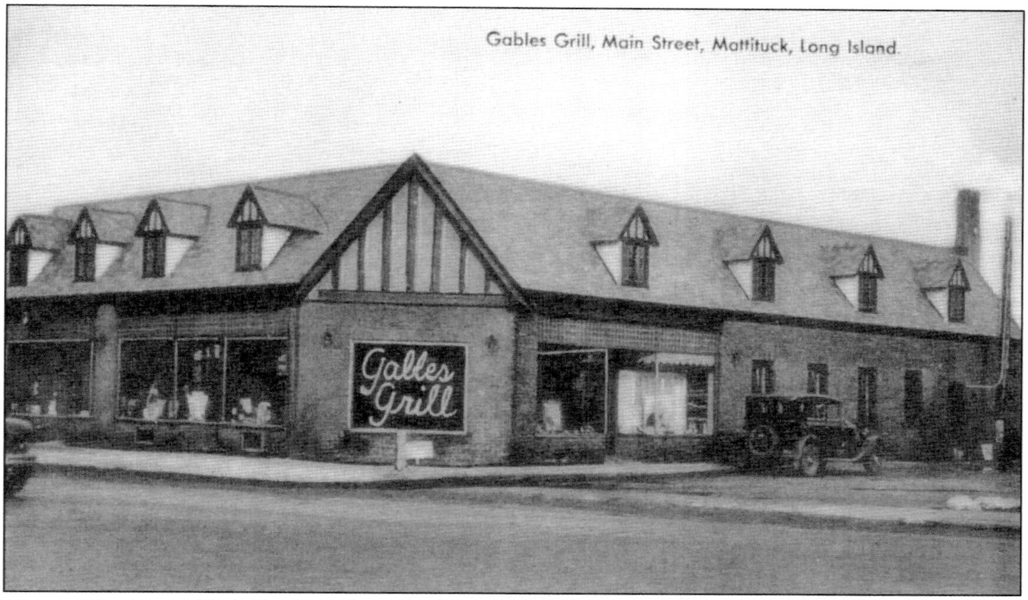

Gables Grill, c. 1935. Harry DePetris built a store on the vacant property opposite the Presbyterian church in 1928 for the A&P. A year later, the A&P moved to Love Lane. DePetris then converted the building into a restaurant called Gables Grill, which featured live music and dancing. The business did not do well during the Depression, so Harry closed it in 1936. (Courtesy of the DePetris family.)

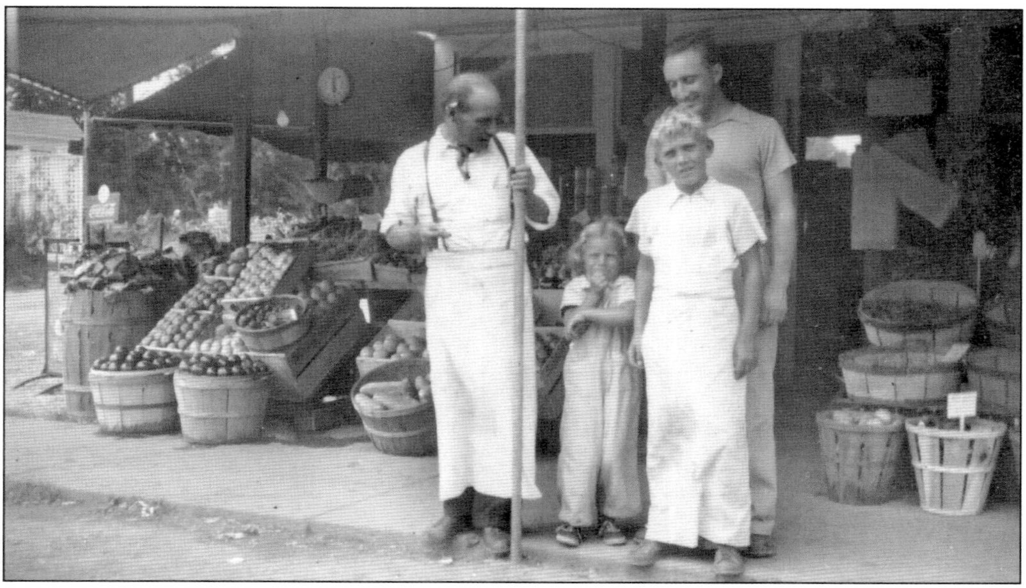

Harry DePetris Fruit and Vegetable Market, 1936. Harry DePetris (left) and his brother-in-law Henry Cantelmi stand in front of the fruit and vegetable market that DePetris built on Main Road across from Bay Avenue in the summer of 1936. After closing the Gables Grill a few months earlier, DePetris decided to return to his former line of business. (Courtesy of the DePetris family.)

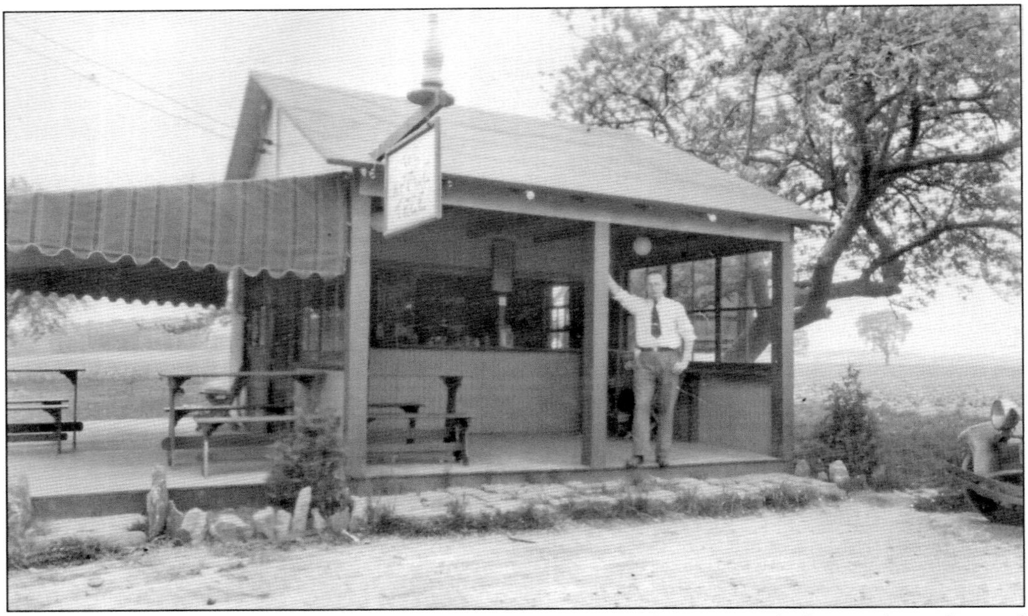

Apple Tree Roadside Stand, c. 1930. The original Apple Tree roadside stand was located at Manor Hill, on the south side of Main Road near the Mattituck-Cutchogue border. The Huttenlocher brothers, Ronald and Victor, started the vegetable and hot dog stand in 1930, with seating for only eight people. The large apple tree behind the stand gave it its name. (Courtesy of the Huttenlocher family.)

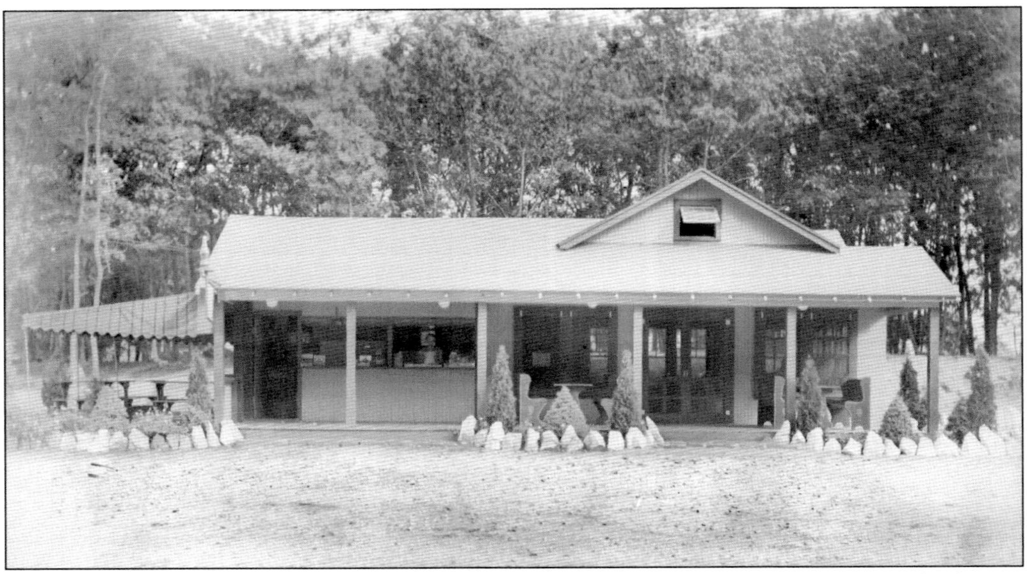

Apple Tree Restaurant, c. 1935. In 1935, the Huttenlocher family moved their refreshment stand to the south side of Main Road, east of the Mattituck bowling alleys. Josephine Huttenlocher, the mother of partners Ronald and Victor Huttonlocher, did all the cooking and baking. Their enterprise grew into a first-class restaurant with seating for 200 people. They employed 13 people and had an orchestra entertain nightly. (Courtesy of the Huttenlocher family.)

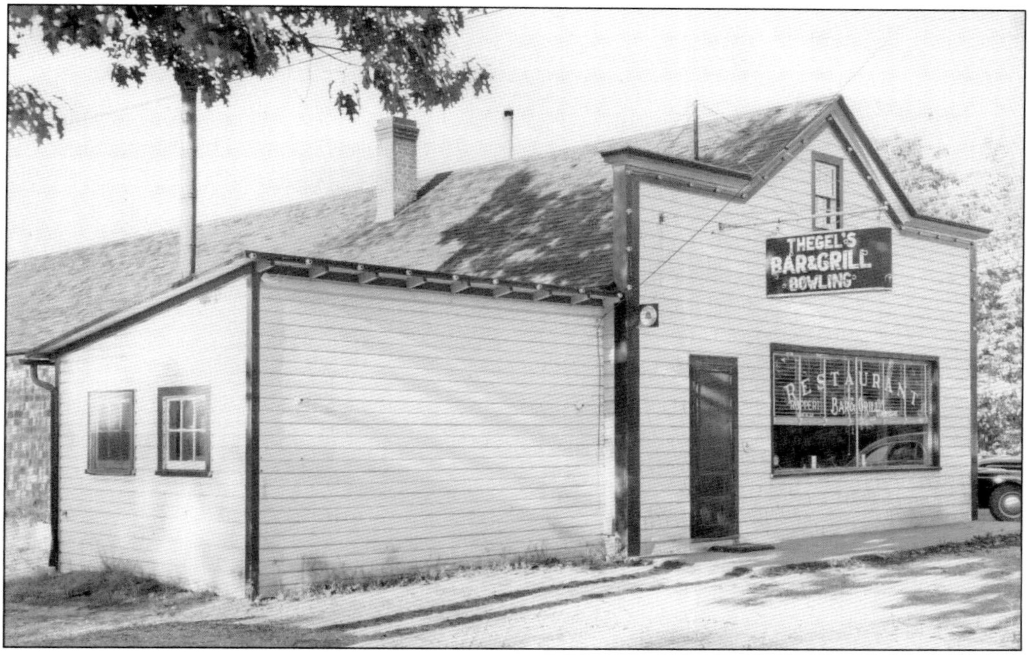

Mattituck Bowling Alley, c. 1940. The Mattituck bowling alley was built in 1929 on the northwestern corner of Main Road and Factory Avenue. The popular sports center burned down in the early-morning hours of March 10, 1955. The alley was owned by Henry J. Gagen of Mattituck and William Albertson of Brooklyn, and Gagen was the manager. In August 1955, a new bowling alley was opened diagonally across the street by Tony Regula. (Courtesy of the Southold Historical Society.)

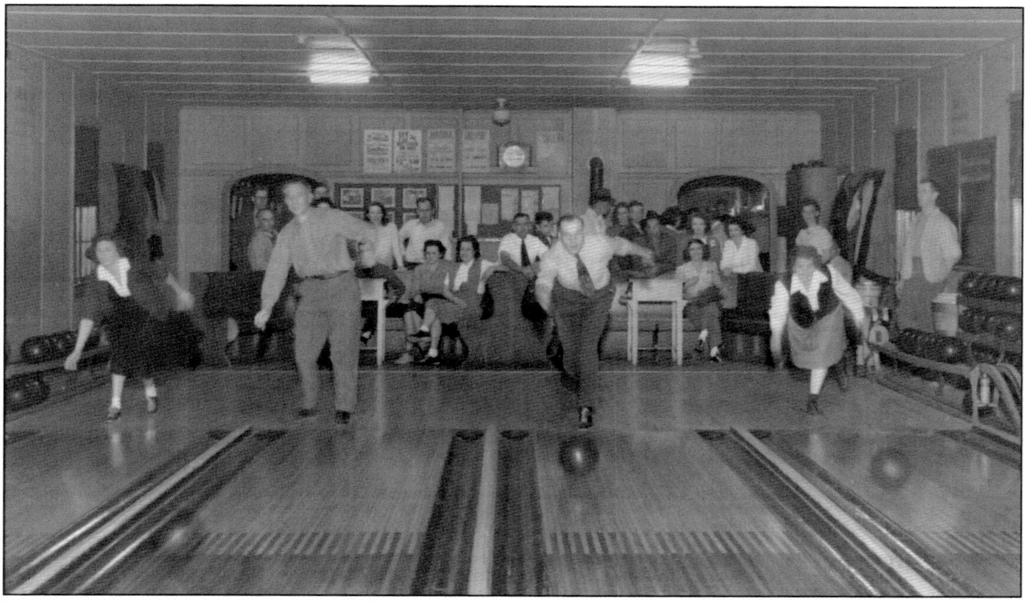

Mixed League Bowling, 1947. The original bowling alley had a restaurant and bar in the front and four lanes in the back. A mixed bowling league is seen here at the alley in 1947, in the era when pins were still reset by hand. (Courtesy of the Southold Historical Society.)

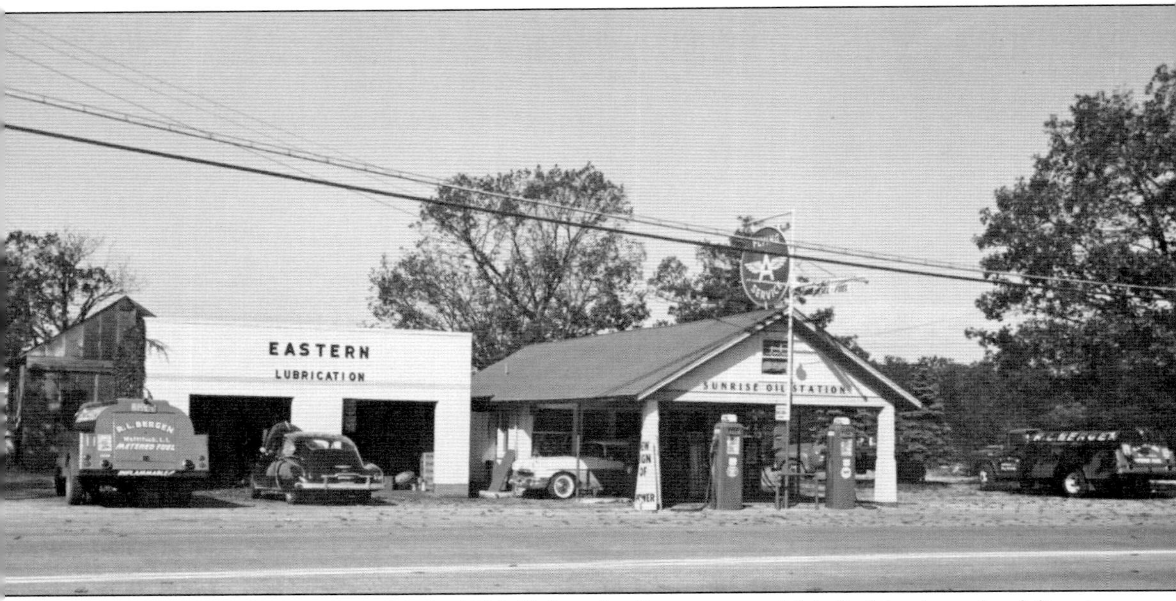

Sunrise Oil Station, 1956. In 1938, Robert L. Bergen started his fuel business by delivering gasoline to farmers from two barrels of fuel in the back of his pickup. His son Donald carried two 5-gallon cans on a yoke up to the farmer's door. Eventually, Bergen bought a larger pickup and an electric pump to pump a gallon per minute. Located on Main Road west of the Mattituck Bowling Alley on Factory Avenue, Bergen's gas station was originally a Tydol station but later became the Sunrise Oil Station. By the 1960s, Bergen's trucks could transport 2,800 gallons, with a pressurized system that could pump 60 gallons per minute. He was very generous with customers who did not have the money to pay for fuel. Behind the station was the trucking business of Steven Hamilton, who shipped potatoes to Boston. (Courtesy of Donald Bergen.)

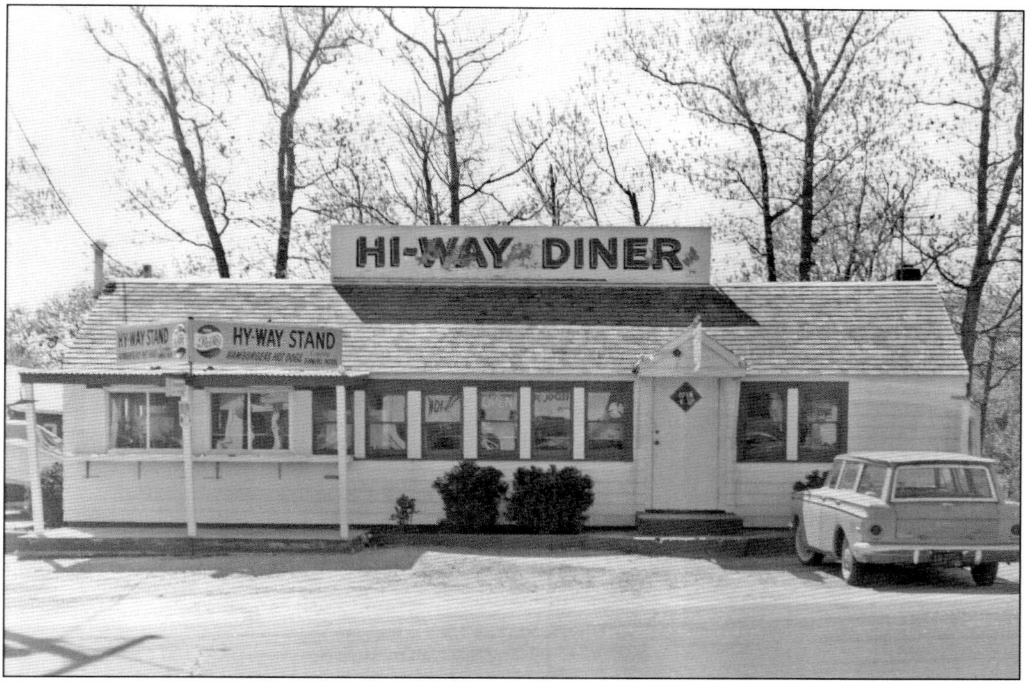

Hi-Way Diner, c. 1955. The Hi-Way Diner was across the street from the bowling alley, on the south side of Main Road. It was originally called Bill's Diner, and was owned by Bill Berliner around 1950. (Courtesy of the Southold Historical Society.)

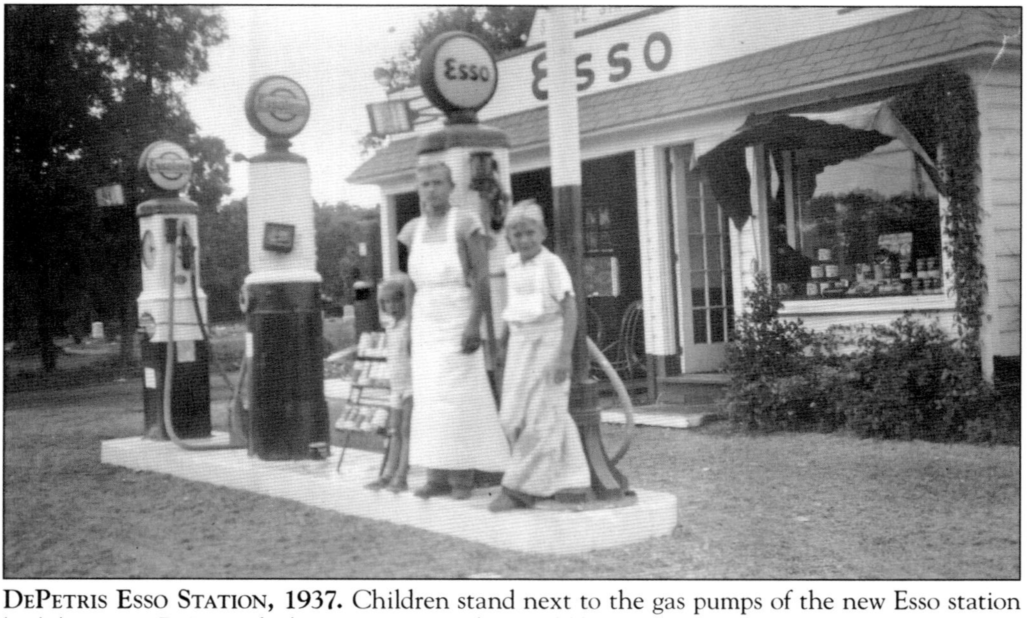

DePetris Esso Station, 1937. Children stand next to the gas pumps of the new Esso station built by Harry DePetris for his son, Enrico, who would be the manager. The station was on Main Road, west of De Petris's vegetable store and east of the New Bethany cemetery. (Courtesy of the DePetris family.)

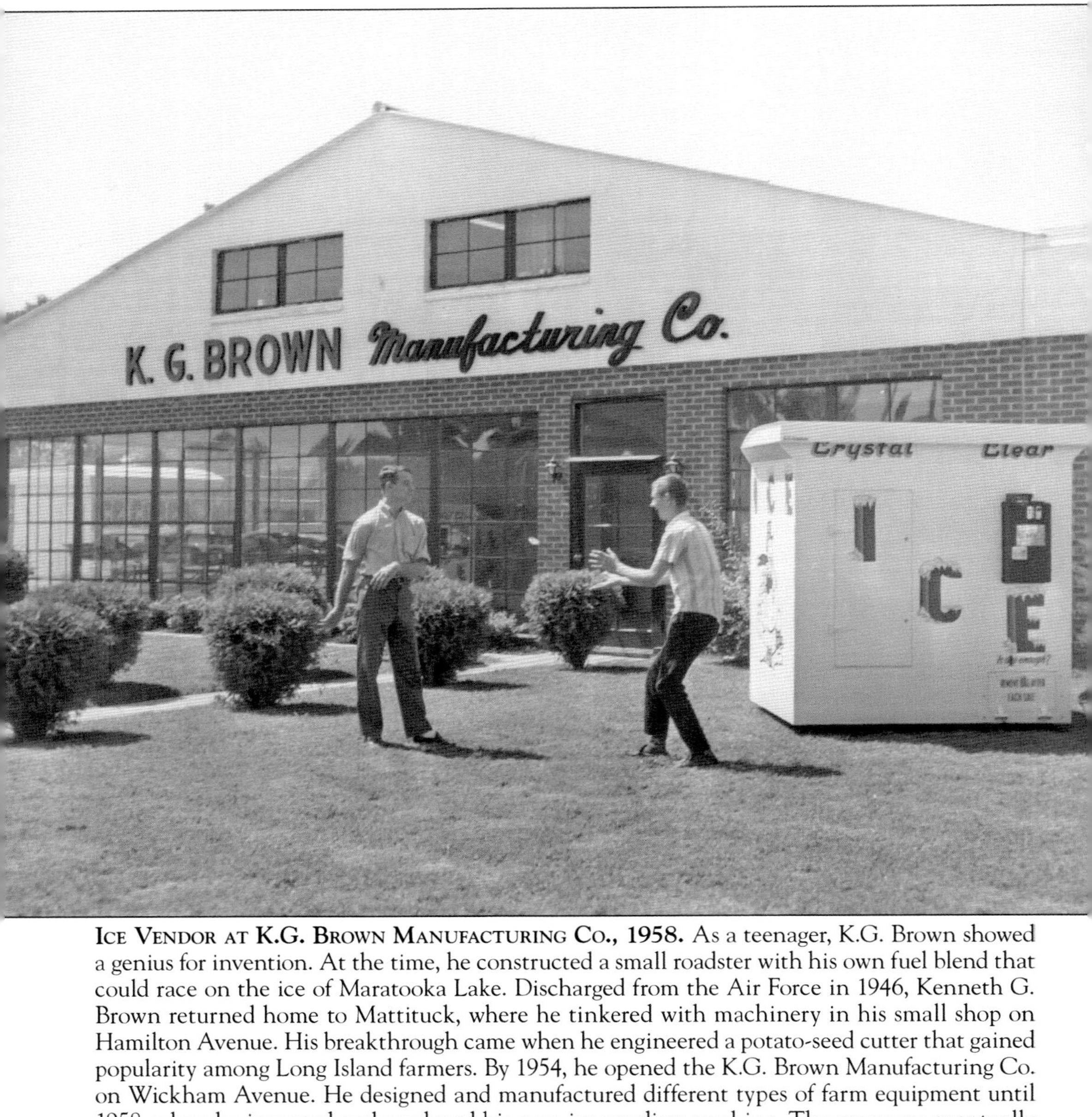

Ice Vendor at K.G. Brown Manufacturing Co., 1958. As a teenager, K.G. Brown showed a genius for invention. At the time, he constructed a small roadster with his own fuel blend that could race on the ice of Maratooka Lake. Discharged from the Air Force in 1946, Kenneth G. Brown returned home to Mattituck, where he tinkered with machinery in his small shop on Hamilton Avenue. His breakthrough came when he engineered a potato-seed cutter that gained popularity among Long Island farmers. By 1954, he opened the K.G. Brown Manufacturing Co. on Wickham Avenue. He designed and manufactured different types of farm equipment until 1958, when he invented and produced his own ice-vending machine. The company eventually focused exclusively on the ice-vending business, and his locally manufactured vendors were sold all over the country. (Courtesy of the Southold Historical Society.)

Mattituck Airbase Brochure, c. 1950. Cedric Wickham agreed to let his son J. Parker open an airport on their potato farm when he returned home from World War II. In 1974, Mattituck Airbase housed one of the best aviation engine shops in the Northeast. Engines came from all over the world for rebuilding. Owners offering aircraft for sale in publications often noted, as a major selling point, "Has a Mattituck engine," implying that the name was the last word in dependability. (MLL.)

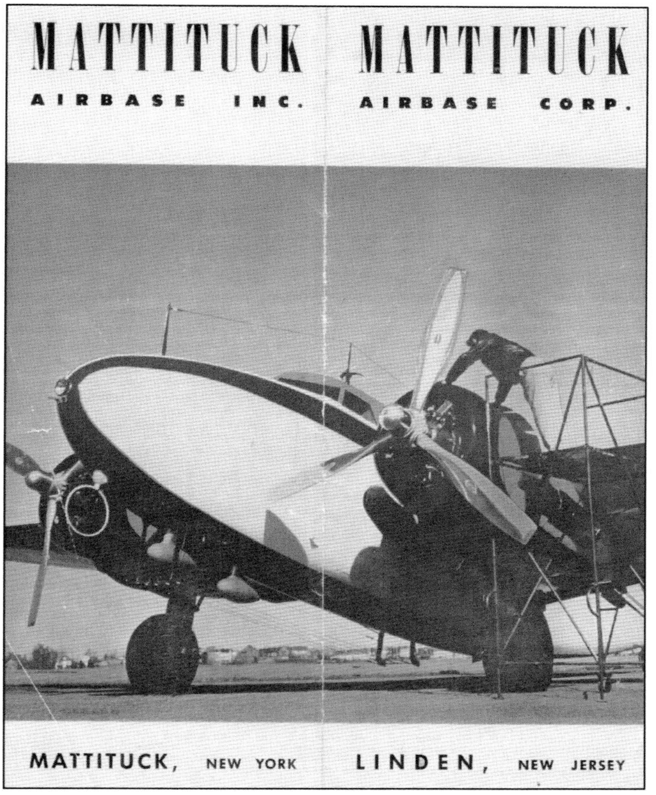

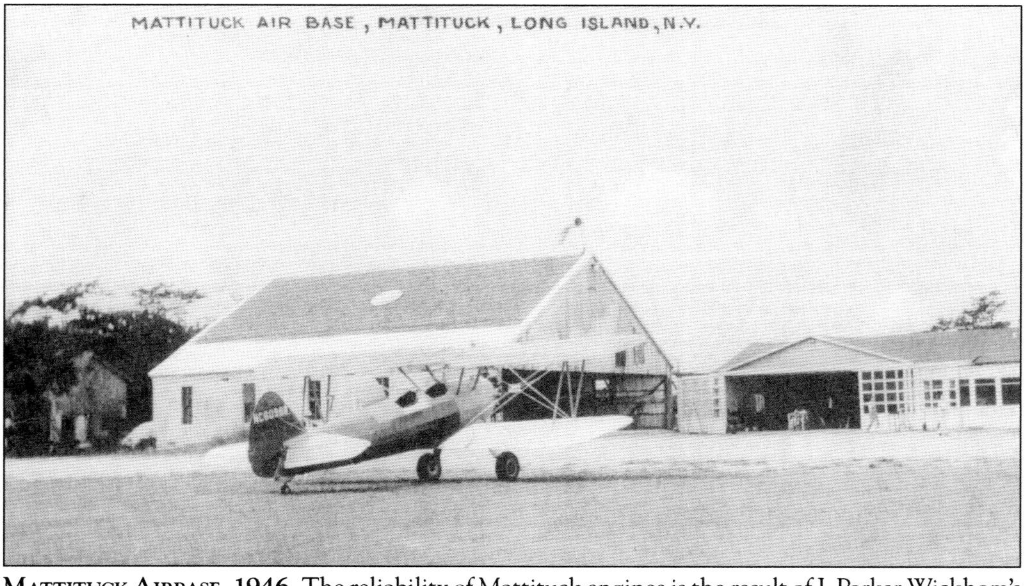

Mattituck Airbase, 1946. The reliability of Mattituck engines is the result of J. Parker Wickham's approach of "one man, one engine," whereby entire engines were assembled by one individual. Mattituck resident and former airbase employee Myron Young recalled, "The engine we made had our name on it, so to speak. If there was a problem with the engine, whenever it came back in, it went right to the guy who built it so he and his supervisor could fix the problem." (MLL.)

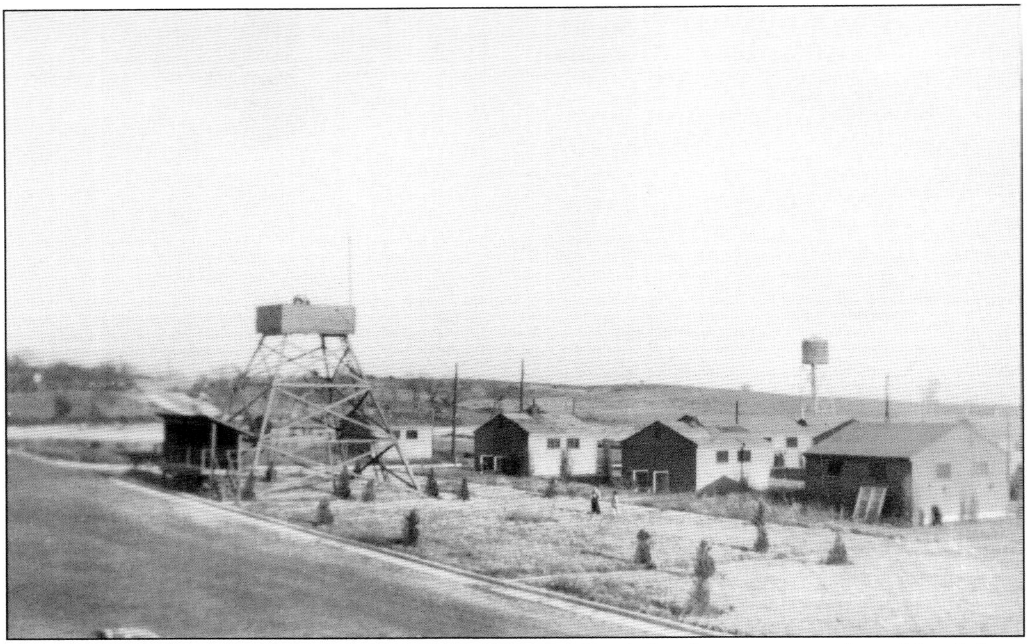

Mattituck Practice Firing Point Camp, 1943. The federal government leased land from Martin Sidor in 1943 to establish a practice firing point on the sound in Mattituck. This Mattituck battery practiced with 40-millimeter automatic weapons throughout different seasons of the year. Red targets were towed on a barge or by a twin-engine plane. The soldiers patrolled the sound shore from Mattituck to Peconic. (Courtesy of the Sidor family.)

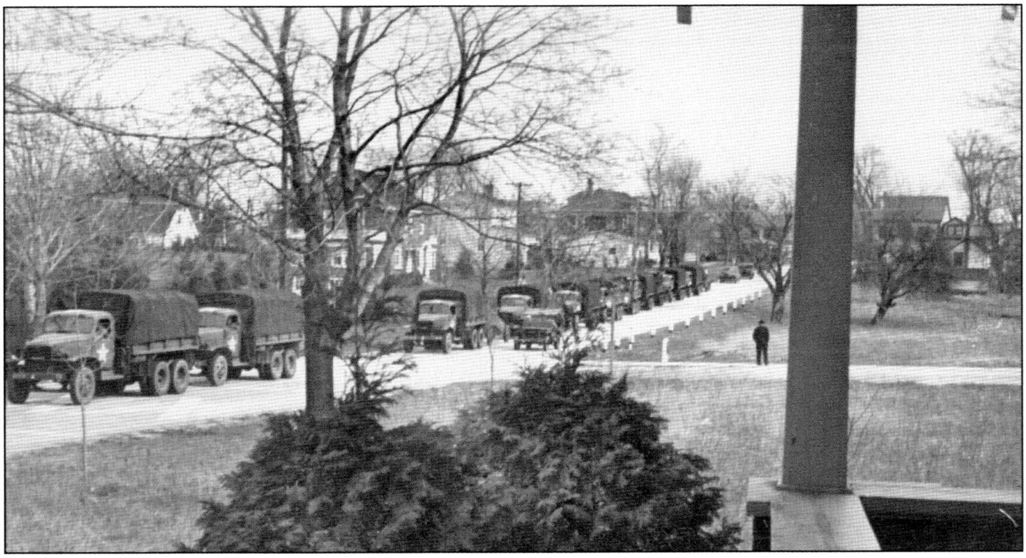

Army Antiaircraft Convoy, 1943. This convoy moves up Wickham Avenue to the Mattituck Practice Firing Camp. The USO held dances for the troops from the Mattituck and Riverhead Firing Points at Mechanics' Hall on Sound Avenue. The good-looking girls from Mattituck-Laurel and the neighboring towns and the handsome troops danced enthusiastically to the music of a fine orchestra. A number of happy marriages resulted in military men settling down in the area. (MLHS.)

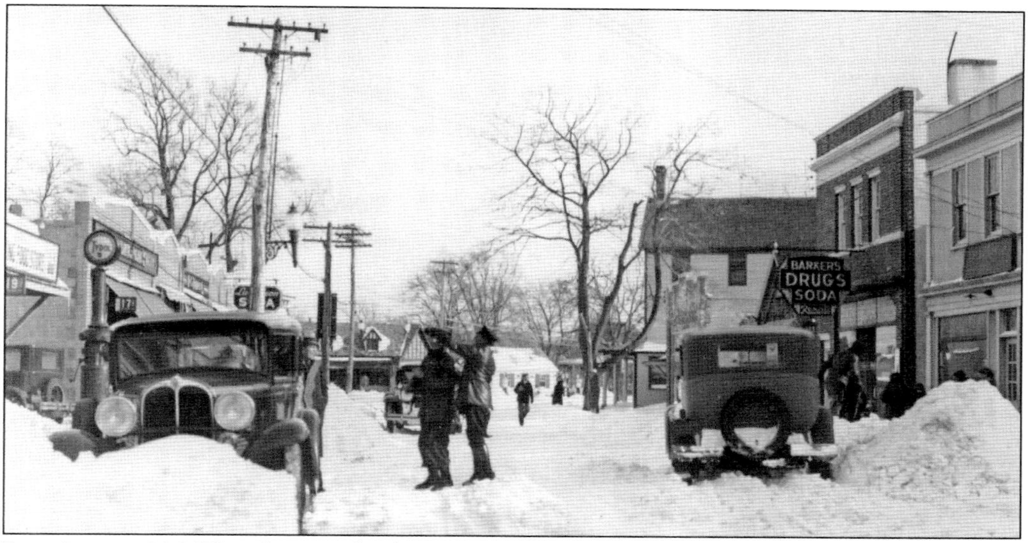

LOVE LANE, 1936. This photograph of Love Lane, looking south on a cold, snowy day, is reminiscent of a scene from Frank Capra's *It's a Wonderful Life*. On the right is the Barker pharmacy, which had been owned and operated by William L. Barker at this location since 1926. Barker came to Mattituck in 1921 after purchasing the Lahy Pharmacy in Library Hall. To the left, on the east side of Love Lane, is the Tydol gas station, run by Rudy Armbrust. (Courtesy of Jim and Pauline Gildersleeve family.)

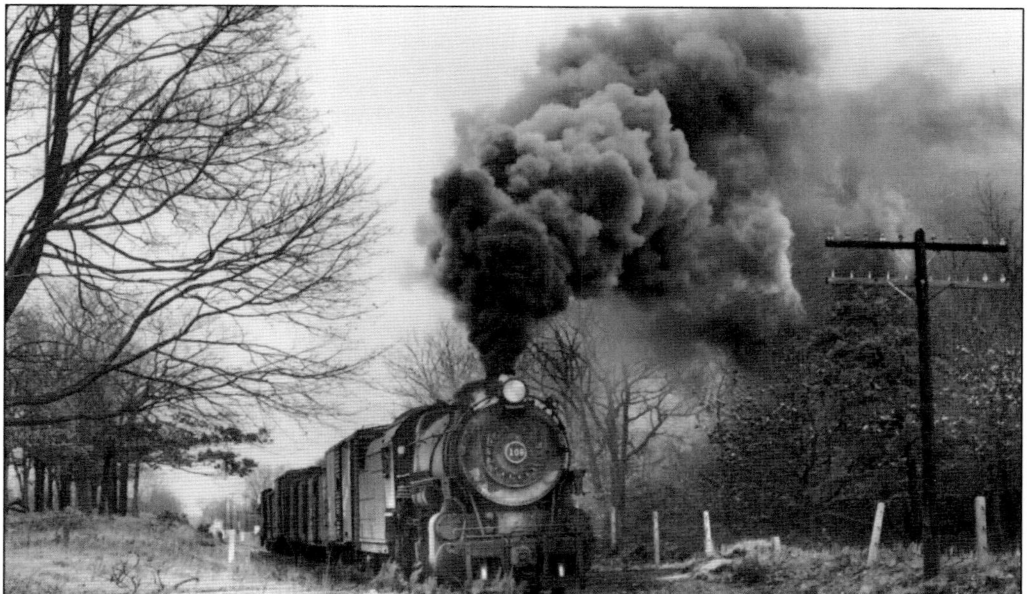

ENGINE 108, C. 1950. Engine 108 roars out of Mattituck Station, belching clouds of smoke as it heads westbound over Factory Avenue. The mighty steam locomotives with their dramatic plumes of smoke that had ushered in the golden age of Mattituck and Laurel at the turn of the century vanished by 1960 and were replaced by truck transportation and passenger trains pulled by diesel engines. Mattituck and Laurel were embarking upon another new chapter in their illustrious history. (Courtesy of Ron Ziel.)

Consistent with our mission to preserve history on a local level, this book was printed in South Carolina on American-made paper and manufactured entirely in the United States. Products carrying the accredited Forest Stewardship Council (FSC) label are printed on 100 percent FSC-certified paper.

MADE IN THE USA